TWO HOURS THAT SHOOK THE WORLD

Also by Fred Halliday

Arabia Without Sultans *†‡

Iran: Dictatorship and Development *†

Threat from the East? Soviet Policy in the Arc of Crisis *

The Ethiopian Revolution (co-author)

The Making of the Second Cold War †‡

State and Ideology in the Middle East and Pakistan (co-editor)

Cold War, Third World *

Revolution and Foreign Policy: The Case of South Yemen, 1967–87

Arabs in Exile: Yemeni Migrants in Urban Britain

Islam and the Myth of Confrontation: Religion and Politics in the Middle
     East*‡

Rethinking International Relations

Revolution and World Politics: The Rise and Fall of the Sixth Great Power

Nation and Religion in the Middle East *

The World at 2000 ‡

*Several of these books have been translated into Arabic (*), Persian (†) and
Turkish(‡).*

FRED HALLIDAY

TWO HOURS THAT SHOOK THE WORLD

September 11, 2001: Causes and Consequences

Saqi Books

British Library Cataloguing-in-Publication Data
A catalogue record for this book is available from the
British Library

ISBN 0 86356 382 1 (pb)

© Fred Halliday, 2002

This edition published 2002

Saqi Books
26 Westbourne Grove
London W2 5RH
www.saqibooks.com

'What can I do, Muslims? I do not know myself. I am neither Christian nor Jew, neither Magian nor Muslim,

I am not from east or west, not from land or sea.'

Rumi

Jalaluddin Rumi, mystical poet, born Balkh, northern Afghanistan, 1207, died Konya, Turkey, 1273.

[This translation, from *Music of a Distant Drum*, by Bernard Lewis, Princeton University Press, 2001, p. 122.]

'What is to be done? *Shto delyat?* We simply cannot return to the claustrophobic, isolationist relativism which our romantics recommend so blithely; each community back to its totem pole!'

Ernest Gellner

Ernest Gellner, born Prague 1925, died Prague 1995.

[*Postmodernism, Reason and Religion*, Routledge, 1992, p. 90.]

The author with Afghan government soldiers in front of Gowhar Shad mosque, Herat, Afghanistan, 1980.

Contents

List of Appendices

Keywords

Afghanistan. Literally 'land of the Afghans', denoting both all inhabitants of that country and more specifically the Pushtun. Founded in 1747 and ruled until 1993 by the Muhammadzai monarchy. From 1978–92, it was ruled by the communist People's Democratic Party of Afghanistan (PDPA) as the Democratic Republic of Afghanistan, from 1992–96 by the *mujahidin* alliance, as the Islamic Republic of Afghanistan, and from 1996 by the Taliban as the Emirate of Afghanistan.

Akhund. Persian, of popular and often derogatory character, for a Muslim cleric. Hence *akhundism*, term used in post-revolutionary Iran by secular critics of the Islamic clerical regime. In English literature, the word occurs in the Edward Lear's poem, 'The Akond of Swat', where it refers to a local Muslim ruler.

Amir al-Mu'minin. 'Commander of the faithful', traditional title of Muslim leaders, taken by Taliban leader Mullah Omar; also one of the official titles of the kings of Morocco.

Anfal. Arabic for 'booty' and the title of a verse of the Quran, often invoked by suicide bombers in preparation for action. Also the name of a campaign launched by the Ba'thist government against the Iraqi Kurds in 1988.

Anthrax. From the Greek *anthrax*, a piece of coal (hence *anthracite*), boil or carbuncle. Since 1876 also a fever caused by minute, rapidly multiplying, organisms in the blood. Treatment by the antibiotic Ciprofloxacin is regarded by many doctors as an expensive, and more risky, response than others, such as the generic drug Doxycycline.

Anti-terrorism. Policies responding to terrorist acts. Cf counter-terrorism.

Arabia. Elastic and often confused word. English term for the Arabian Peninsula, in Arabic *al-jazira al-'arabia*. See *Jazira*. The English term 'Saudi Arabia' is in Arabic *al-mamlaka al-'arabiyya al-sa'udiyya*, 'The Arab Kingdom of Saudi Arabia'. The older English term '*Araby*' and comparable terms in other European languages can be used to cover the Arab world, as well as Iran, real or imagined, as a whole. Hans-Werner Henze's recent song cycle, *Sechs Lieder aus dem Arabischen*, translated as 'Six Songs from the Arabian' derives its title from one of the six items, a Persian poem by Hafez.

Asian. Literally, any inhabitant of the continent of Asia, from Turkey to Japan, and comprising all of the Middle East, South Asia, Southeast Asia and East Asia. Since the 1980s contemporary British usage, an inhabitant of, or person originating from, South Asia, of indeterminate religion (i.e. Hindu, Muslim, Buddhist, Sikh, Jain or Christian).

Asymmetric Conflict. Term developed by social scientists and US strategists in the 1970s, above all in response to Vietnam, to denote a war between fundamentally dissimilar powers, the orthodox state having an advantage in firepower, and economic resources, the guerrilla opposition having greater endurance and tactical agility. The aim of the latter is to undermine the dominant state through political pressure on its regional allies and on its domestic, political and financial system. For a classic analysis see Andrew Mack 'Why Big Nations Lose Small Wars: the Politics of Asymmetric Conflict' in *World Politics*, vol. 27, no. 2, 1975.

Ayatollah. Persian for 'Shadow' or 'Sign' of God, highest clerical title in Shi'ite Islam.

Ba'thism. A militant nationalism, drawing on fascist ideas of war, leadership and blood, as well as racial superiority, in this case Arab, but also on communist forms of state and party organisation. Ideology of the Arab Ba'th Socialist Party, in power in Iraq since 1968 and in Syria since 1963.

Bioterrorism. Came into use in the 1990s to denote the use by terrorists of biological weapons, e.g. anthrax, botulism, plague, smallpox.

Blowback. Somewhat evasive term, said to be a CIA slang, for activities carried out by former Western clients, such as the Afghan guerrillas, who later turn against the West. Examples of exculpatory passive: 'the pen *was* lost', '*it* slipped' rather than '*I* lost it', '*I* knocked it over'.

Brigade 005. A special military unit, composed of Arab militants, used for operations in support of the Taliban inside Afghanistan. Notorious for the violent suppression of opponents of the Taliban, especially the Shi'ites.

Containment. Term popularised after World War II as an alternative to all out war, to denote Western policy towards the USSR, one of military resistance to its expansion, but longer-term erosion of its ideological and political dynamic. Classically formulated by American diplomat George Kennan in his 1947 *Foreign Policy* article, 'The Sources of Soviet Conduct'.

Corkscrew Journalism. Instant comment, bereft of research or originality, leading to a cycle of equally vacuous, staged, polemics between columnists who have been saying the same thing for the past decade, or more. The term originated in the film *The Philadelphia Story* (George Cukor, 1940).

Counter-terrorism. Policies designed to prevent, if necessary by anticipatory action, terrorist acts.

Crusade. From the French *croix*, 'cross', a campaign by Christians to defeat Muslims and reoccupy the Holy Land of Palestine in the eleventh-thirteenth centuries. First used in English in 1577. Associated at the time, as in the occupation of Jerusalem in 1099, with the massacre of Muslim and Jewish inhabitants. First used in 1786 to denote aggressive movements against a public enemy. The Arabic/Muslim term *salibi*, 'crusader', has been used in recent times, but rather little before, as a term of invective against Western states. Its use by Muslims outside the Mediterranean is a product of activism in the late 1990s. See also Hulagu.

Denial. Literally, to declare not to be true; in psychoanalytic theory, the denial of some form of reality, such as an unwelcome event or a particular trauma suffered by an individual. More loosely used in the 1980s and 1990s to refer to the refusal of individuals, and collective groups, to accept responsibility for their own crimes or for conflict.

Deobandi. A conservative Islamic movement, named after the town of Deoband, in India, where it originated in the nineteenth century. The ideological inspiration for conservative Pakistani groups, and for the

Taliban. Opposed to the liberal trend founded by the college at Aligarh, Pakistan.

Enlightenment. Process of change in European thought associated with secularism, rationalism and cosmopolitanism, much abused in recent years by political theorists in the West. Islamist discourse tends to appropriate the term, arguing that Islam provides its own light, *nur*, and that enlightenment, *tanwir*, can be reached through religion. By contrast, in Israel, the Jewish *haskala* is now denounced by Judaic fundamentalists: hence the abusive use of the term by Ariel Sharon in his reference to the 'enlightened', *maskel*, European states who appeased Nazi Germany in 1938.

Evil-doers. Old Testament term, much favoured by George Bush II. *Cruden's Complete Concordance to the Old and New Testaments* gives 17 references, e.g. Job 8.20 'neither will we help the evil-doers', Isaiah 1.4 'Ah sinful nation, a seed of evil-doers'.

Faqih. In Islamic terminology, an interpreter of *fiqh*, or Islamic law. In modern Arabic political usage, a verbose or irresponsibly unrealistic person.

Fard. Arabic for 'duty'. Islam distinguishes between *fard al-'ain*, the five duties incumbent on all Muslims, also known as the five 'pillars' (*arkan*) of Islam, and *fard al-kifaya*, an obligation – such as *jihad*, returning greetings or attending funerals – which is performed by some on behalf of the community as a whole.

Fath. Arabic for 'conquest', a term with Quranic resonances. Reverse acronym for *harakat al-tahrir al-falastiniyya*, the Palestinian Liberation Movement. Separate from the broader umbrella Palestinian Liberation Organisation (PLO), of which it is a dominant member.

Fatwa. Technically, a judgement by an authorised Islamic judge, or *mufti*, more generally, any polemical point of view by a self-proclaimed source of authority.

Folks. Bushspeak for a terrorist enemy, as in 'those folks who did this'. Other examples of unhegemonic West Texas judicial terminology: 'dead or alive', 'possy', 'outlaw' and 'turn him in'.

Globalization. Term popularised in the 1990s to denote a range of concurrent international trends in three main spheres: liberalisation and increase of trade and investment in economics, democratisation and the increased linking of societies in politics, and the breaking down and intermingling of societies and cultures. Experts dispute the extent and distribution of each of these, their interaction, and the degree to which the trends involved are a continuation of earlier forms of global interaction, based on North-South inequality, going back decades or even centuries. Arabic renders the term as *al-'awlama*, 'world-becoming'. Persian oscillated between *jahangiri*, 'world-grabbing' and the more positive *jahanshodan*, 'world-becoming'; the latter has, for the moment, prevailed.

Great Game. Used to designate the nineteenth century rivalry in Central Asia between Britain and Russia, which ended with the 1907 convention defining relations in Persia, Afghanistan and Tibet. Loosely and rather inaccurately applied to the situation in the Trans-Caucasian and Central Asian regions after the collapse of the USSR in 1991.

Grief Gap. Term used to denote the distance between US and other Western reactions to the 11 September 2001 attacks, and the response in many other parts of the world.

Ground Zero. US Military term for point of impact, at which a major explosion occurs, used of the site and wreckage of the World Trade Centre, New York, 11 September.

Gulf War. Term applied to both the 1980–88 Iran–Iraq war, sometimes called 'the first Gulf war' and the 1990–91 Iraq-Kuwait war. Should also be applied to the precursor of both, the 1969–75 Iran–Iraq conflict, which ended with the Algiers Agreement between the Shah and Saddam Hussein in 1975. It was the renunciation by Khomeini of that agreement, in particular the commitment not to interfere in the internal affairs of each country, that laid the ground, if not the legitimation, for the two later wars.

Halal. Literally 'released' from prohibition. The Hebrew equivalent *kashar* implies something that is fit, or suitable.

Hamas. Acronym for *harakat al-muqawama al-islamiyya*, the Islamic Resistance Movement, a Palestinian branch of the Muslim Brotherhood, founded in 1982. Also the name of a more moderate, and quite distinct, Algerian political party.

Hawala. Arabic for a promissory note or bill of exchange, general term for system of informal money transfers. Also an Urdu and Hindi term.

Hearts and Minds. Term originated in British counter-insurgency campaign in 1950s Malaya, to describe the winning of popular support away from communist guerrillas.

Hijab. Arabic for 'cover', conventional word for woman's veil.

Hizb al-Tahrir. The Party of Liberation, a Sunni fundamentalist group founded in Jordan in 1953 by the Palestinian *sheikh* Taqiuddin al-Nabhani, and with following in the Arab world, Central Asia and western Europe, especially Britain, which aims to restore the Caliphate.

Hizbullah. The 'Party of God', a Quranic term, revived in modern Arabic politics, first in Yemen in the 1960s then in Lebanon by Shi'ite militants in 1980s. Hizbullah has widespread support in Lebanon and is represented in its parliament. In July 2000 it achieved its main strategic goal in pushing Israeli and Israeli-backed forces out of Lebanon.

Homeland Defense. Taken from Soviet usage in World War II and applied to US defence policy in the late 1990s, to justify the National Missile Defense Programme. Since 11 September, it is used to denote bodies responsible for internal security in general.

Hulagu. Mongol leader who sacked Baghdad, and destroyed the 'Abbasid Empire, the second of the two great Arab Islamic empires, in 1258. A term used by Saddam Hussein, in 1991, to describe George Bush senior. Saddam did not at that time use the term 'crusader'.

Ijtihad. From the same root as *jihad*, independent judgement in the interpretation of texts within Islam, especially associated with Shi'ites. The conventional Sunni position is that the 'gate of *ijtihad*' was closed centuries ago.

Intifada. Arabic for 'uprising', a level of mobilisation below *thawra*, revolution. Used of the 1948 and 1952 popular demonstrations in Iraq, and the 1970–71 state-directed peasant risings in South Yemen, but mostly associated with the Palestinian movements of 1987–92 and 2000–2001 against Israeli occupation.

'Iqab Allah. From the same root as 'sanctions', *'uqubat*. 'The punishment of God', a phrase used by Osama bin Laden to refer to the 11 September attacks in the USA, and then taken up by protesting crowds in the Arab world.

Islam. Literally 'submission', the religion revealed to the Prophet Muhammad between 610 and 632 AD, now the faith of well over one billion believers, around 90 per cent are Sunni, and 10 per cent Shi'ite, with some smaller other groups, such as Ibadhis, in Oman. Over fifty countries are members of the Islamic Conference Organization, an inter-state body set up in 1969 after an arson attack on the al-Aqsa mosque in Jerusalem. The core texts of Islam are the Quran, the word of Allah as revealed to Muhammad, and the *hadith*, or sayings attributed to the Prophet.

Islamic Art. As readers of the *International Herald Tribune* correspondent Souren Melikian's frequent and scholarly articles will know, this is a factitious term, without historic, artistic or theological basis, invented by museum directors and sales room promoters to cover a wide variety of different cultural and geographic works.

Islamism. Term used as an alternative to 'fundamentalist' and the French *intégriste*, to denote a movement that used a return to a supposedly traditional Islam as the basis for a radical political programme. Examples would include the Iranian revolution, the Muslim Brotherhood, Deobandism and the Taliban.

Jahiliyya. 'Ignorance', generic Quranic term for times before the arrival of Islam, used in modern times by fundamentalists to denote the non-Muslim, specifically western, world.

Jazira. Arabic for 'island' and 'peninsula'. The conventional word for the Arabian Peninsula, or what in English, but not in Arabic, is termed 'Arabia'. Used as a name for the pan-Arab satellite TV station based in Qatar since 1996. Also used by Osama bin Laden for Saudi Arabia, a name he rejects, *jazirat Muhammad*, 'the peninsula of [the Prophet] Muhammad'. The use of this inclusive term by the al-Qaʻida leader would seem to imply, (i) that *all* of the Arabian Peninsula is one territory, with no distinction between Saudi Arabia, which is four-fifths of the territory, and the other six states, Yemen, Kuwait, Oman, Bahrain, Qatar, the Emirates; and (ii) that the whole of this territory, not just the holy cities of Mecca and Medina and their environs are sacred territory (see **Mecca**). The former assumption is seen by non-Saudis as an expression of expansionism, the latter has no legal or scriptural foundation.

Jerusalem. From the Hebrew *ir ha-shalom*, city of peace, claimed by both Israel and Palestine as their political capital. Arabic *al-Quds,* 'the blessed', corresponds to the ancient Hebrew *ir ha-kodesh*. Another political term that can mean a number of different things. The geographical area denoted by the term has expanded greatly in modern times, from the small historic centre, site of Christian, Jewish and Muslim shrines of 1900 to the expanded city and suburbs of to-day. The religious significance of this city for all three religions has ebbed and flowed over past centuries: it is, above all, a function of contemporary political concerns.

Jihad. Arabic for 'effort', comprising military, political and spiritual activities. Normally used by Islamists for 'struggle', in contrast to the Arabic secular term *nidal*. From this root come both *mujahid*, one who struggles for Islam in one way or another, in modern terms a political and military activists, and *ijtihad*, independent judgement within Islam.

Kemalism. Ideology of Mustafa Kemal Pasha, 'Ataturk' or 'Father of the Turks', after the establishment of the Turkish Republic in 1923 as a secular and unitary state. The six pillars of Kemalism are: republicanism, populism, nationalism, secularism (Turkish *laiklik*), statism and revolutionism. Kemalism remains the ideology of the Turkish state and military to this day, contested by Islamist parties and Kurdish opponents alike.

Kufr. General term, used in the Quran, for enemies of the faith, non-Muslims, apostates. Not a precise equivalent of the Christian term 'blasphemy'. Now used as generic term of abuse against anyone whose views the speaker disapproves of. One who practises *kufr* is a *kafir*, generally an unbeliever. The word was taken by Dutch and Portuguese sailors in the seventh century and became a term of (European) racist abuse, as *kaffir*, in South Africa.

Magus. A Zoroastrian priest, practitioner of obscure skills, hence *magic*. Used in Christian tradition to refer to three wise men, *magi,* who visited Jesus at his birthplace in Bethlehem. In modern Arabic, an anti-Persian term of abuse, e.g. by Saddam Hussein of Khomeini during the Iran–Iraq war. *Magian* is an alternative term for Zoroastrian and Parsee.

Mecca. In Arabic *Makka al-mukarrama*, blessed Mecca. An ancient trading and pilgrimage city in the Hijaz, western Saudi Arabia, population 700,000 (2000). Site of the Ka'bah, literally 'cube', a stone covered with black cloth which stands at the centre of the Great Mosque, allegedly built by Adam and later rebuilt by Abraham and Isaac as a replica of God's house. The pilgrimage to Mecca, *hajj*, at least once in a lifetime, is one of the five duties or pillars, *arkan*, of Islam. The city has an exclusion radius of around 30 kilometres, beyond which access is now limited to Muslims. As positive figure of speech in English, a place or goal which people aspire to visit (e.g. tourist sites, dance halls), first used in 1823.

Middle East. Geostrategic term coined in 1902 by US Admiral Mahan. Now adopted, without any significant questioning, at a time when other Western concepts are being questioned, e.g. 'Far East', 'Central Europe', 'British Isles', in main Middle Eastern languages. Thus, *al-Sharq al-Awsat*, the title of a major Arabic daily published in London, and the Persian *khavar miane*.

Muhajirun. Literally 'emigrants', those followers of Islam who fled from Mecca to Medina. In contrast to the *ansar*, supporters, who were from Medina itself. Term used in modern times by a range of Islamist groups.

Mujahid, pl. mujahidin. One who wages *jihad*, used in modern political discourse to denote nationalist and Islamist fighters, e.g. during the Algerian war of independence (1954–62), the anti-monarchical resistance against the Shah (1971–79) and the Afghan anti-communist war (1978–92).

Mullah. 'Master' or 'lord' (cf. Hebrew *rabbi*, my master or teacher). General term in Shi'ite Islam for a Muslim clergyman, or *'alim*. South Asian term *maulana* signifies a respected clergyman.

Muslim. A person who adopts Islam. The archaic term 'Mohammedan'/ 'Mahometan' is incorrect: a mistaken analogy with 'Christian', a follower of Christ, it suggests that the Prophet Mohammad was divine.

Mutawi'un. Literally 'volunteers', enforcers of belief, the religious police known in Saudi Arabia, and in Afghanistan, as the Force for the Enforcement of Good and the Prevention of Evil (a phrase taken from the Quran). A brutal, authoritarian and intrusive irregular force used to employ dissident tribesmen and harass women, foreigners and others in public spaces.

Northern Alliance. Loose group of non-Pashtun guerillas opposed to the Taliban, and comprising *mujahidin* who held power in Kabul from 1992 to 1996. Manily Tajiks and Uzbeks. Their leader, Ahmad Shah Masud, was fatally wounded in an assassination attack two days before 11 September 2001. It is reasonable to surmise that these events were connected.

OMEA. 'Of Middle East Appearance'. Term used by US authorities in racial profiling.

Operation Enduring Freedom. Term finally given to the US campaign against its opponents, after abandonment of earlier versions, such as Infinite Justice (this latter was said to be offensive to Muslims, since Allah is the only source of such an action).

Osama bin Laden. Self-appointed leader of al-Qa'ida. Born in Saudi Arabia in 1957, son of Yemeni millionaire building contractor Muhammad bin Laden. Attended Thagh elite secondary school in Jeddah, then studied management, economics and Islamic studies at the King Abdul Aziz University in Riyadh. He is associated with the 1982 Sunni uprising in Syria, and with the funding and organization of Arabs in Afghanistan in the 1980s. He returned to Saudi Arabia in 1989 but following a dispute with Saudi rulers, over their response to the Kuwait crisis in 1990, he moved to Sudan, and from there, in 1996, back to Afghanistan.

Pakhtu/Pashtu/Pushtun. Linguistic community organised into tribes comprising over 40 per cent of the Afghan population, and that of the neighbouring North-West Frontier Province in Pakistan. Main cities are Kandahar, Jalalabad in Afghanistan and Peshawar in Pakistan.

Pakhtunistan/Pashtunistan/Pushtunistan. Territory claimed by successive Afghan governments in Pakistan since the latter's independence in 1947. Afghanistan has contested the border defined in 1893, the Durand Line.

Pakistan. State formed in 1947 after the partition of British India into Muslim and, predominantly, Hindu states. The word itself is said, variously, to be based on the Urdu/Persian for *pak*, pure, or on the initial letters of some of the major provinces comprising it, Punjab, Kashmir and Sindh. An important goal of the founders of Pakistan was to free South-Asian Muslims from what they termed 'Arab imperialism'.

Pariah. Tamil for a caste who perform unclean activities, particularly leatherwork and shoe-making, later outcast. In international relations of the 1990s, term for states with whom the USA has major security conflicts: Iran, Iraq, North Korea and Afghanistan.

PDPA. People's Democratic Party of Afghanistan, a communist party founded in 1965. In power from 1978–92: leaders Nur Muhammad Taraki (1978–79), Hafizullah Amin (1979), Babrak Karmal (1979–86) and Najibullah (1986–92). Taraki was murdered in October 1979 by Amin, who was killed by Soviet forces in December 1979; Karmal was ousted by Soviet pressure in 1986 and died later in exile in Moscow; Najibullah fell to the *mujahidin* in April 1992, lived for four years in the UN compound in Kabul, and was captured, tortured and hung, along with his brother, when the Taliban took Kabul in September 1996. From 1978–79 dominated by the *khalq* (People) faction, and from 1979–1992 by *parcham* (Flag). Persian name *hizb-i dimukrat-i khalq-i afghanistan*.

Pundit. From the Sanskrit *pandita*, a learned man, specifically an adviser on Hindu law to the British courts in India.

Al-Qa'ida. Arabic for the 'Base', or the 'Foundation', the organization headed by Osama bin Laden. The existence of this organization was announced on 23 February 1998, as part of a World Islamic Front comprising groups from Egypt, Pakistan and Bangladesh. The term has no apparent antecedents in Islamic or Arabic political history: explanations range from a protected region during the communist era in Afghanistan, to it being an allusion to the Bin Laden family's construction company, to the title of a 1951 Isaac Asimov novel, *The Foundation,* which was translated into Arabic as *al-Qa'ida*, and which describes the destruction of a mighty empire, Trantor.

Ramadan. Ninth month of the Islamic calendar. A time of fasting and abstinence from sexual activity from dawn to sunset. Associated with family and social visits, at nightime, often with special foods and social gatherings. Also associated with some of the bloodiest battles in early Islamic history, notably that of *Badr*, the October 1973 Arab–Israeli war (the Egyptian offensive was named 'Operation *Badr*'), and with heavy fighting in the Iran–Iraq war of 1980–88.

Ranger. Pre-1776 term for a US irregular soldier, now used for special intervention forces. Not the exact equivalent of the UK's SAS, as they are more numerous, less elite.

al-Sakina. Arabic word for 'harmony' and oneness with Allah, suggestive of mystical and, possibly, sacrificial state, used more recently by Islamic youth training groups in the UK.

Salafis. The *Salafiyya* was a movement founded in the late nineteenth century that revered the 'pious ancestors', *salaf al-salihin*, of Islam. Originally a term denoting modernising and reformist trends, associated with al-Afghani and Abduh, from the 1970s onwards it came to denote a conservative, Islamist, trend in the Arab world, especially the Arabian Peninsula.

Salman Paq. Town near Baghdad said to house Iraqi nuclear facilities, repeatedly attacked by Western air forces. Named after Salman al-Farisi, a close *ansar* or companion of the Prophet, and the first Persian to convert to Islam, who is buried there.

Second World War Language. Global conflict, 1939–45. Source of several terms used, or revived, in later conflicts: e.g. 'appeasers', 'the Allies', 'home front', 'blitz', 'Churchillian' . . .

Shari'a. From the same Arabic root as *shari'*, street. A generic term for divinely sanctioned Islamic law, now a talisman invoked by fundamentalists without historic or canonical authority: often confuses those, 80 out of 6,000 verses of the Quran that are concerned with law and, by dint of being the word of Allah, divinely sanctioned with the broader body of Islamic law, *fiqh. Shari'a* is thereby used to comprise the Quran, the Hadith, Sunnah and subsequent jurisprudence: this entails, however, that it is not divinely sanctioned.

Shi'a. Literally 'faction', the followers of Ali, the cousin and son-in-law of the Prophet Muhammad who fell into conflict with the successors of the Prophet and formed a separate sect, now make up around 10 per cent of the world's Muslim population. Sub-groups include Twelvers, Ja'fari, Ismaili and other communities. The dominant religion in Iran, Azerbaijan.

Silver Bullet. American expression for a one-off complete solution, from Lone Ranger stories, according to which only a 'silver bullet' can kill the hero. Rather misused, to suggest invincibility of the enemy, as in the phrase by Secretary of Defense Donald Rumsfeld, that there will be no 'silver bullet' in this crisis.

6+2. UN negotiating process, initiated in 1993, under which the six states bordering Afghanistan (China, Pakistan, Iran, Turkmenistan, Uzbekistan, Tajikistan) plus the USA and Russia joined a negotiating process to end the conflict in and around Afghanistan. See Appendix 2.

SOS. 'Save Our Souls', a maritime distress signal, more recently used as 'Supporters Of Shari'a' by preachers at London Finsbury Park Mosque.

Steganography. Concealment of secret messages in computer graphics or text.

Suicide Bombing. Tactic used by terrorist and military groups in a number of countries during the twentieth century, notably *kamikaze* ('divine wind') airplane pilots in World War II, Tamil Tiger guerrillas in Sri Lanka, the Hizbullah in Lebanon and Islamists in Palestine. A distinction needs to be made by cases where this tactic is used against the soldiers of an enemy state (Japan, Lebanon) and where it is used against civilians associated with that state (Sri Lanka, Palestine, 11 September). The Arabic expression, *'amaliyya istishhadiyya*, 'sacrificial operation' became commonly used in the 1990s. Those who dissented referred to such actions as *'amaliyya intihariyya*, 'suicidal mission'. The Quran prohibits suicide, but not (verse 2:51) sacrifice in the cause of a just struggle.

Sunni. From *sunna*, literally 'tradition', the majority current in Islam, counts around 90 per cent of its followers. Less receptive to interpretation and innovation. Strongly adheres to text and to the revival of political authority.

Taghut. Quranic term for 'idol', object of pagan worship, to be destroyed by the faithful. Applied by modern Islamists, notably Khomeini, to describe political opponents, e.g. the Shah, Bani Sadr, Jimmy Carter, Saddam Hussein. Hence the generic term *taghuti* for secular elite and their associated lifestyle. Wrongly used by many Arab writers for tyrant, *taghin*.

Talib, Persian plural **Taliban**. Literally a religious student, term used for the movement, based on recruits from Deobandi *madrasas* in Pakistan to the Taliban movement in 1994. Contrast to 'Students (*daneshjuan*) Following the Imam's Line', the group of Iranians who seized the American embassy in Tehran on 5 November 1979.

Terrorism. Arabic *irhab* (literally intimidation), Persian *terorizm*. Denotes the use by political actors, opposition forces or states, of deliberate fear to promote political ends. First used in 1795 to denote the terror of the French revolutionary state against its opponents, used in a similar way by the Bolsheviks, notably Leon Trotsky, to legitimate their actions. Has come in the second half of the twentieth century to refer almost exclusively to acts by opposition groups: assassinations, kidnapping and hijacking of planes, occasionally ships and buses, with civilians, bomb attacks on buildings and civilians in public places.

Ulema. Plural of *'alim*, someone proficient in *'ilm*, knowledge or science, a man of learning, the equivalent of the clergy in Islam. Also known as *mullahs*. Islam does not have an equivalent of the Christian sacrament of ordination, or a clear clerical hierarchy.

Umma. Muslim word for community, used 62 times in the Quran. Denotes the Muslims and other communities. The Quran suggests that in paradise the Muslim *umma* will be a minority of all these present. In modern political discourse it can denote the Arab world *al-umma al-'arabiyya* or the community of all Muslims. Contemporary usage suggests aspiration to unity of all members in one political community. Broader than the terms nation, people, country. Also gives Arabic for 'internationalism' *al-umamiyya*, nationalisation *ta'mim*, and for the United Nations *al-umam al-muttahida*. Same root as Hebrew term *am*, people.

Wahhabism. The official ideology of the Saudi state since its formation in 1902, more broadly, movements supported, or allegedly supported, by Saudi Arabia. Founded by Muhammad Ibn Abd al-Wahhab (1703–87). Followers of the strict Hanbali school of Islamic law, Wahhabism is one of the three main components of conservative Sunni Islam, along with the Muslim Brotherhood and the Deobandis. Ibn Abd al-Wahhab branded all who disagreed with him, including other Muslims, especially Shi'ites as 'infidels' and declared *jihad* on them. In their 1802 conquest of Iraq, and in their revival in the early part of the twentieth century, they destroyed Shi'ite shrines and tombs. The descendants of Ibn Abd al-Wahhab are today called the Al Shaykh, the 'Family of the Shaykh', in contrast to the politically dominant Al

Saud. In Russia the term *vahabobchik* is now an all-purpose word for Muslim opposition groups.

YSP. Yemeni Socialist Party, in Arabic *al-hizb al-ishtiraki al-yamani*, founded in June 1965 as the National Front for the Liberation of South Yemen. Came to power in South Yemen in November 1967, and transformed into the YSP in 1978. The only Arab regime to support Soviet style 'scientific socialism'. Initially supported revolutionary movements against North Yemen, Oman, Ethiopia and Saudi Arabia. Weakened by factional disputes of 1969, 1978, 1986, this last involving several thousand casualties. Merged with conservative North Yemen in May 1990, and defeated in the inter-Yemeni civil war of April–July 1994. Retains semi-legal existence within Yemen.

Zion. A hill just south of the gates of Jerusalem, then applied to the city as a whole and later to the physical, but in some cases spiritual, land claimed by Jewish nationalism. Hence **Zionism** the movement pioneered by Theodor Herzl in his 1896 *Der Judenstaat (The State of the Jews)* and by the founding Zionist conference at Basle in 1897. The term is used in a variety of ways, some quite specific, referring to the movement to establish a Jewish state in Palestine, others denoting generally sympathetic if not unquestioning support for the Israeli government of the day, some of a fantastical, racist, kind purporting to identify a worldwide conspiracy as in the anti-Semitic forgery *The Protocols of the Elders of Zion.*

In small tribute to the late Raymond Williams, sociologist, historian and critic of culture and his Keywords: A Vocabulary of Culture and Society, 1976. *Thanks also to the* Evening Standard, *23 October 2001; Cyril Glassé, the* Concise Encyclopaedia of Islam, *London: Stacey International, 1989; the* Shorter Oxford English Dictionary; *and Henry Yule and A. C. Burnell,* Hobson-Jobson.

Introduction:
Political Violence and the Claims of Reason

On Sunday 16 September, five days after the attacks on New York and Washington, I was invited by the BBC World Service to take part in a two-hour special worldwide phone-in on the events. The programme, 'Talking Points', had received 30,000 emails before the broadcast even started. During the two hours that followed, we heard from no fewer than forty-seven different people, through phone calls and emails, from many continents, beliefs and points of view.

The programme began with accounts from two people who had been in the World Trade Center during the attacks: they told of the rush to escape, of people falling over each other, of friends they had suddenly made and whom they had lost again within minutes, of the unfolding horror. One told how when, after 45 minutes, he got down to the ground he had a choice to turn one way or the other, into Liberty Street or into the well between the towers: no one gave any guidance. On instinct he went into Liberty Street. If he had turned the other way he, like all the people who did so, would have been crushed as the tower collapsed. We heard from people who, five days after the event, did not know if missing relatives might be alive: a Dutch mother whose son Peter Verweij had been there, an English teenager whose father had worked on the 92nd floor of Tower 2. We heard too from many other people across the world. Some, such as two Afghans living in, respectively, Australia and California, were for the first time facing hostility. Some callers in India, Israel and elsewhere denounced the involvement of Muslims in terrorist acts. Many Muslims called in. Some condemned the hijackers. Some pleaded with the listeners to the BBC to try to understand why there was such resentment against the West and America, to address what they saw as the deeper causes of this event and of the global reaction to it. An American woman living in Ramallah, said that although she wanted to be with her family in New York, BBC listeners should recognize that there was widespread criticism, 'regions of resentment', of US policy. Some callers appealed for love, some for prayer. An American caller wondered at the European reluctance to act. An Iranian exile wanted Iran to be identified as the main source of terrorism. The reactions did not follow religious lines. A Croatian denounced America, saying it had been a global bully and now 'it had got a bloody nose'. A caller from Pristina, in Kosovo, pointed out that in what was now an almost entirely Muslim region there was 100 per cent support for America. One caller thought that, if they wanted to, the FBI could take Osama bin Laden to their headquarters in two hours. And so it went on.

The events of 11 September 2001 and their consequences are, by any standards, a global event: the explosions themselves killed people of many countries, not least hundreds of Muslims, be they Pakistani and Arab professionals in the World Trade Center towers or the up to 200 Yemeni doormen and workers on the ground. The explosions were watched, with incredulity and fear, across the world. The longer-run consequences are worldwide, affecting military security, the everyday security of people in their homes, workplaces and travel, the world economy and, not least, relations between peoples, cultures and religions. The events have precipitated a global crisis that will, if we are lucky, take a hundred years to resolve. They are far from being the first acts of violence intended to cause terror, by states of all shades and often of purported peacefulness. But they were in certain senses unique in form and consequences, and acquired a greater impact, occuring as they did, at the start of a new, initially hopeful, age. Political terrorism is a product of modernity itself: but the events of 11 September have punctured a huge hole in the optimism of the new millennium and of that modernity.

On the BBC phone-in programme I was asked by the presenter,

Robin Lustig, if I had anticipated such an event. I had studied the politics of the Middle East and its conflicts for over thirty years. I had visited many of the countries involved: Afghanistan, Iran, Iraq, Kuwait, Saudi Arabia, Yemen, Palestine and others. I had written and lectured on fundamentalism, terrorism and regional conflicts. In March 2001, I had argued on al-Jazira television with a supporter of bin Laden, Abu Qatada: he defended the destruction of the Buddhist statues in Bamyan on the grounds that they were un-Islamic. He also asserted that the world had no right to protest on this occasion, as they had not done so in 1969, when the al-Aqsa mosque in Jerusalem was set on fire, or when the Ayodhya mosque in India was destroyed in 1993. Terrorism 'from below' is a crime, so too is terrorism 'from above'.

I had, by dint of being brought up in Ireland, just south of the border with the North, a long-standing and very uneasy acquaintance with political violence and the uses to which it is put, be this by those nationalist and religious forces that are opposed to states and also by states themselves. I was ten-years-old when the 1956 IRA bombing campaign, organized from my town, began. I had heard tell of 'progressive atrocities'. I well recall the nationalist who in Belfast in 1969, told me that the Protestants had the right to self-determination, 'provided they went and did it somewhere else'. In 1976 the Director of the Institute for Policy Studies, for which I worked in Washington DC, Orlando Letelier, and another colleague, Ronni Moffitt, were murdered on their way to work by DINA, the Chilean secret police.

My answer to Robin Lustig's question was, nonetheless, no: I had not anticipated such an event and would not claim to have done so. Moreover, I think that human affairs often cannot be accurately predicted, that for all the attempts to amass data and find precise methodologies, political and social processes are in many ways unpredictable. Intelligence and academic or political analysis may predict certain events, such as invasions. The great intelligence failures of the twentieth century were of this kind: Stalin's failure to predict the German invasion of Russia in 1941, Israel's failure to predict the Arab attack of 1973, the Arab and Western failure to predict Iraq's invasion of Kuwait in 1990. But other events – revolutions, the collapse of communism, September 2001 – are of a different character and go to the heart of the unpredictability of political events and the role of human will and deception within them. History always surprises. The French Revolution of 1789 and the Bolshevik of 1917 were such sudden upheavals.

What is possible, however, is to try to explain and to analyse such events. This book is one among, no doubt, many such contributions and works. I have done it in large measure by drawing on research and writing I have already published. Chapters 1 and 12 address two of the central issues involved in these events: the explanation of what happened on 11 September, and the analysis of the argument on 'Islam and the West'.[1] The remaining chapters were published before September 2001 but I hope they will contribute to the explanation and analysis of some of the many questions involved in this crisis.[2] Thus Chapter 1 is followed by two chapters on political issues central to the crisis, fundamentalism and terrorism. Two subsequent chapters deal with the question of hostility to Muslims: they identify a pervasive hostility to Muslims in the modern world but question the account, often phrased in historical and cultural terms, that many people, including many Muslims, give of this. These chapters on anti-Muslim prejudice are followed by four that examine specific political questions raised by the present crisis and the ensuing discussion: the Arab–Israeli question and the politics of respectively, Kuwait, Iran and Saudi Arabia. These studies of particular Middle Eastern conflicts and countries are not designed to give a comprehensive overview of the modern Middle East or of what, in Chapter 1, I term 'the greater West Asian crisis'. But they are part of the critique of stereotype that besets these issues: they are an attempt to go beyond some of the simpler presentations of this found in both the West and the Middle East, and to show what is going on *within* these societies.

The last three chapters tackle broader questions in international relations that are equally present in the assessment of 11 September. One examines and questions the assumptions of much contemporary discussion of the USA: it is not a defence of the USA but rather an argument for a more accurate, engaged and internationalist debate with America. Next to the nonsense about 'Islam', that about America and the formation of its foreign policy is one of the biggest areas of confusion in this crisis. The chapter on globalization looks at this process, the overall context of the contemporary crisis: globalization does not explain, let alone excuse random acts of violence, but it is a context that accounts for some of the response – a pervasive anti-American rancour and resentment – to 11 September found in many parts of the world. Finally, in Chapter 12, I return to the issue of cultural conflict and question much of the argument presented about this in both East and West.

This collection is a necessarily partial and provisional response to 11 September. Three broad principles underlie it. First, whatever the responses of states and of other organizations to this crisis, it is essential to begin with what is the prime responsibility of political and social analysis, namely, not prediction, but *explanation*. If such an explanation leaves open questions to which we do not have an answer, if it spurs its own debates and research agenda, that is to be expected. Secondly, a response to these events can and should be based not on supposedly distinct cultural or civilizational values, but on an *internationalist* approach: by this is meant one that takes into account the different global interests and reactions involved, but, more importantly, starts from principles that are shared by different cultures and peoples. These principles include accuracy in history and media reporting, a commitment to the values embodied in the UN Charter and its major human rights conventions, a commitment, however inchoate in moral or legal terms, to identify what forms of violence are illegitimate, by states and their opponents, and an awareness of some shared moral values, of which the commitment to personal security and peace of mind is not the least. Thirdly, and above all, any response, in writing or action, can and must be based on *reason*. Too easily challenged by proponents of cultural difference or by careless critics of the Enlightenment and modernity, this is the prerequisite to any intellectual response to 11 September, to dealing with the ills to which it draws attention and to resisting, over the decades and perhaps centuries to come, those who use violence, fear and demagogy to further their ends.

In regard to international relations as an academic approach, this involves the claim, which I strongly support, that ignorance about how international relations work, is a pervasive common ill. Here, it often seems, any fantasy or conspiracy theory goes. Freud once argued that the aim of psychoanalysis was to reduce extreme hysteria to everyday common misery. The function of reasoned argument and an engaged scepticism towards emotive claims in international affairs is to do just that. To that end, amid the uncertainty and clamour of the time, this book is intended to be a contribution.

In part such a call for reason involves a focus on the responsibility of intellectuals. Too often those with authority, voice, learning, choose not to resist but to profit from and inflame conflict. We see this in the Muslim world, in the Balkans, in Ireland. Four categories of intellectuals are especially evident in such exacerbation: TV and press reporters, historians, novelists and, not least, clergymen. In country after country, they have, in the 1990s, betrayed their calling. Where deliberate provocation ends, careless reporting, and lazy headlines, can do the same job.

Reason also involves, in regard to the conflicts of the Middle East or elsewhere, less indulgence of claims and rhetoric based on religion. To a student of international relations and someone whose job it is to examine real world causes and legitimate claims, too much credence is given, on all sides, to the claims of religion. It is common but trite, 'pious' in the worst sense, for people to hold forth, pontificate indeed, about the value of tradition, the sacred character of this and that and the irreconcilable claims of religion. Too much indulgence is given to terms like 'sage', 'venerable' and 'divine'. Many a priest, rabbi and mufti, for example, is engaged in such activity: a sceptical, informed look at so-called claims to Jerusalem would be in order here. So too would some qualification of arguments based on rhetoric about historic 'hurt', 'damage' or 'resentment'. We are or should be concerned with the problems of this world, with human welfare, with saving life, with nutrition, food, habitat, equality, peace. All of these, the stuff of the United Nations Develoment Program (UNDP) human welfare and development indicators, are absent from disputes about supposedly holy places, be they in Jerusalem, Kosovo or Ayodhya. An equal outpouring of fractious particularism is evident over many years in Ireland. In the case of Jerusalem let us not forget that it was disputes in 1853 between two groups of Christians over the keys to the Church of the Nativity in Bethlehem that sparked the Crimean war. The outside world and the significant body of sensible, religious and secular, people within all communities, and within their diasporas, should be more impatient on such matters.

The global consequences of 11 September 2001 will take many years to work themselves through and may well long outlast the life of those reading this book. In addition to the identifiable military, economic and intelligence responses, which lie beyond the scope of this volume, there will involve a response at the level of reason and emotion, an analytic assessment ongoing into the future and a sustenance of human spirit, above all hope.

Faced with the paucity of historical and political analogies, it is nonetheless reassuring in these times to reach beyond, to texts of religion, albeit interpreted in secular vein, and to literature. Some have invoked Armageddon, the final battle in the Christian tradition, which this is not; some the Irish poet Yeats in *The Second Coming* on his foreboding of the collapsing centre: 'Things fall apart. The centre cannot hold; mere anarchy is loosed upon the world... The best lack all conviction while the worst are full of passionate intensity.' Others invoked W. H. Auden's poem *1 September 1939*, which, amid great anxiety and on the eve of war, evokes the supreme value of love: 'Waves of anger and fear circulate over the bright and darkened lands of the earth.' Chapter 99 of the Quran, *Surat al-zalzal*, the Verse of the Earthquake, speaks of a terrible event out of which good will come, and the perpetrators of evil are punished. Perhaps most fitting in the light of the global repercussions of these events, are antidotes to rhetoric from East and West about cultural clash: the words of the thirteenth-century poet, Rumi, cited on page 5, and those of the seventeenth-century English poet, John Donne. The issues raised by 11 September confront everyone on this earth. 'No man is an island entire of itself; every man is a piece of the Continent, a part of the main . . . any man's death diminishes me, because I am involved in Mankind,' Donne wrote in 1624; to which one might add, with adaptation of his conclusion, 'Do not send to know for whom New York burns. It burns for us all.' A battle, global in intent and in extent, was joined well before 11 September 2001. Its course is by no means certain.

1

September 11, 2001 and the Greater West Asian Crisis

The crisis unleashed by the events of 11 September is one that is global and all-encompassing. It is global in the sense that it binds many different countries into conflict, most obviously the USA and parts of the Muslim world. It is all-encompassing in that, more than any other international crisis yet seen, it affects a multiplicity of life's levels, political, economic, cultural and psychological. In an attempt to get an initial intellectual hold on this momentous process, a first reaction is to reach for grand historical analogy. In terms of world history there is mention of Sarajevo 1914, where a single terrorist act, in this case the assassination of Archduke Ferdinand of Austria and his wife, precipitated World War I and with it the end of the imperial order in Europe; of Operation Barbarossa and Pearl Harbour in 1941, the attacks of, respectively Germany on the USSR and Japan on the USA; of Cuba 1962, when, in the aftermath of the 1959 Cuban revolution and attempts by the USA to overthrow the new regime, Soviet intermediate-range missiles were placed on the island of Cuba and, in the confrontation between Washington and Moscow, the world came nearer to a nuclear exchange than ever before.

Each of these events was global in cause and consequence. In each case, the explosion had roots deeper than strategic rivalry. The

ensuing clash of states was preceded by social and ideological conflict. Yet none of these historical analogies matches the peculiar
timbre of 11 September 2001, at once the most spectacular case
ever of the policy espoused by anarchists from the 1880s onwards
of 'propaganda of the deed', an iconic destruction against the clear
blue sky, and an event that, at one stroke, launches a roller-coaster
of grief, fear and uncertainty. It is easy and portentous to say, as
many have, that 'everything has changed' since 11 September. This
is, however, a proposition that is as hard to disprove as it is hard to
prove. Even the most cataclysmic of events can lead to exaggeration: the world did not change, the sun did not darken, the novel,
hope or happiness did not die after Auschwitz, the Gulag, Sabra
and Chatila, Sarajevo, Rwanda. The world learnt something, or at
least some of it did: as a result, some things, not least the political
systems, the histories, the cultures, the hopes and fears of mankind
continued. The same will be true of 11 September 2001. Yet enough
has changed, and will continue to change, for this to be recognized,
already, as one of the landmarks of modern world history.

If the causes of this event can be traced back into the history of
the Arab and Muslim worlds and of Western interaction with them
and with the non-European world as a whole, the consequences of
11 September will stretch far into the future. It is a measure of the
very pervasive and far-reaching impact of these events that they are
not just concentrated in one geographical area or on one aspect of
life, the military or the economic. These consequences can be identified on at least five levels: the military engagement of the USA
and its allies in Afghanistan and possibly other countries; changes
in relations between states, in terms of diplomacy, resolution or
exacerbation of local and regional conflicts; a distinct, reformist if
not revolutionary, shift within developed countries in arrangements
for security, intelligence, surveillance and compliance; the long-run,
global, social and economic consequences of the crisis that has
followed 11 September; and the cultural, philosophical and psychological aftermath of violence and insecurity felt in all societies.
One of the effects of 11 September is, however, greatly to increase
insecurity not only in those countries suspected of being associated with terrorism, but also in all other states, an insecurity of the
economy and market being compounded by a personal one. It is
rightly said that risk has become a pervasive feature of modern life
in regard to food, sex, travel. In many countries political security
did not exist before 11 September. But in many it did, and was a

good, personal and public, to which all people could reasonably aspire. Moreover, for those already in war or insecurity on 10 September, 11 September may well have made things worse. For the rest of us, living in or visiting any city or country that had hitherto avoided such violence, the sound of an overflying aircraft causes anxiety. A sense of assumed security in much of modern life has, for some long time at least, been significantly eroded.

To this pervasive insecurity is added the unique, opaque, character of the conflict. The terrorists have not exhausted their options: as in planning for nuclear war, so too in this kind of offensive, a plan for a successful, surprise, 'first' strike may be accompanied by an equally well-hidden second-strike capability. Some of the things that have followed 11 September are processes that were, in some degree, already in train: they include the worldwide recession, growing hostility to immigrants and refugees in developed countries and an assertion by the USA of military hegemony. But 11 September has also reversed some trends hitherto prevailing: the most obvious is the shift from the certainties of neo-liberal market policies to the intervention of Organisation of Economic Cooperation and Development states (OECD), above all the USA, in their economies. Subsidies, infusions of money into markets, tax incentives have all followed, as has a more invasive attitude to tax havens and money laundering. It will take years to assess the consequences.

The governments of the world talk, as they must, and as, under Article 51 of the UN Charter, they may, of a war against an enemy: but this is an enemy that is not a strategic threat and against which there can be no easy or predictable end. Therefore, this is not a war, in the sense of a great mobilization with a clear strategic or calculable end. One of the casualties of 11 September has been those doctrines painstakingly laid out to justify war to a sceptical population of the developed world: Caspar Weinberger in 1985, Tony Blair in Kosovo in 1999. Weinberger, then US Secretary of Defense, laid down six conditions for military action by the USA. Some of these conditions are met in this case (a challenge to the US national interest, Congressional support) but one, namely, 'clearly defined political and military objectives', most certainly is not. Blair, in his April 1999 speech justifying the intervention in Kosovo, listed five criteria: some, national interest and the exhaustion of diplomatic options, coincided with Weinberger's criteria. But again, military operations that could in his words be undertaken 'sensibly and prudently', seem elusive in this case.

There is no clear strategic goal and most certainly no clear exit. Indeed, as US strategists quickly recognized, there is not only no 'silver bullet' but also no criteria, other than universal peace and tranquillity, that would signal an end to this conflict. Here too it is important to avoid exaggeration. This is not the first war of the twenty-first century: the inhabitants of Grozny, Juba, Prestovo, Colombo, Kabul, not to mention Srinagar, Nablus and Medellin, would have reason to question that. Those who seek to use this event not to condone the carnage in the USA but to question anterior political and moral neglect of other conflicts are right to do so: yet among the greatest casualties of these events may precisely be those caught up in such conflicts. The response to such moral inconsistency should and can be to bring indignation and diplomatic concern with these other questions up to the level expressed after 11 September with regard to the events in New York and Washington. It is illogical and immoral to allow real or alleged Western neglect of other conflicts, in the Balkans, Central Africa or Palestine, to lessen indignation at the brutality and folly of 11 September. No balance sheet of such neglect, especially with regard to the Muslim world, can ignore what was done in the 1990s, not least in Bosnia and Kosovo.

Explanations

11 September 2001 was, therefore, an event, possibly unique in its form and impact, that raises many broader issues, which will confront all of us in the years to come. The first question is cause: why this group of young men, most from the Arabian Peninsula, planned this action. Here a distinction may be made between the longer-term and more immediate, or conjunctural, causes. Much is made of the long-term antecedents. Some involve the Crusades, the attacks by Western Christians on the Muslim world that began in the eleventh century, others the Islamic concept of struggle, *jihad*: bin Laden says the conflict has been going on since the 1920s. In his statement delivered in October 2001 (Appendix 5), bin Laden invoked the '80 years' time frame: he did not say exactly what he meant – the collapse of the Ottoman Empire or the British takeover of Palestine. Some of his associates have invoked the expulsion of the Arabs from Spain in 1492. But the image of the Crusades means little to those outside the Mediterranean Arab world, and

the term Crusader War (al-harb al-salibiyya) has only recently entered the generic Islamic vocabulary. In 1991 Saddam denounced George Bush Sr as Hulagu, the Mongol emperor who destroyed Baghdad in 1258, not as a Crusader. *Jihad* is quite an inappropriate term, for the proper, Quranic reason that the armies of Islam sought to convert those they conquered to Islam, whereas, whatever else is involved, this desire to conquer is irrelevant in the contemporary context. Khomeini, for example, distinguished between *jihad-i asghar*, the smaller or military struggle, and *jihad-i akbar*, the greater struggle, or *jihad ba nafs*, the struggle with the self. *Jihad*, literally 'effort', can mean any form of exertion by Muslims, from fighting to economic mobilization to prayer and mystical introspection.

There are two more immediate historical contexts for 11 September, one colonialism, the other the cold war. The legacies of both, followed by the inequalities associated with globalization, have produced, in the Middle East as elsewhere, a generalized resentment against the West. Colonialism created the state system in the Middle East after 1918, but it also left behind a set of unresolved issues that have bred conflict and a kind of rancour, towards the USA and others, ever since. These issues include the Palestine question, the Kurdish issue and the status of Kuwait, and indeed the very sense of thwarted relations with the outside world. As no claim was made for responsibility in the US attacks no one can be sure what the exact significance, if any, of 11 September was, but in a broader framework it is a date that resonates in three ways: as an echo of 'Black September', in Arabic *Aylul al-aswad*, the 17 September 1970 attack by King Hussein of Jordan on the Palestinian forces in his country; as a throwback to the day in 1683 when, it is said by some, the Ottoman armies were defeated at the gates of Vienna; and as the date on which, in 1973, in one of the most signal crimes of the cold war, one abetted by the USA in aftermath if not in origin, General Pinochet launched his bloody coup against the elected Popular Unity government in Chile. One may doubt if the last of these, far from the Islamic world, or the second, an obscure date in Ottoman history, meant anything to the hijackers of the US east coast. But these resonances do suggest that the event has to be seen in a broader contest of conflict between the developed and non-European worlds. If nothing else, for the first time in five hundred years of European and 'Northern' interaction with the South, the latter had struck in significant degree against the territory, cities and hegemonic symbols of the dominant state. That this took place in a way that was itself criminal and destructive boded no good for the majority of the world's population. That in the statements of al-Qa'ida it confined its appeals to one portion only of the non-European world and was indeed racist towards non-Muslims in general, and Jews in particular, was itself part of the crime. Colonialism, the long arc of centuries of Western interaction with the rest of the world, is of limited relevance.

The age of colonialism (roughly 1870–1945) was succeeded by that of the cold war (1945–90). Some commentators suggested that 11 September marked the real end of the cold war in that it marked the start of a new global conflict replacing that of the post-1945 era. For others, the conflict between the West and the Islamic world was itself a new cold war, a new global rivalry replacing the old. It is tempting to recall here that the first, original and probably forgotten usage of the term 'cold war' was indeed in regard to the conflict between Christianity and Islam in Spain, in the writings of the Castillian author Don Juan Mañuel (1282–1348): 'War that is very strong and very hot ends either with death or peace, whereas cold war neither brings peace nor brings honour to the one who makes it.'[1] But these invocations of total war are flawed. The latter – 'Islam'– Western relations as cold war – is mistaken: the contemporary conflict with some Muslim states and with most Muslim opinion is not a global conflict at all, as was the cold war, not least because 'Islam' does not in any way appeal to the populations of the developed Western states and lacks strategic military or economic potential. The former – 'Islam–West' as substitute for the cold war – is misleading in that the rise of the fundamentalist groups is not subsequent to, but an integral result of the cold war itself.

The cold war indeed contributed to this crisis and in particular to the destruction of Afghanistan from 1978 onwards, but in a way that should give comfort to few. One can here suggest a 'two dustbins theory' of cold war legacy: if the Soviet system has left a mass of uncontrolled nuclear, chemical and biological weapons and unresolved ethnic problems, the West has bequeathed a bevy of murderous gangs, from the National Union for the Total Independence of Angola (UNITA) and Cuban exiles in the Caribbean and Miami to the *mujahidin* in Afghanistan, who are now on the rampage. There is an intimate relation between the rise of the armed Islamists and the crushing of the Left in the cold war.

In two countries in particular, the transnational Islamist militias associated with bin Laden were used first not against the West, but against the local forces of the left, the PDPA in Afghanistan and the YSP in Yemen, both ruling pro-Soviet forces brought down in the early 1950s by their enemies. The People's Democratic Party of Afghanistan (PDPA) took power in 1978 and fell, after the withdrawal of Soviet aid, in 1992; the Yemeni Socialist Party (YSP) ruled in the South Yemen from 1967 to 1990 and was defeated in the 1994 civil war.

Here of course there has been another striking example of the denial of responsibility that is so pervasive in the wake of 11 September. This denial is found in East and West: the leaders and intellectuals of the Arab world and, more broadly, of the Islamic world have been criticized, rightly, for a failure to counter the half-arguments and demagogy of the Islamists. Their failure is one that stretches back before 11 September and was indeed a contributory factor to it, as it has been to the confused arguments thereafter. But there is a striking Western responsibility here too, for stoking up Islamist movements in the cold war period and in helping to promote the kinds of autonomous terrorism that culminated in the Taliban and in al-Qa'ida. Much is made, after 11 September, of the West's culpability in abandoning Afghanistan. It is said that after the cold war, the West 'abandoned' Afghanistan. Here there is much validity, but with two corrections. First, it was not the West or the East that sparked the explosion of Afghan society in the late 1970s: it was Afghans themselves. The conflict began, and will end, as an Afghan civil war. In so far as this is the case, part of the responsibility must lie with the Afghan communists, particularly the dominant *Khalqi* faction of the PDPA who ruled after April 1978 and who did so much to provoke Afghan society. Afghanistan was an example even more extreme than anything seen in Iran, Algeria, Egypt or Turkey of a revolt against the modernizing secular state.

Secondly, it was not abandonment by the West in 1989 but three other things that played a decisive role in the subsequent violence. One was the decision, taken soon after the PDPA came to power in 1978 and reinforced after the Soviet forces went in in 1979, to arm and finance the *mujahidin*. It would have been much wiser to allow the reformist–communist regime to stay in power. This was followed by a catastrophic decision, taken by the USA in 1988, to sabotage the international agreement associated with the Soviet withdrawal of forces. For eight years the UN Secretary-General had worked, along with diplomats from other countries, to get a negotiated withdrawal by the USSR. In the end, in Geneva 1988, the USSR agreed, but on condition that the West and Pakistan stop arming the *mujahidin*: Article II of the agreement signed in Geneva stipulated just that. But from the very day of the signing, the Reagan administration broke the agreement and continued its policy of promoting the *mujahidin*. This illegal decision, taken as part of the USA's global cold war strategy, was the root of the subsequent chaos and fighting, which led to the triumph of the Islamist guerrillas in 1992. The third fateful decision taken by Pakistan and Saudi Arabia and, at least to some degree, condoned by the West, was to create the Taliban and support their drive to power in 1994–96. The first two of these three policies were direct products of the cold war.

The West Asian crisis

So much for the long-term causes – colonialism and the cold war – of 11 September 2001. The conjunctural causes are to be found in the formation of what may be termed a new integrated West Asian crisis. The necessarily imperfect term 'West Asia' is used to denote an area that, in addition to the countries of the Arab world and Iran, also covers Afghanistan and Pakistan. There has, in several countries, been a weakening, if not collapse, of the state, in the 1970s and 1980s in Lebanon, more recently in Afghanistan and Yemen. It is in these countries, where significant areas are free of government control or where the government seeks to conciliate autonomous armed groups such as al-Qa'ida, that a culture of violence and religious demagogy has thrived.

This crisis has three general features: the first is the new pattern of linkages between hitherto separate conflicts, the second is the crisis of the state in this region and the third is the emergence of a new, transnational and fundamentalist Islamism. A central confusion concerns the interrelationship between the different centres of conflicts. It is common in Western parlance to talk of 'the Middle East' problem, or crisis, meaning by this the Arab–Israeli question. This is mirrored in some Middle Eastern rhetoric. In parallel vein, nearly all Arab opinion attributes a pervasive, if not determining, role in the modern history of the region to the establishment of the state of Israel. Israel, for its part, looks at the policies of other states, in the current context most obviously Iran, solely in terms of the Arab–Israeli conflict. No one who studies the history of the region can doubt that, since the end of World War I, there *has* been some connection between the different conflicts and movements in the region: you cannot write the history of Arab nationalism without including the role of Palestine. You cannot assess US strategy in the region as a whole without taking its relationship with Israel into account, as was, indeed, the case with France, until the 1960s Israel's closest ally. We see now, in rising Arab anger with the USA over Palestine, combined with growing sympathy for Iraq, another such interconnection. In this sense, Saddam Hussein was and is right when he talks of 'linkage' between the two areas of conflict, Palestine and the Gulf. It was indeed recognition of the truth of Saddam's claim that jolted the Republican administration of 1991, Secretary of State James Baker in particular, into pushing forward with Arab–Israeli negotiations at Madrid in 1991.

But this claim of linkage should not be taken too far. Saddam uses it for calculated reasons, to paint himself as a champion of the Palestinian cause, something he never was, and to distract attention from his gross violations of human rights at home and acts of aggression against his neighbours. The Middle East consists of over two dozen states, with very different problems and capabilities, and cannot be reduced to one single conflict, whatever the connections between these may be. Israel played no significant role in the Iran–Iraq war of 1980–88 or the Iraqi occupation of Kuwait. The denial of rights to the six million Palestinians has very different causes from the denial of the rights of the thirty million or more Kurds. The conflict in Lebanon that exploded in 1975, for all that it was inflamed by Israelis, Syrians and Palestinians, was rooted in the shifting relations between Lebanese communities themselves: the rise of the Shi'ite militia Hizbullah, for example, was a response to Israeli *and* Palestinian intrusions, but also the outcome of changing demographic and social balances within Lebanon and the desire of the Shi'ites for greater recognition in that country. Another constant of Middle Eastern politics and external concerns is the price of oil, which is determined by many factors, some to do with the global economy, some with climate, some speculative, some political. The oil price, from, say 1970 to 2000, has little to do with Palestine or, for that matter, Afghanistan: the 1973 oil price rise used the October Arab–Israeli war to take advantage of market conditions. Interconnections have to be recognized, but it is better to avoid simplistic reductions of one conflict to the other, whatever friends and interlocutors in the region tell us. The Arabs cannot blame everything on Israel, the Israelis should not seek to analyse Iran's defence policies uniquely through their own security interests. But that they do so is part of the reality of the region.

This rhetorical linkage is compounded by something new and central to 11 September 2001 and its aftermath, the way in which the historically distinct conflicts of Afghanistan, Iraq and Palestine have in recent years come to be more and more connected. Militants in each, secular nationalist (Saddam) as well as Islamist (Osama bin Laden), portray the cause of resistance to the West and its regional allies in the Muslim world as one. They also, most importantly, see an opportunity in connecting these crises to mobilize support in pursuit of their major goal, retaining, or taking control of their own countries. Two or three decades ago the connections were much weaker, even between Palestine and the Gulf. Now these two epicentres are tied, with extension to Bosnia in the north-west and Afghanistan and Kashmir to the east and south. This is the new, rhetorical and militarized political geography of the new greater West Asian crisis.

The state: present and absent

This West Asian crisis developed, however, in a context not only of conflict within West Asian regional states and between them and the West, but also of a crisis of the state itself. Indeed, in three significant ways, the institution that lay and will continue to live at the heart of this crisis was the state. In the first place, the goal of the fundamentalist and militant movements that have ravaged West Asia in recent years is not religious, in the sense of faith, nor cultural, in the sense of values, but political: it is to take power from those who control the states and, once they have power, to hold on to it. This is a goal that is shared with secular guerrilla movements that exist in the Middle East and elsewhere: the aim of the Palestine Liberation Organization (PLO), as of the Kurdish Workers' Party (PKK) and of nationalists guerrillas in Ireland or Spain, is to take political power. This link between fundamentalism and the state is examined in greater detail in Chapter 3. The main target of 11 September is not US power or a somewhat carelessly defined 'civilized' or 'democratic' world, but the states of the Middle East themselves. Osama bin Laden, with his regressive social and political ideals, particularly hostile to women and Shi'ite Muslims, is above all a threat to them. Suffice it to say that it is this goal, a clear political one, that determines what fundamentalists, including al-Qa'ida and others, do. This is the logic and the strategic function of 11 September: bin Laden's denunciation in his 7 October statement of *hypocrite* regimes speaks to this. The term 'hypocrite', *munafiq*, is a Quranic term used by Islamists to denote those who appear to back the national cause but do not.

Secondly, the rise of fundamentalism itself is intimately related to the character of states. In some countries, such as Iran, Algeria, Egypt, Turkey, fundamentalism has taken the form of a revolt against the state. Here a relatively strong modernizing state has been challenged by movements of social and political opposition. In one case, Iran, they succeeded, elsewhere they did not. However, in some other countries, where the state was much weaker, a different pattern was followed. Herein lies one of the specific characteristics of the al-Qa'ida organization: it has arisen and been sustained in countries with very weak states. Colonialism, significantly, did not touch some of the countries in the region and it is here that no effective modern state was ever created: Afghanistan and the larger northern part of Yemen are two such examples. In such cases it was not revolt against a modernizing state but rather the historical *absence* of a state that provided the context for modern wars and for the growth of transnational armed militias. The fundamentalists, armed and financed from other states, were able to establish themselves in these countries and, most significantly, to form alliances with the weak states at the centre. The latter could not control the countryside or the fundamentalists, but did deals with them and used them in their struggle against other, rival forces and especially against the Left. In Afghanistan, the Taliban used al-Qa'ida against the Northern Alliance, as the fundamentalists were earlier used against the ruling communists. In Yemen the regime of President Ali Abdullah Salih used the Islamist militia against the Yemeni Socialist Party in the conflicts of 1990–94: it was these same elements, tied into the ruling elite by allegiance and marriage, that were later to attack foreign tourists in January 1999 and blow up the USS *Cole* in Aden harbour in October 2000.

The state is, however, central in another and most controversial dimension, namely the organization of the terrorist groups themselves. It is easy, too easy, when faced with any terrorist group to claim with certainty that it is acting at the behest of, as the agent of, a foreign power: this may be but a way of avoiding discussion of the causes that led to the outbreak of this violence in the first place. For their part, terrorist groups seek to conceal the degree of support that they do get from states, in finance, training and operation. In the absence of evidence this question must, therefore, remain an open one. The record of terrorism in the Middle East in recent years suggests, however, that in many cases the degree of state involvement in acts of violence by apparently independent or underground groups is greater than at first sight appears: not all, but many, terrorist groups have received support from states, even if these groups originated in an autonomous manner. Thus the opponents of the regimes in Iran and Iraq sought support from other states; the PKK in Turkey got support, in varying intensities, in Syria, Armenia and Greece; the factions in Lebanon sought aid from, depending on their orientation, Israel, Iran and Turkey. Al-Qa'ida began life as the ally of the opposition fighters in Afghanistan: but, like the latter, it received support from two regional states, Pakistan and Saudi Arabia. Once the Taliban came to power in Afghanistan, in 1996, they formed a close alliance with al-Qa'ida. Indeed, it would appear that, as the Taliban themselves lacked sufficient financial and military support, they found in al-Qa'ida an ally of considerable importance, military and organizational, in sustaining themselves in power. For all the appearance of being independent of states, those responsible for the events of 11 September and their antecedents were closely associated with at least one state, and were indeed participants in its consolidation.

States will remain central to this conflict. The outcome of the conflict resulting on 11 September will be decided by states and by their ability to survive and sustain this conflict. The gravest impact of the anthrax attacks in the USA in October 2001 was that they challenged the central claim of the state to authority, its ability to protect its citizens. There is no doubt as to the ability of the Western states, at whatever price, to survive this conflict. Whatever the cost or duration, this is the intention and the capability of the USA and its allies. Less certain is the outcome in a number of Arab and Muslim states involved in the crisis: Pakistan, Saudi Arabia, Yemen may all be affected by upheaval from within, if not immediately, then over months and years. Here the time-frame could be a long one. 11 September was an earthquake, which weakened the structure of many states: they may not fall immediately or at all, but their propensity to be overthrown is that much greater. An analogy suggests itself with 1948, the first Arab–Israeli war: the Arab world lost that war and its regimes survived. But over time the shocks of 1948–49 hit Arab states, as the discrediting of regimes and the rise of a more militant nationalism challenged established rulers: most spectacularly in Syria in 1949, in Egypt in 1952 and in Iraq in 1958. The Bolshevik revolution of 1917 found no immediate successors: these were to come three decades later in the outcome and longer-run impact of World War II. The last case of pro-Soviet communists coming to power was in 1978 in Afghanistan. The timescale for assessing the aftermath of 11 September in West Asia is not the weeks or months of military action, but the years of political and social tension that may follow.

Transnationalism and Islamist violence

This brings us to the third conjunctural cause. Mention has already been made of the political purpose that underlies the Islamist project. Yet this alone cannot explain the form, or strategy, of the movement that attacked the USA in September 2001. As will be discussed in Chapter 2, Islamism – a political current within the Middle East and elsewhere, that aims to establish a state and society based on religious principles – goes back at least to the 1920s. It is a response to the modern challenges faced by these societies: colonial domination, the rise of mass parties of a secular character, be they nationalist or communist, and the moves by modernizing states, starting with Turkey and Iran, to introduce a secular realm of law, education and politics. In the post-1945 period, the 1950s and 1960s, such movements received encouragement from the cold war, but it was the Iranian revolution of 1979 – which for the first time brought an Islamist movement to power – that gave the movement a new impulsion.

Iran was, however, to mark both the triumph and also the limits of such movements. In the short run Khomeini's triumph of promoted similar movements elsewhere, be they in Sunni countries, such as Egypt and Saudi Arabia, or amongst Shi'ites, in Afghanistan and Lebanon. Iran itself sought to promote the export of its revolution, to three countries in particular: Iraq, Afghanistan and Lebanon. In the first, despite an eight-year war, it failed. In the second, its followers were much weaker than the Sunni groups supported by Pakistan, whom

Khomeini used to refer to with the derisory term *Islam-i amrikai*, 'American Islam'. Only in Lebanon did Hizbullah have some success, as the leading opponents of the Israeli occupation forces in the south. However, in Lebanon as in many other countries of the region, the Shi'ites made up only a part of the population; therefore, Hizbullah became a political and military force within a broader Lebanese framework. When the Israelis pulled out in July 2000 its military campaign halted.

The Iranian revolution did not, therefore, spread to other countries; as time went by, the experience of the Iranian people themselves led to a questioning within that country of the very purpose and cost of revolution. Elsewhere, Islamist movements became more prominent, but at the cost of resorting more and more to violence, rather than to the popular mobilization and Islamist programme that had marked Iran. In Algeria and Afghanistan the very *raison d'être* of these movements took an increasingly virulent form: divorced from any established institutions or leaderships, basing themselves ever more on terror, this second generation of Islamists became a force without strategy or limit, caught in a cycle of violence. They also came to resort to violence not only against their secular opponents, but against those of other Muslim communities, notably the Shi'ites. In the Arabian Peninsula this took the form of anti-Shi'ite rhetoric and discrimination, in Afghanistan and Pakistan it resulted in massacres of Shi'ites by fundamentalist Sunni groups.[2]

Herein lies the background to the emergence of the particular brand of militarized Islamism espoused by the Taliban and al-Qa'ida. In terms of the greater west Asian crisis, this represents the fusion, in a form never seen before, of movements based in the Arab world, and those influenced by South Asian Islamism. There had been links between these two parts of the Muslim world before, as in the influence upon Egyptian thinkers like Sayyid Qutb by the Pakistani Islamist al-Mawdudi. However, the fundamentalism of the Arabs and the Afghans was initially different: the former were descendants of the austere Islam promoted in the eighteenth century by the Wahhabi movement, brought to power with the creation of Saudi Arabia in 1926; the latter were influenced by a conservative strand of Indian Islam, called Deobandi, after the town in which the anti-liberal strand had its training school. The Deobandis were initially weak in Afghanistan, but through a Pakistani group that promoted their ideas, *Jamiat-ul Ulema-i Pakistan*, they came to have significant influence over young Afghans, especially those in the refugee camps of Pakistan. A climate of militant fundamentalism amongst these young men, living in *madrasas* or religious schools from an early age, without contact with family or women, bred the recruits for what was to become the Taliban.

The recruitment of Arabs to fight the Soviet forces in Afghanistan, tied these militants to the networks of Pakistani politics and created a new explosive organizational mixture. By the time of the collapse of the PDPA regime in 1992, large numbers of Arab militants were in Afghanistan, linked to the conservative forces there and the Deobandi networks in Pakistan. The creation of the Taliban in 1994, by Pakistani intelligence services working with Saudi funds, provided a framework for the Arabs to find an ally, in taking power in Afghanistan and working to do so elsewhere.[3] Three elements therefore came together: a reassertion of the most traditional strands in Islamic thinking, a brutalization and militarization of the Islamist groups themselves, and a free-floating transnational army of fighters drawing support from Pakistan, the Arab world, south-east Asia and Chechnya with its base in Afghanistan. In the context of the greater west Asian crisis, and the revolt against the states of the region, as well as their western backers, there now emerged an organised and militant challenge.

Analytic issues: culture, violence, USA

Cultural clash

Thus three issues – the greater West Asian crisis, the conflicts besetting states, the emergence of a harsher transnational Islamism – lie at the core of this new global imbroglio. Working out how these forces have interacted and will interact is hard enough. But, as will be examined in greater detail in Chapter 12, in addition to the crisis of history mentioned above, discussion is made more confined by invocations of culture, by talk of a 'clash of civilizations' and of an incompatibility of Western and Islamic values. This worldview is not just a product of Western hostility to the Muslim world, or some stigma imposed by the 'West' on Muslims: there are some, too many, be it said, in the Muslim world and in the Muslim community in Western Europe who also espouse this demagogy and who have been quick to respond in such vein to the events of 11 September. They welcome facile analyses even more than many nationalists in the West, yet the argument will not be settled, nor these events explained, by invoking cultural clashes or by trawling around

45

in holy texts for quotes for and against violence and resistance. All religions have, if people chose to dig them out, texts and precedents that legitimate violence, terror and senseless sacrifice by individuals. In Judaism and Christianity, the Book of Deuteronomy and Judges, in the Quran, *Surat al-anfal* and *Surat al-tawba*. This is why the well-intentioned project of recent years, backed by many in the West and the Muslim world, of 'dialogue' between faiths and civilizations is insufficient. Coexistence is better than war, but as soon as you admit the fundamental difference and legitimacy of cultures, and implicitly of those, usually bearded old men, who interpret them, you are caught in a spider's web. To this issue I shall turn in Chapter 4. The normative framework for dealing with these issues, of conflict between states and of differences within them, need not be cultural or civilizational at all, but universal, being based on international law and the principles of the UN. This makes no distinction between 'Western' and other peoples and eschews the kind of exclusive language to which too many politicians and clergymen resorted in the aftermath of 11 September.

The politics and the use of violence, culture and text, are contingent instruments, not causes. When they wish to do so, people of all cultures can resort to and justify atrocities. This is why the instrument of terrorism has been used in modern times by, among others, Fenian Catholics, Hindu assassins, Zionist gunmen, Buddhist fanatics and Islamist militants. They were not guided by texts. They were guided by other, extra-textual concerns, to find what they wanted in the texts. The confused, rhetorical invocation of cultural clash is found on both sides. It takes two to have a 'clash of civilizations'[4] and there are those on both sides who are using the present conflict to promote it. Samuel Huntington's theory rests on two propositions that are not trivial, but are not about cultural clash: the inevitability of inter-state conflict and the need for the USA to promote its own cultural values. This theory misses, however, the most important cause of the events of 11 September, which will also define the consequences in the Muslim world of what is to come, namely, the enormous, long and very violent clash *within* the Muslim world between those who want to reform and secularize and those whose power is threatened or who want to take power in the name of fundamentalism. It is not, as Huntington asserts, that Islam has 'bloody frontiers': those of Hinduism, Zionism, secular nationalism are no better. It is rather that within Muslim societies a war has been in train for decades, and found on 11 September a dramatic transnational expression. This internal war has been the basis of the conflicts going on these past decades in Pakistan, Iran, Egypt, Turkey and, most violently of all, Afghanistan. Religious fundamentalism in all societies has, as we have seen, one goal; this goes for the *haredim* in Israel, the ranting Bible-thumpers of America, Islamic fundamentalists in the Middle East and Hindu chauvinists in India. The goal is not to convert other people to their beliefs, but to seize power, political, social and gendered, within their own societies. Their greatest foe is secularism: this is the internal clash that led to the World Trade Center atrocity.

Violence and terror

These events highlight questions of history, causation, the state and culture. They also draw attention to the issue of violence and its related phenomenon, 'terrorism'. Here two prevalent and dangerous discourses seem to be in play. On the one hand, the perpetrators of 11 September and other acts of sudden violence against civilians hold to the view that extreme, indeed any violence is justified in pursuit of a political goal. This fulfils two political goals of terrorism – to demoralize the enemy and to mobilize supporters. On the other hand, many states in the world, in the Middle East and elsewhere, such as the Russians in Chechnya, hold to the view that extreme violence is justified in defence of their state. There are shades of such a discourse in statements that have come out of the USA in the aftermath of 11 September.

This approach to terrorism is confused and unnecessary: it presupposes an opportunist definition. These are not questions of arbitrary definition: the USA has to face its own violation of international norms. The denunciation of 11 September by George Bush opens up the discussion of other groups that he and his predecessors may have supported (the Afghan *mujahidin*, the Nicaraguan *contras*, more recently the rebels in southern Sudan), who certainly committed acts of terror and whom many also see as terrorists. The opportunist approach is not, however, confined to states. The Left, for its part, has long been too insouciant on this issue.

There are legitimate rules of force that apply to opponents of states and to states alike. Certainly, all cultures and all states accept the principle of just resistance to oppression. In his defence before the court after the failed attack on the Moncada barracks in Cuba in 1953, *History Will Absolve Me*, Fidel Castro listed a long line of Western theologians and thinkers who had justified resistance, from

John Salisbury, Thomas Aquinas and Martin Luther to the US Declaration of Independence. All cultures equally allow, as does Article 51of the UN Charter, for self-defence by states. But states are the greatest perpetrators of violence and terror. It should not be forgotten that the word 'terrorism' began life not as applied to the tactics of rebels, but as an arm of state policy, in the French and Russian revolutions. The Bolshevik leader, Trotsky, had some sensible things to say about the folly of terrorism from below, but justified terror by the revolutionary state.

There are, however, broad principles, some enshrined in historic discussions, some in international law, including the Geneva conventions and its protocols, which provide a basis for discussion of this issue. They limit the violence that dissidents and states can legitimately use. Here there is, whatever demagogues of East and West may say, no barrier between Western or international codes and those of the Muslim world. All religions contain passages that can be cited to justify terrorism and barbaric acts in war. But for those who want to use or find them, there are also principles of constraint. The Islamic tradition has a concept of 'legitimate' or 'just' war, *al-harb al-mashru'a* or *al-harb al-'adila*, just as Christianity has its concept of 'just' war. In contemporary Arabic there is a clear distinction between struggle that is legitimate, *jihad*, and that which is aggressive, illegitimate or motivated by robbery, *ghazu* or *'adwan*. The Quran (e.g. *suras* 9:13 and 22:40) contains legitimation for going to war, but also warns against the illegitimate use of force. 'Fight in the cause of God those who fight you. But do not transgress limits: for God loves not the aggressors (*mu'adun*).'[5] Similarly, within the Islamic sources, the Quran and the sayings of the Prophet, the Hadith, there is considerable discussion of the conduct of war: on the treatment of women and children, prisoners of war, the degree of force that is legitimate. These principles, framed in different historical idioms, now overlain by international law and convention, take terrorism out of the realm of the subjective: one person's terrorist *is not* another's freedom fighter.

US policy

Mention has already been made of the supposed cultural clash between the Muslim and Western worlds. There is, however, another cultural issue present, if more inchoate, in the discussions of 11 September, namely, attitudes not towards the East, the Islamic world, but towards the West, the USA. It is this issue, as much as that of relations with the Muslim world, that will underpin events in the aftermath of 11 September and that has underlain debate on every major international crisis of recent years, from Kuwait to Kosovo. The issue of attitudes to the USA was, one may assume, present in the minds of those who attacked New York and Washington on 11 September: they evidently hated the state, the country, the culture, its laws and, above all, its people and all who chose to work in or, as tourists, visit it. Yet more important than the question of attitudes to America in the cause of the attacks is that of their relevance to the response: for the widespread international sense that America either deserved or in some way provoked such an attack is one of the most evident consequences of 11 September.

The USA is a country with a record, at home and abroad, that arouses criticism and indignation, in some cases rightly so: Vietnam, Nicaragua, the neglect of Palestinian rights, Cuba, the grotesque irresponsibility of its gun laws and its media, the insidious role of religion and money in public life, to name but some. Yet such criticism has to be matched, and often is not, by a recognition of what that country means and will mean for the world as a whole. Too much discussion of the USA, in Western Europe as much as elsewhere, is guided by a set of lazy prejudices, condescending in continental Europe, more fetid (in variant left and right variants) in the British case, demagogic and rancorous without proportion in many of the developing countries. This animosity is too rarely marked by an informed or measured assessment of that society.

For all its faults, the USA is, to date, the most prosperous country in human history, the one to which many people, possibly half of the world, would like to emigrate and work, whose vitality in a range of fields, from music to medicine, outstrips all others. It must be doing something right. It has in regard to many issues, gender and immigration among them, a record that puts most of Western Europe to shame. Much is made, especially in recent days, of American militarism and belligerency: this is, the discourse of cowboy culture aside, a myth. No other major country has a record as cautious and restrained as the USA: it had to be dragged into World War in 1941, as it was dragged into Bosnia in 1995. The USA fought these wars in the 1990s – Kuwait 1991, Bosnia 1995, Kosovo 1999 – all in response to aggression against Muslim people. Sneering at American aggressiveness comes strangely from other countries given their record in modern times: Britain and France, who trampled over half of Asia and Africa, Russia and China, not to mention Germany, Italy and Japan.

This denunciation of America is detached from any concrete, informed assessment of US policy in the period since the cold war. Under the Clinton administration, the US record was far from perfect but in a range of issues, from international economic and human rights policy through to specific areas of conflict, it did engage in a constructive manner. Moreover, the idea that all the ills of the world can be blamed on the USA, or on its state or citizens, is simplistic indeed. Indeed one of the widest complaints against the USA is not that it did too much, but that it did too little.

At this point the argument often shifts to something more diffuse, 'globalization'. But this is itself hardly a cause or a legitimation of what occurred on 11 September. As discussed in Chapter 10, globalization is a complex process, in some ways one that has been in train for decades if not centuries, and can hardly be attributed to the recent policies of any state. The resentment at globalization comes on top of the experience of colonialism and the cold war. It need hardly be added, moreover, that the actions and associated statements of those involved in the New York attack bore little connection with the cause of the world's poor: the organizers and the leadership of al-Qaʻida came in large measure from a country, Saudi Arabia, that had for three decades profited, with no second thoughts, from squeezing the economies of developing countries by overpricing oil. Their own statements (see Appendices) were masterpieces of prejudice and particularism, confined in their appeal as they were to members of a faith that amounts at most to a fifth of the world's population and denouncing all others, including, presumably, most of the population of Latin America, Africa, South Asia and East Asia as infidels. The anti-imperialism of racists and murderers is a perverse programme.

What 11 September means, and will mean, is as yet obscure. That it is a decisive, confusing and frightening moment in world history, is not. The analysis of this chapter is one, provisional, attempt to explain what happened, and to address some of the questions involved. The chapters that follow are contributions to an elucidation of some of the underlying issues.

2
Fundamentalism and Political Power

Introduction

Even if we live outside societies that are ruled by, or significantly affected by, fundamentalist movements, the rise of fundamentalism nonetheless poses difficult questions, both for foreign policy and for ethical evaluation. Indeed, one of the things I would like to suggest here is that if our political responses have been uncertain, many of the moral ones have been even more so. Fundamentalism promises to make a major impact on the world in the years to come and will almost certainly not soon go away or subside. We could do worse than to begin now to engage in a more searching discussion of this phenomenon and recognize how far we are not prepared for it. The fundamentalists have a rather clear and determined view of what they are about. It is time for those of us who are not fundamentalists to produce a response that is equally clear and indeed determined. Whatever else, this is a phenomenon that should not be underestimated.

My discussion of 'fundamentalism' therefore aims to examine, in a critical vein and from the perspective of a secular, democratic and rational position, a major political phenomenon of our times: fundamentalism requires understanding but also poses challenges to the peace and freedom of many societies. The issues raised here are ones with which Charles Darwin at least would be familiar, and I trust that he would respect the tone in which this talk is given. Indeed, the very term 'fundamentalism' is one that originated partly as a response to his work. If the reaction was in particular to the discovery of the origin and evolution of species, it was more generally to the claim of natural science and critical thought to reinterpret and indeed challenge holy Scripture. That battle, which exploded in the 1920s within the USA and which has given us today's term 'fundamentalism', with its associated doctrine of creationism, is still with us. This conflict endures both in its particular form, *vis-à-vis* the origins of the human race, but also *vis-à-vis* the broader intellectual issues at stake.

It is from this perspective that I wish to approach the question of what is termed 'fundamentalism'. I want to offer some thoughts on why and how this phenomenon is so important in the modern world, but also to stress its contemporaneity in two other respects. One is to argue that, for all their invocation of tradition and their calls for a return to some past, fundamentalisms are responses to the contemporary world and are, to a considerable extent, framed in terms of contemporary ideas and concerns. Secondly, I want to examine some of the ways in which the contemporary world that we inhabit, in Western Europe, may respond, indeed, needs to respond to this phenomenon, and some of the political and moral choices that fundamentalism poses. We have come, belatedly, to recognize, in regard to culture, religion and ethnicity, the need and right to a 'politics of difference'; but this right to difference must apply as much *within* as *between* cultures, religions and ethnic communities.

The rise of fundamentalism: programme and explanation

When we talk of fundamentalism in the contemporary world, we refer to a range of movements in different countries that share certain common characteristics and that are, in particular, characterized by a combination of two elements, of no necessary relation to each other but that are, in the case of fundamentalisms, contingently if repeatedly linked. One is the invocation of a return to holy texts, read in a literal way; the other is the call for these doctrines to be applied to social and political life. These two elements are present in fundamentalism and distinguish it both from other movements of authoritarian politics and from cases where, in a non-fundamentalist or non-literalist way, movements seek to apply religious doctrines to politics (as in the influence of Catholicism on Polish and Irish nationalism or the radical Church in Latin America). This rough definition has wide applications: we may think first of the Islamic movement in Iran, which came to power in 1979 and which has ruled the country ever since. But we may also think of fundamentalist movements in other Muslim countries, in Egypt and Algeria in particular, which similarly seek to establish what they term an Islamic state. They do not refer to themselves as 'fundamentalists' although the Arabic translation of the term, *usuliyya*, is used in political language today, along with other terms, notably *mujahidin* (fighters for *jihad*), by those who support them, or *mutatarrifin* (extremists), by those who do not. In the case of Islamic movements, the French *intégriste* (originally a Catholic term, now suggesting a claim to legislate for all social activity) and the English term Islamist (denoting the application of Islam to politics) are at least equally appropriate. But even if much of the emphasis has been on the Islamic world, the term 'fundamentalist' has been applied much more broadly. It encompasses the strain already mentioned in Christianity of Protestant evangelical sects, which emerged in the 1920s and called for a return to a literalist reading of the Bible. Like any term, 'fundamentalist' may be partly understood by looking at its opposite, in this case Christian 'modernist', i.e. with regard to the reading of the holy texts.

In the third of the great monotheistic religions, Judaism, there are also trends that are conventionally categorized as fundamentalist, involving to some degree a combination of scriptural loyalty and socio-political programme that is comparable with but not identical to those of their associates in Islam and Christianity. This is most evident among parties of the religious Right in Israel, the *haredim* (ultra-orthodox, literally 'anxious', hence 'observant'), and also among the newer religious militants, notably Gush Emunim and others: in varying ways they seek to extend the authority of Judaic law within Israel and to establish a state based on the appropriate legal texts, in this case the Halakha.

Yet if fundamentalism is in origin very much a product of the monotheistic religions, not least because it is they who have the clearest idea of a holy writ to which to return, it is not peculiar to them. In India there has emerged over the past two decades a strong

Hindu fundamentalism, which seeks to establish Hindutva, a Hindu state, and Ramraja, a state based on the teachings of the god Ram. The declared aim is to revive the holy state of Bharat, which has for centuries been defiled by the enemies of Bharat – Muslims, Jews, Sikhs and, rather in last place, the British. Nor has Buddhism been immune to such phenomena, as the politics of Sri Lanka for one have shown.

As with any political term – communism, fascism, populism, nationalism – we are not dealing here with a single object; these movements are not similar in all respects. Indeed, beyond the theological differences with which they define themselves, there are major differences between them, in content, context and goal. Christianity, for example, has far less to say about matters of personal hygiene and diet than have Judaism, Islam or Hinduism. The scope of holy law is also very different, the Torah and the Shari'a having more to say than Canon Law. Christianity and Islam have centuries of political power and, indeed, imperial conquest to invoke, whereas Judaism has never enjoyed such temporal success. In some contexts, it is the clergy who play a leading role – this is true for Judaism, Protestantism and Iranian Shi'ite Islam. In others it is very much a lay leadership, indeed, a political leadership invoking religion, that has come to the fore, as in the Islamist movements of North Africa and in the Hindu movements. Needless to say, the protagonists of all of these movements would take strong objection to any comparisons between their own, supposedly unique return to 'true' values and the fanaticism of others.

In that sense, the issue of comparison depends to some extent on the questions being asked; yet since we are looking at these movements as social and political movements in the contemporary world it is valid to stress some of their shared characteristics. Here I would mention four. In the first place, all these movements seek to derive their authority from a call for the return to holy texts, to writings allegedly derived from god. This is, in its literal sense, the meaning of the term 'fundamentalism'. For Christians, Jews and Muslims these texts are clear enough – the Bible, the Torah and Talmud, the Quran, Hadith and *fiqh* or legal texts. For Hindus who lack such a text and indeed lack a monotheistic god, the job has been more difficult but is now in hand: for what is taking place in Hinduism is a reform designed to make it more like the monotheistic religions – a single god, Ram, whose hitherto androgynous sexual identity has been masculinized, a set of holy texts, the Ram legends, congregational worship and, an essential part of the mono-theistic concept of a proper religion, the subjugation of women. The argument of all these movements is that these texts provide in themselves the basis for defining a proper life and, what is most pertinent in present circumstances, for defining the way society and the state should be organized. Yet what in practice occurs is a read-ing, by contemporary authorities and for contemporary uses, of these texts. Hence the endless debates about interpretation, or what in Islam is called *tafsir*, as if renewed erudition and authority can somehow tell us what these texts 'truly' or authentically enjoin about the position of women, the correct form of government, what to eat or drink, and when the world will come to an end or when it began.

The second, related feature of this resort to 'fundamentals' is the claim that within them the constitution of a perfect state for the contemporary world can be identified. Muslim fundamental-ists make much of the Shari'a, despite the fact that Shari'a, in the conventional sense of legal prescriptions contained in the Quran, amounts to only about 80 verses out of 6,000 and covers only a few topics of potential legislation: the term itself, literally 'the right way', is mentioned but a few times. The invocation by Muslims of the early Islamic government of the Prophet is equally forced: even assuming that a system of government that evolved for seventh-century Arabian cities was appropriate for today, one would have to ask how valid it was, given that three of Muhammad's four ini-tial successors died unconstitutional, violent deaths. The Judaic invocation of the biblical past is little more substantial: the king-doms of Saul, David and Solomon lasted for around 80 years in all, before giving way to the wars between Israel and Judaea. This is hardly the historical authority needed to claim a territory in perpe-tuity or a sufficient basis on which to legitimate a state re-established over two thousand years later.

The third common feature of these movements is that, for all their apparent otherwordliness, they aspire to one thing above all, namely political and social power. In the case of Judaism it is not clear how far the *haredim* aspire to control the state directly: but through their participation in the political arena, through using the proportional representation system, parties and other activity, they seek to extend the control of rabbinical power across much of society, just as Gush Emunim seek to make a stand on certain key issues, notably land. In the case of the other three – Christianity,

Islam, Hinduism – this political claim is much clearer: they are not movements of conversion nor movements of theological innovation, but movements that aim to win power, through elections, force or insurrection, and to establish appropriate states. Fundamentalism is, in this sense, a means of attaining and, once attained, maintaining political power: it is, of course, for this reason above all that it is of concern to all of us.

This brings me to the final shared dimension of these movements, namely their intolerance and, to a considerable extent, their anti-democratic character. For although they claim to speak in the name of the people and to pursue their goals through democratic means, they are, by ideology and by organization, authoritarian and potentially dictatorial political groups. They reject the premises of democratic politics, including tolerance and individual rights, and claim an authority that is not derived from the people: it is derived from the will of god, inherent in scripture and interpreted by self-appointed, exclusively male, leaders, whether clerical or not. They all include as an important part of their ideology hostility towards those who are not of their faith and, almost more importantly, towards those of their faith who do not share their particular orientation. All are happy to condemn the rest of us, 'unbelievers' and so on, to gruesome and unending pain. Given the way in which religious identity has become intertwined with ethnicity in the twentieth century, fundamentalist movements have also come to include racist views within their overall ideology – against Jews (on the part of Muslims and Christians), against Arabs (on the part of Jews), against Muslims (on the part of Hindus), etc. In the society they envisage, there is usually some place for those who do not accept their views, but this is at best an ambiguous, subordinate status, and the imposition of social practices advocated by these fundamentalists is regarded as legitimate on all who live in that society. Alongside protestations of tolerance, there is frequently, in their literature, an aggression and contempt for those who are different – whether it be the hatred of Christian fundamentalists for their secular fellow citizens, the diatribes of Islamists against the corruption of the West, the 'conspiracies' of the Jews, the *jahiliyya*, or ignorance, of the contemporary world; or the vitriol that Hindu fundamentalists now pour on Muslims in India, as traitors, illegal immigrants, perpetrators of a historic violation of Bharat and so on; or the hostility of Jewish fundamentalists to assimilators, secular Jews, Christians, Arabs and the like.

All of these movements make a great noise about the aggressiveness and conspiracies of their enemies, and proclaim themselves as victims. But there is often a strong dose of projection in all of this. The Western, Christian and post-Christian world is making much at the moment of how aggressive 'Islam' is and how it threatens the West: but the most elementary study of the history of the world over the past three centuries would suggest that the boot is rather on the other foot, as it remains in many parts of the world. In Bosnia, it has been the anti-Muslims, Serbian Orthodox and Croatian Catholics, who have done most to poison inter-communal relations. But Islamists have their own share of the blame. Islamist rhetoric about Jews is frequently racist. In the response to *The Satanic Verses*, Muslims have recently been exercised about the question of blasphemy; but perhaps all concerned with this issue should study the Quran more carefully, for it tells us that Christ was not the son of god, that he was not crucified and that he did not rise from the dead – all propositions that in the Christian world conventionally constitute forms of blasphemy. In India, the Hindu chauvinists, ranting on about what the Muslims have done to India, have coined their own intolerant rhetoric: '*Musulmanan ke do-hi shtan, Pakistan aur kabristan*' ('For Muslims there are only two places, Pakistan or the grave'). This yard call for the Muslims to be chucked out to Pakistan sits quite easily with the Hindu militant demand that Pakistan be abolished and reincorporated into India. There is also something chillingly disingenuous in the Hindu argument that Muslims are quite free to live in their state provided they accept the cultural, i.e. Hindu-defined, religious character of Bharat and its political system. Everyone accuses the other of fanaticism and extremism, when not of terrorism: all the fundamentalisms mentioned so far demonstrated fair examples of these, in the past and in modern times.

Alternative explanations: scriptural and contingent

If we can now turn to the question of explanation, there are, in broad terms, two possible approaches, what I would term the 'scriptural' and the 'contingent'. By the scriptural I mean those who look at fundamentalisms above all in terms of their relation to holy texts and to the religious arguments that follow from the interpretation and organization of a religious movement. Such an approach may be found within theology, but it also arises in social science debates on the significance and indeed determining influence of religious beliefs in social and political behaviour: Max Weber, for one, had much to say on this. Thus, to examine these movements in terms of the impact of, say, Islamic jurisprudence or an Islamic world view or the Protestant ethic or Jewish or Hindu tradition would be to take this approach. Fundamentalism is, in this approach, to be seen as a return, a revival of something already there, this return being explained by the renewed interest in holy texts, often out of some fear of corruption or innovation within the religious community concerned. In many ways, this scriptural approach to fundamentalism parallels the traditional or perennialist approach to nationalism: the ideas, the doctrine, the past are seen as largely determining the present. Needless to say, this is the explanation of the fundamentalists themselves, all of whom claim that they are returning to a 'true' interpretation and to a past that was always, in some almost archaeological sense, 'there', waiting to be rediscovered. It also follows from this that fundamentalism is not specific to the contemporary world: in addition to the authoritative, original periods and doctrines invoked by fundamentalists, there have throughout the history of the major religions been plenty of movements of return to the scriptures – Wahhabism in Islam and Methodism in Christianity, to name but two.

The alternative approach, which I have termed the 'contingent', emphasizes the modernity and contingency in these movements. First of all, it draws attention to the contemporary causes of these movements, which, though they vary from country to country and religion to religion, are features of the modern world. Thus, fundamentalisms in many developing countries emerge as a reaction against the failures of the modernizing, secular state, which has been perceived as corrupt, unable to solve economic and social problems and often dictatorial. This goes as much for the Shah's Iran as for the FLN in Algeria or the Congress Party in India. Equally, these movements are a response to very real issues confronting these countries – mass urbanization, unemployment, a sense of continued foreign domination. Many arise in countries that have experienced, or continue to experience, foreign domination – they can include elements of nationalism and third-world anti-imperialism. They offer a simple, apparently clear solution to the problems of the modern world. They also arise in a context that is itself one of modernity: the nation state, the modernized state apparatus, the social and legal claims of that state over its citizens. In some cases fundamentalism is associated with social groups that are on the decline, in others with newly formed urban masses, or, in the case of Afghanistan after 1978, with a threatened rural population reacting to the increased claims of the centralizing state. In the case of Israel, fundamentalism, for all that some have questioned the possibility of a Jewish state before the coming of the Messiah, involves a campaign to determine certain policies of this state and to shape the character of its newly constituted immigrant population.

This modernity is evident too in the language and ideology of the fundamentalists. Despite all the invocation of the past and of traditional symbols, the language and policies of fundamentalisms can be seen as a form of contemporary ideology, using traditional or classical themes for contemporary purposes and borrowing eclectically from modern secular ideologies – hence my designation of this approach as the 'contingent' one. The general functions of political ideologies are well known: establishing an identity, who 'we', the people or community, are, and, equally importantly, who 'we' are not; the proffering of a legitimating history, including heroic acts, treacheries and oppressions; a morality of struggle and often of sacrifice; a programme for mobilization and assuming of power; and, as the final stage, the providing of a model for building a new society, within which are a set of principles designed to legitimate the denial of power to those who want to challenge the new order. In the past century or so we have seen many cases of this – liberalism, fascism, communism in their various guises – but perhaps the most appropriate approach, as several writers, among them Sami Zubeida and Ervand Abrahamian, have pointed out, is that of populism. This is a broad, trans-class ideology, stressing the 'virtue' of the people and the corruption, financial and moral, of the oppressors. Equally central to populism is a form of nationalism and hostility to foreigners, defined in a variety of ways, and a fondness for conspiracy theories. Modern secular society and not least its constitutive ideology 'liberalism' are objects of particular scorn. All of this, and more, is to be found in the ideologies of fundamentalism. Such ideologies are, particularly in their Islamic and Hindu varieties, programmes for mobilizing political support, for the conquest and retention of political power. In the case of Judaism and Christianity the emphasis is less on foreign domination and more on the need to fight the dangerous, corrupt, secular elements within their own societies. Yet these two trends also have a very strong nationalist element: Christian and Jewish movements count among the most patriotic, as well as intransigent elements in their own societies, and their adherents, deploying religious righteousness, have been among the strongest proponents of national assertiveness, the use of force, the destruction of their enemies. It is not for nothing that, in contemplating nuclear war, so many American writers during the cold war fell back on the religiously sanctioned idea of Armageddon.

No modern idea or context is more influential than that of the nation and nationalism: what an apparently religious identification signifies is in many cases an ethnic one, a mobilization of religiosity – of idea, worship, dress, identity – in a context of national conflict. This is as true of the Muslims of Palestine and Bosnia as it is of the Hindus in India. Yet it is the national that defines and mobilizes the religious, not the other way around. Indeed, in the Indian case, what we have seen quite clearly from the 1920s onwards, with the founding of the RSS, is the elaboration of a programme, based on European ideas of nationhood, for the creation of a Hindu nation, an Aryan race and culture derived from Sanskrit, which will purge Bharat of the corruptions of centuries.

This leads me to the issue of interpretation and use of scripture. For where the scriptural and contingent approaches perhaps diverge most is in their analysis of the way in which these movements use texts. For the former, fundamentalism constitutes a 'return' to the texts; for the latter, it means using the texts and shaping the interpretation to meet contemporary needs. Even the more pious would concede that the holy texts contain many ambiguities and possibilities for alternative interpretation, what the more secular among us would call contradictions. Most great works of human thought and literature do. Among Christians, 'Turn the other cheek' is juxtaposed with 'An eye for an eye, a tooth for a tooth', for example. The Quran enjoins that there should be no compulsion in religion (la ikrah fi al-din), but also makes clear in quite punitive terms, remote from freedom of choice, what will happen to unbelievers. Judaism is ambivalent on attitudes to gentiles. Hinduism contains much that can be used to enjoin an ethic of non-violence and tolerance, as Gandhi for one realized to great effect; it also has a mythology and language replete with the warlike and the bloodthirsty, as today's militants are quick to tell us. What the ideological interpretation would suggest is that the terminology, the injunctions, the very content of these texts are a resource that populist movements, consciously or not, use for contemporary purposes. There is, in this sense, no one 'true' Islam or Christianity or Judaism. It is possible in Islam to justify, for example, any general form of society – not just capitalism or socialism but also feudalism and slavery. It is possible to cite parts of the Quran that favour equality of men and women – it is also possible to cite plenty of passages that favour male supremacy. Much energy has been spent within Judaism on the interpretation of the term 'Zion' – whether it is a state of mind and spirit or, if a place, whether a part of or all of Jerusalem or a nation state, with particular borders. What is important is that, in modern circumstances, it is contemporary wishes, not some immanent true interpretation, that determine what use is made of these texts. Hence Zion has come to mean for the Jews something that is by no means specific to them, namely a nation state, with a clear territory, population and language. In the same way the term *ge-ula* – redemption – has both spiritual and instrumental variants. Equally, one can go through the religious texts and see how words, of apparently ancient provenance, are used for contemporary purposes. What they 'mean' is not what those who used them a thousand or two thousand years ago meant, but what the ideologues of today want them to mean.

It should be evident that, as between these two forms of interpretation, the scriptural and the contingent, I favour the latter. They are not necessarily exclusive: even the most ardent supporter of the contingency school would concede that part of the energy and character of these movements derives from its theological character. The energy and money put into religious education – in *madrasas*, *yeshivas*, Bible classes, temple meetings – is evidence enough of this. Yet neither the causes nor the content, let alone the programme and consequences, can be adequately explained by this. We are looking at well-organized, modern, determined political movements, for whose members the almighty is a suitable, quite possibly sincerely worshipped legitimation.

The Iranian case

At this point I should like to depart from the general, comparative discussion of fundamentalisms to look in more detail at the case of Iran, the most prominent case of a fundamentalist movement and the one country where a thorough-going fundamentalist movement has been in power, since 1979. I was in Iran before and after the revolution and interviewed many of its leaders. I have stood on the streets of Tehran and seen tens of thousands of people march by, shouting, '*Marg bar liberalizm*' ('Death to liberalism'). It was not a happy sight; among other things, they meant me.

There is no need to rehearse at length the originality of this revolution, compared with others in the tradition that began in France in 1789. Not only was it carried out by a clerical leadership, who called for the return to a model of government derived from the seventh century, but in other respects too it appeared to reject the assumptions of all other post-1789 revolutions. It rejected material development (Khomeini once said that economics was a preoccupation of donkeys), it denied the sovereignty of the people (this came from Allah) and it rejected any legitimation in terms of antecedents – only the Prophet and his immediate successors counted, and all that had come since, with some tiny exceptions, was to be renounced – corrupt, decadent, *jahil* (ignorant). There could be no more dramatic example of the apparent break between fundamentalism and modernity.

Yet on closer examination it is not quite so. The causes of the Iranian revolution include several factors, of a more or less secular and indeed material kind, that led to the fall of the Shah's regime: the growth of an explosive situation in the cities, with mass migration, rampant corruption, inflation; the failure of the regime to allow for legitimate forms of political discontent, and the prior suppression of the mass secular forces, nationalist and communist, that had dominated the Iranian political scene in the decade after World War II; the success of Khomeini in leading and organizing a mass political movement, focused on a set of simple and widely held goals – the ousting of the Shah, and the ending of Western, particularly American, influence in the country. For all the appearance that Iran underwent a return to the past and that its revolution was 'traditional', it was in some respects modern, indeed perhaps the most modern social revolution seen in any country. It took place not among the peasantry, but among the urban poor and middle classes, and it achieved its aims not in the main through violence, but through political means, the mass opposition protest and the political general strike. The paradox of the Iranian revolution was that it was *both* the most traditional *and* the most modern of social revolutions.

This is evident too in the very ideas, the political ideology that Khomeini put forward. Khomeini's religious outlook was based not just on a literalist reading of the Quran, but on certain trends within Iranian Shi'ism: on the one hand, *irfan*, or mysticism, which enhanced a certain disdain for the immediate and the material, and on the other, the interpretation of Shi'ism, historically the sect of those in opposition to government, to mean not so much abstention from the world and from politics as a contestatory engagement with it. This included something that most theologians had previously rejected, namely the idea that there could be an Islamic government on this earth even before the return of the twelfth Imam. Khomeini's theory of *hokumat-i islami*, or Islamic government, rested on what was in effect a new, innovatory solution to the problem of how a sincere Muslim can affect politics in the absence of the Imam, namely his theory of the vice-regency of the legal authority, or jurisconsult, *velayat-i faqih*. In this theory, the legal interpreter, in the first instance Khomeini, was authorized to wield religious authority and establish an Islamic government, with an authority derived from god.

This apparently purely theological solution was of course to be understood not just as a theological breakthrough, but also as something that served a much more immediate, material concern, namely how to acquire and maintain political power. It justified the takeover of the Iranian state by the clergy and the depreciation or denial of other forms of authority. If one looks at the subsequent history of the Iranian revolution, not as a scriptural but as a pragmatic, political one, with ideology used to justify the mundane and universal goal of keeping state power, then much becomes clear. The mullahs have seized and kept control through the mechanisms found elsewhere – mobilization for war, discretionary use of welfare, repression of internal opponents, demagogy about foreign threats and conspiracies abroad. Such dramatic actions as the seizure of the US diplomatic personnel in 1979 or the condemnation of Salman Rushdie in 1989 need to be seen not as aberrations or irrationalities but as calculated acts of a regime bent on maximizing support. The political logic of the Rushdie affair may be more evident if placed in the context of the history of such condemnations: it is worth recalling that perhaps the four most important political trials in Western history were all on charges of blasphemy – Socrates, Jesus Christ, Galileo and Spinoza.

This material and modern set of preoccupations is also present in the very ideology of the regime. If one looks at the terminology and policies enunciated by Khomeini, it all begins to look much more familiar, particularly in the light of third-world populist movements of the post-war epoch. Khomeini's central set of concepts, *mustakbarin* and *mustaz'afin*, literally 'the arrogant' and 'the weak', correspond to the people/elite couplet found in other populisms. Populist terms used to disparage the elite – corrupt, linked to foreigners, decadent, parasitic – all recur in Khomeini. The main political slogans of Khomeini – Islamic republic, revolution, independence, economic self-sufficiency – are the standard goals of nationalism in developing countries. His term for imperialism, *istikbar-i jahani*, 'world arrogance', is immediately recognizable the world over, and not a bad description at that. The denunciation of opponents as 'liberals' was taken from the communists. One might suppose that these borrowings would be subordinated to an other-worldly theological perspective, but what Khomeini actually said and did once he came to power illustrated, if nothing else, the primacy of Realpolitik. Thus, although he started by renouncing patriotism and the Iranian identity, he began invoking Iran and the concept of fatherland once the Iraqi invasion of 1980 had begun. Most interestingly of all, in the last months of his life, he enunciated a new principle of political behaviour, based on the primacy of *maslahat*, or interest: according to this, what mattered were the interests of the people and the state, not the formal prescriptions of religion. In situations of conflict between the two it was the interests of the state that prevailed even over basic religious duties such as prayer; no clearer enunciation of the implicitly secular principle of *raison d'état* could be given.

Responses and questions

So far this discussion has sought to analyse the spread of fundamentalism and to suggest certain common causes and features of this phenomenon. It would be wrong to exaggerate the import of these movements. The majority of Muslim countries are not about to be overrun by fundamentalism, and the wave of Christian fundamentalism has had an intermittent history: in the USA it lost on the great issue of its choice in the inter-war period, prohibition, and the actual influence of the so-called Moral Majority on the USA of the 1980s was less than many had feared, not least because

its chosen political leader, the twice-married, non-churchgoing sep-
tuagenarian Ronald Reagan showed little other than electoral
interest in its concerns, and then proceeded to make his peace with
the Soviet Anti-Christ. In Eastern Europe the most religious-influ-
enced movement of protest, Solidarity, not by the definition used
here a fundamentalist movement but having a related appeal, came
to power in Poland only to lose it again to the reformed communists and to see its legislation on reproduction largely ignored by
the population. However, some of these are movements, which, by
dint of the crisis of the countries in which they originate, and their
own determination, may be with us for a long time. In Iran and
Sudan, Islamist fundamentalists are in power. They may well come
to power in Algeria and could do so in Egypt. In Israel Judaic fundamentalism can certainly have a nefarious impact. In Western
societies fundamentalism still has its strongest hold in the USA,
where, in its evangelical form, it allegedly commands the loyalty of
around 40 million people: it may not be about to come to power,
but it continues to make a lot of trouble trying to legislate on what
women can and cannot do and on related 'single' issues. In Europe
so far radical Right and Left movements have been secular, indeed
anti-Christian, but few can predict how things will develop in the
East in the years ahead.

Here we come to the question of response – at two levels, the
political and the philosophical. Politically it is not possible to ignore the threat that these movements pose to the citizens of the
countries in which they live and, by extension, to the world. The
revolution in Iran and the rise of fundamentalism elsewhere has
led to the deaths of many people, as would, on a perhaps greater
scale, the victory of the Islamic Salvation Front (FIS) in Algeria. A
policy response needs to be evolved on the basis of at least three
principles. First, we have to recognize the sources, indeed, the legitimacy of protest of these movements and to address the social,
economic and political issues to which they are a response. There
can be no solution to the crisis in Algeria without a change in the
economy that will provide jobs and a reform of the increasingly
corrupt state. Equally, we must recognize how a range of issues
sharpens the national and religious militancy of peoples: in the
case of the Islamic world, Western neglect on the questions of Palestine and Bosnia, to name but two, has stimulated religious
anti-imperialism. In many cases the rise of fundamentalism, be it

in Gaza or Bosnia or among Muslims communities in Western Europe, is a response to the oppressions these communities feel and the apparently inadequate response of secular forces, whether within the countries concerned or internationally. The racists and alarmists talk much of a fundamentalist fifth column inside Western Europe: we should look first at how and why people who were encouraged and invited to come and work in Europe have turned to a more religious and militant definition of their identity in the face of the problems they have encountered. The problem of 'Islam' in Western Europe is above all a problem of their Christian fellow citizens and of governments, not of any Muslim threat to the larger society: there are around six million Muslims in a Western Europe of over 250 millions.

Secondly, we need, in our own analysis and coverage, to get away from the simplification and stereotyping that equate Muslims with Islamists: most Muslims are not Islamists, any more than most Hindus, Jews or Christians are fundamentalists. 'Islam' is not, in any serious sense, a threat to the West, militarily or economically: Islamic states have not been a military threat since the seventeenth century, and if there is an economic challenge today it comes from the Far, not the Middle East. There is no one Islam or for that matter Christianity, nor should the term 'Muslim' be used to denote ethnicity. What is often lost in contemporary discussion is the very diversity and variety of these religions, both in the possible readings of their holy texts and in the culture, the literature, the meanings that have been present within them. If Islamic civilization, for example, has a dogmatic, orthodox, stern strain within it, something it shares with the other religions, it also has much that is sceptical, hedonistic, cosmopolitan, humorous and humane. The patriarchs of each religion conspire with their stereotyping enemies to confuse this, much as in the past dogmatists argued that the only 'real' socialism was that of Joseph Stalin or Enver Hoxha. It is only when, and if, this very diversity within the communities is recognized, as well as a diversity and multiculturalism between them, that the claims of fundamentalisms to be authentic expressions of a national culture can be repulsed.

Beyond politics there are, however, philosophic and moral issues that underlie these questions, and it is a matter of note, and indeed concern, that at the very moment when a new set of dogmatic, self-assertive movements arises, there should be such confusion in the camp of those that they do not encompass. By this I mean, in broad terms, the camp of those committed to a set of individualistic, critical, democratic and, of necessity, secular values. This confusion takes at least three broad forms. One, derived from the critique of Western domination and ethnocentrism, can be broadly termed the critique based on cultural relativism – 'what right have we to impose "our" values on other people?'. The second, much à la mode at the moment but hopefully on the way out, is post-modernism, in the form of those who argue that we cannot be sure of any rational enlightenment values – they advocate a 'deconstructed', restless indeterminacy of analysis and ethic, a politics of 'difference'. Finally, from within the camp of contemporary moral philosophy, we hear the argument that we cannot be sure of any general moral principles, let alone ones that should be universally defended as between traditions and communities, and that all we can do is fall back on procedures for adjudicating disputes – this latter is, in broad terms, the argument of Alasdair Macintyre, Stuart Hampshire and Raymond Plant, all people of weight.

In the context of what is happening in societies and communities threatened by fundamentalism, or for that matter dictatorship or militant nationalism, these ruminations prompt a degree of perplexedness and indeed irritation. If you are languishing in the jails of the Islamic guards in Iran, forced to wear mediaeval clothes on the streets of Tehran, being shot for your commitment to secularism in Egypt or Algeria, being driven out of your home and possibly killed in Bombay or having your land stolen by people who claim it was given to them by god, then it is little comfort as you protest in the name of universal values to be told you are ethnocentric or not post-modernistically playful enough or that, sorry, after all, we cannot be sure that the rights you ask to be defended are properly founded. There is, in this atmosphere of agnosticism, both a failure to grasp the issues at stake in much of the world and an irresponsibility bordering on a late twentieth-century version of the *trahison des clercs*.

It is certainly evident that the modernist enlightenment project, as envisaged earlier in the twentieth century, was inadequately and often crudely worked out. We are not living in a world where some undifferentiated progress is inevitable or where secularization and disenchantment are universal. Many of the claims of reason were overstated, when not repressively imposed. The greatest crimes of the century were not committed by religious fundamentalists. The very term that lies at the heart of this debate, 'secularism', may also benefit from re-examination: originally formulated in the 1840s as an alternative to religious and ecclesiastical authority, it has been taken too much for granted within democratic societies. But these enlightenment concepts remain a foundation on which it is possible and, I would argue, necessary to build, as much as are our concepts of democracy, individualism, rights and tolerance. We should be prepared to redefine and defend them. Let us be quite clear about it: the fundamentalists of all hues are themselves unrelenting and determined in pursuit of their goals and are quite prepared to silence and, in some cases, to kill those who get in their way, and in addition, for what it is worth, to send us all to hell. On the side of those who are not fundamentalists there should be some greater element of clarity, intransigence and indeed combativity, before it is too late.

3
Violence and Communal Conflict: Terrorism 'from Above' and 'from Below'

Article 4 – Fundamental guarantees

1. *All persons who do not take a direct part or who have ceased to take part in hostilities, whether or not their liberty has been restricted, are entitled to respect for their person, honour and convictions and religious practices. They shall in all circumstances be treated humanely, without any adverse distinction. It is prohibited to order that there shall be no survivors.*

2. *Without prejudice to the generality of the foregoing, the following acts against the persons referred to in paragraph 1 are and shall remain prohibited at any time and in any place whatsoever:*

    (a) violence to the life, health and physical and mental well-being of persons, in particular murder as well as cruel treatment such as torture, mutilation or any form of corporal punishment;
    (b) collective punishments;
    (c) taking of hostages;
    (d) acts of terrorism;

> *(e) outrages upon personal dignity, in particular humiliat-*
> *ing and degrading treatment, rape, enforced prostitution*
> *and any form of indecent assault;*
> *(f) slavery and the slave trade in all their forms;*
> *(g) pillage;*
> *(h) threats to commit any of the foregoing acts.*

('Humane Treatment', Geneva Additional Protocol II, 1977)[1]

Since the latter part of the 1960s the issue of 'terrorism' has played a significant role in political life and discussion in many countries, and in international relations. The Arabic term *irhabiyya* (terror- ism) also came into common usage at that time. Persians had long used *terorizm* (or *irhab*). The lives of many people have been af- fected by actions classified as 'terrorist'; many more bear the psychological and physical marks of involvement in such actions. 'Terrorism' is not, therefore, a matter that can be avoided, a fig- ment of the imagination of political opponents and repressive regimes. Yet it has become, above all in the Middle East, a subject of such distortion and myth that it is next to impossible to estab- lish a balanced discussion of it. Some Western writers on the subject have sought to abandon the term altogether on the grounds that the term is so overloaded with emotional and polemical associa- tions that it cannot be used. They argue that there remain, however, two other phenomena that can be analysed: 'terror', a goal or in- strument of political and military conflict, and political violence, of which 'terrorism' is a part.[2]

As far as is possible, this is a line of argument I would support. It is possible, and preferable, to write about a range of political and military phenomena, everything indeed covered by the term 'terrorism', without using the term. Yet the term 'terrorism' has become so widespread and some of the actions it denotes so con- tentious that it may, nonetheless, be worth trying to assess some of the general issues involved. One of the casualties of the prevailing discourse on terrorism is the possibility of moral judgement. On the one hand, crimes by states are used to absolve the crimes of those opposed to them. Yet, as Geneva Protocol II stipulates, in all political conflicts those opposed to the state as well as the state itself are bound by moral and legal conventions. On the other hand, when states talk of 'terrorists' the crimes of opposition groups are used to deny the legitimacy of protest or of the right to resist and rebel: yet the latter is a central feature of Western and Islamic thought and has been given further meaning by modern concepts of democratic and national legitimacy.[3]

The challenge facing anyone who seeks to analyse 'terrorism' as a political phenomenon is, therefore, to take the phenomenon seriously, not to accept prevailing mythologizing, but to try to establish an independent terrain on which to discuss it. Attempting to find a middle ground is not possible: there is no middle ground where political violence is concerned any more than there is with racism. We need an independent position and the function of a comparative and historical perspective is precisely to help establish that independent ground. The aim of such an examination is two-fold: on the one hand, to use a critique of the prevailing discourse on terrorism to open up discussion of the varying uses of political violence in the contemporary Middle East and elsewhere; secondly, to bring into the open the moral judgements and possible moral principles that are relevant to the study of political violence, and above all to allow discrimination as to when it is legitimate for states and those opposed to them to use force.

Anybody who has been involved in the Irish or the Middle Eastern situations or any of the other comparable cases of ethnic and religious conflict realizes the complexity and danger of this question of 'terrorism'. It is a very difficult one, starting with the obvious fact that there is no agreed definition of the word 'terrorism'. One argument sometimes invoked states, that 'one person's terrorist is another person's freedom fighter'. This is a relativist fallacy: it means that if you believe that someone's cause is just, then whatever he or she does in pursuit of that cause is itself justified. There are, there must be, violent actions which everybody whatever their cultural background can agree are illegitimate. But because of the wide range of actions covered the act of definition is a complex one, as it is with any other social concept – religion, fundamentalism, or even war. Indeed one scholar has identified no fewer than 109 different meanings of terrorism.[4]

A second reason for the difficulty of discussion is the degree of mythologization and exaggeration we confront. To say that the issue of terrorism has been taken out of context and has been exaggerated and distorted is in no way to detract from the moral and human seriousness of the terrorist phenomenon. There does, however, seem to be a tendency to inflate and distort the question. The USA during the 1970s and 1980s made much of the issue, and presented it as a unitary, worldwide threat.[5] Governments in the Middle East have also made much of the issue to discredit their opponents, and conceal their own uses of political violence, domestically and internationally. Israel has long done this, in an attempt to discredit the Palestinian cause: Benjamin Netanyahu, in particular, made a career out of self-serving demagogy about 'terrorism'. Arab governments have also used the issue of terrorism to justify their own repressive policies, and to identify all political opponents with the cause of political violence. The Turkish government has used the term 'terrorist' to justify its refusal to develop a political solution to the Kurdish question. Yet there can be no legitimate criticism of the uses of political violence by opponents of a state if it does not permit a full and open examination of the right to rebel, and of the conditions under which such a right may apply. We can extract the issue of 'terrorism' from such a political agenda through two paths, conceptual clarification and historical perspective. It may then be possible to address a third issue, that of the role which terrorism in its current, selective usage denotes in bringing about political change.

Conceptual clarifications

Let me begin with the conceptual problem. The word 'terrorism' dates from the French Revolution, like many other now fashionable terms including 'nationalism', 'guerrilla' and 'counter-revolution'. It was originally used in 1794 to refer to the use of terror by governments against their own populations. That is where the concept originally comes from, an origin worth remembering. It was in this sense too that Leon Trotsky, whilst Commissar of War in the post-1917 Bolshevik government, used it to justify the use of political violence against the enemies of the state.[6] Trotsky argued that socialism could not be built in Russia under conditions of imperialist intervention without revolutionary violence and repression. Etymologies and meanings change, and the term certainly has developed many different meanings since. Yet it is important in any evaluation of the use of violence in politics, and in adjudication of crimes against humanity committed in the contemporary world, not to lose sight of what one can term 'terrorism from above'. The castigation by the governments of the USA, Israel, Egypt or Turkey of 'terrorist' opponents may not always be without justification: in their usage, however, it precludes assessment of actions in which they and their clients have also been involved. At the same time recognition of this use of illegitimate violence should not lead to denial of the crimes committed by those not in power, which we can call 'terrorism from below'. Today it is in this latter sense that the term is generally used: individual acts of violence separated from a war or civil war context but carried out for certain political ends. Today we are talking about political terrorism, not about lunatics or haphazard assassinations. We refer to kidnappings, hostage taking, hijackings, bombings, and so on. Terror is, therefore, capable of being used by those with state power and those without, as an act on its own or as part of a wider war or civil conflict.

If we look in more detail, there are four different aspects of the concept of terrorism, or four different meanings which we have to take into account. Once again it needs to be stressed that what we choose to call 'terrorism' is a matter of convention; it is not something that is automatically 'given' by facts or by history. The first, very important aspect is what is called enforcement terror, that is, the terror of governments. This is what I would term 'terrorism from above'. It has been said many times, but it loses none of its force to say it again, that the great majority of the acts of terror committed in the modern world and in history have been committed by those in power against those who are out of power. This is as true for what states have done within their own territories as internationally. This does not provide an answer to the question of moral assessment of hijacking or bombs in supermarkets, but it does provide a moral corrective to some of the selective judgements that are made by academic experts and state officials. Even if one takes the case of the states that do carry out acts of terror outside their own frontiers, one had better start by looking at what they do to their own citizens, which is often much worse.

There are, secondly, acts of violence that are isolated, separate from the situation of a country at war and hence intended to cause terror itself rather than contribute to a broader conflict. By extension and in its narrow Western and Israeli 1980s sense, terrorism refers to acts of violence carried out internationally, in other words carried out in a third country, outside the context where its political causes can be located: an IRA action in a country other than Britain, a Palestinian action outside of the Middle East, an Islamist bomb in New York, a South Moluccan action in Holland. These would be regarded, in contemporary usage, as being acts of 'international terrorism' in the narrowest sense. This is the sense, for example, in which the US State Department's Counter-Terrorist Office was set up. Such actions have recurred. Yet the problem with this usage is that, in practice, it can be selective and self-serving. During the 1980s this usage was not used to identify acts of violence committed by states, the USA or its allies, in other countries – Israel in Lebanon, the USA and Pakistan in Afghanistan, the US-backed *contra* in Nicaragua. The term 'international terrorism' also contains the suggestion that somehow terrorism is itself organized internationally, that there is some worldwide network, aided or tolerated by certain states, which explains the incidence of terrorism, negatively defined, in a range of countries. That there are links – military, financial, political – between different groups using political violence and that some states have aided them is indisputable. The idea of a unitary or co-ordinated 'international terrorism' is, however, a myth.[7]

The term 'terrorism' is also used much more broadly to describe the violent actions in a civil war or conflictual situation of any group of which you disapprove. The Geneva Protocol II of 1977 clearly identifies forms of violence that are impermissible in civil conflicts. The problem with this is that it too easily confuses the discussion of the uses of political violence by conflating the identification of violence with the legitimacy of the cause in which it is committed. First, political violence is a recurrent part of political change. People sometimes say that the British and the Americans had a 'peaceful' path of development. In reality, the history of both Europe and the USA is marked by the spilling of blood, civil wars, and the rest. That is how, in part, these states were established and how the boundaries between them were fixed. If other countries are now going through that experience, it may be alleviated or it may be condemned, but as a historical fact violence as part of political change is very widespread indeed. Moreover, in the context of many third world liberation movements and nationalist movements violence and acts of what in the narrow sense can be called terror have occurred. Therefore, the use of the term terrorist today is very often used to denote any liberation movement or nationalist movement of which states or people in the West disapprove. To avoid this slippage we need always to distinguish between a criticism of certain forms of violence, or of the resort to violence itself, and the validity of a cause itself.

There is a fourth aspect of terrorism which, looking from outside the Western framework, is important to bear in mind. This is 'terrorism' as a globalized anxiety and pretext, a *grande peur* of the late twentieth century. Here terrorism is a public concern, reflected and promoted as a state issue, as a subject of seminars in universities, as a subject of alarm and alarmism, rather like witchcraft, promiscuity or spies. In this sense, the issue of terrorism has been inflated to cover many other phenomena and to justify and direct political action. There is distortion in the degree of emphasis laid on certain acts of violence internationally. So the degree of selection involved in focusing on one aspect of violence and ignoring others constitutes 'terrorism' as an ideology, as a set of political values, a set of political programmes which bear some relationship to the reality but which clearly serve other social functions as well.

This mythologization of terrorism is similar to other forms of orchestrated public anxiety, just as in other contexts the harassment of individuals accused of 'un-American' or 'un-Islamic' activities, or immorality, or spying, serves broader purposes. It can be used by states to justify general repression of political dissent. It can also occasion spontaneous hostility to forces that are not involved in the acts concerned. Such was the use of the Reichstag fire to foment anti-semitism in Germany in 1933. Such too was the widespread anti-Islamic response within the USA to actions – the Oklahoma bombings of 1995, the explosion of TWA 800 off the coast of New York in 1997 – that had no connection to Muslim groups or individuals. The issue is not to deny that acts of terrorism from below do occur, but rather to disentangle analysis of such acts from the broader context in which the issue of terrorism is discussed.

So, within the general category of 'terrorism' there are these four themes: the use of violence by states against their subjects; isolated acts of violence; the question of violence in liberation and nationalist movements; and, finally, the inflation for political ends of terrorism as an issue.

Terrorism from below: three historical phases

We can now attempt to place the issue of 'terrorism from below' in some historical perspective. There are certain things that a historical perspective will *not* do. It will not enable us to define what we mean by terrorism. We have to define that ourselves in order to look at the history. It will not give us a morality of terrorism; that is something we have to derive from our own principles. A historical view of terrorism will certainly not give us a theory of the 'terrorist personality', the very pursuit of which is an intellectually nonsensical activity, although one out of which a lot of people have made money and reputations and received research grants. Nor will it give us a general theory of the causes of terrorism: there is no such a thing.[8] However, it may help us to put today's phenomenon in perspective and to see what measures, what responses, we can come to.

The history of terrorism from below can be divided into roughly three phases.[9] There is what you could call the pre-history of terrorism, that is, the history of terrorism up to the end of the eighteenth century, which is essentially the history of assassination, before bombs and, obviously, hijackings. This was found, for example, among the Zealots of Palestine, and among the *hashashin* – the assassins in the Middle East; it was found in ancient Rome and ancient Greece, occurred in subsequent societies as well, and of course has a continuing history. The point about the first or 'pre-historical' period is that the victim was often assumed or alleged to be guilty. Consequently, there was a theology or morality of assassination: it was said to be justified. Many are the states that erected statues to assassins: the Athenians erected a statue to the tyrannicides Harmodias and Aristogeiton. While many of the assassinations that have taken place in the twentieth century lack any such justification, it is nonetheless worth remembering that the issue began with what allegedly was justified terrorist activity.

The second phase of terrorism is the nineteenth century, involving acts of violence, in Europe and North America, particularly by anarchists and later by nationalists. This is part of the radical politics of early modernity. One can argue that the high point of this second phase came between two assassinations: the assassination of Tsar Alexander II in 1881 and the assassination of Archduke Ferdinand of Austro-Hungary in 1914. Those were the two most politically spectacular assassinations, the ones with the greatest consequences. It was between those two that one saw the high point of 'propaganda of the deed', of men like Ravachol setting off explosions, of anarchists in Paris, of Johan Moste in New Jersey talking about bombs, though not doing much about it. This period also saw the rise of nationalistic assassination movements – in Ireland, Iran, Egypt, India and elsewhere. Among the nationalist movements were the two nationalities that have probably the oldest history of terrorist actions and which still maintain violent or 'physical force' elements in their tradition, the Irish and the Armenians. And it should not be forgotten that World War I was sparked by the assassination in Sarajevo.

The third period of terrorism is the period since World War II. We are dealing here again with different phenomena – in broad terms, actions by three kinds of group: the secular Left, nationalist movements and religious fundamentalists. The first group, the secular Left, comprises organizations active in the 1960s such as the Weathermen in the United States, the Rote Armee Fraktion in Germany, the Brigate Rosse in Italy, the Angry Brigade in Britain, and the various Japanese Red Army factions. These carried out bombings and similar activities in developed, democratic capitalist countries. They achieved nothing and they had, more or less, disappeared by the late 1970s. This wave of terrorism by groups of the far or anarchist Left is no longer with us on the same scale. A related post-war phenomenon was that of the urban guerrillas in Latin America, particularly in Uruguay, Argentina and Brazil: they too were more or less defeated by the mid-1970s. As their critics on the Latin American Left pointed out, the resort to armed resistance in the absence of a significant mass movement led to isolation for the guerrillas and increased repression from above.[10] In the 1990s there was a revival of terrorist activity by ideologically more diffuse minority groups whose main aim appeared to be the disruption of life in urban communities: the Aum Shinrikyo (Supreme Truth) sect which unleashed nerve gas in a Tokyo underground in March 1995, killing twelve people and injuring several thousand, and the Oklahoma bombing by American right-wing militia elements in the same year. This 'new terrorism' has as yet not taken either a pervasive or effective form.[11]

Acts of terror by movements struggling for national independence comprise the single most important category and the one that was very much the subject of the widespread discussion of 'terrorism' in the 1980s. In the post-war period this began with the struggle of the Jews in Palestine for independence after World War II, and the attacks on British and Arab victims as part of that struggle. There have been many others which were equally successful and whose regimes were later generally accepted internationally: Kenya,

Cyprus, South Yemen and, of course Algeria. Other nationalist forces have also used terrorism from below: the Palestinians, the Basques, the Moluccans and those in Northern Ireland who pursued a struggle in the name of a united Ireland, 'physical force' as distinct from 'moral force' republicans, together with their 'loyalist' opponents.

A further development of terrorism since the 1970s has been that of actions by religious groups. Outside the Middle East this is easily presented as a function of Islam or, if not of the Islamic religion as such, then of political militants, Islamists, invoking Islam. Such anti-Islamic stereotyping is easily reinforced by the rhetoric of Islamist groups such as the Armed Islamic Group (GIA) in Algeria, who call for an indiscriminate use of violence against all who collaborate with the 'apostate' (*mortadd, kafir, mulhid*) regime. In opposition to this rhetoric, three points need to be made. First, the incidence of political violence by groups invoking religion is by no means specific to Islam: Christianity, Judaism, Hinduism, Buddhism have all been invoked by those using violence from below and above. In Northern Ireland Christians of two sects – Catholics and Protestants – have invoked religion to justify their crimes. In Israel fanatical Jewish groups have advocated violence by the Israeli state when it has suited them, and independently when it has not. Baruch Goldstein, who killed twenty-nine Palestinians in Hebron in 1994, claimed to be doing the work of God. In India, there has been an ominous rise in the use of violence by Hindu chauvinist groups, using again both state and unofficial means to terrorize their Muslim and Christian fellow citizens.

Secondly, it is nonsense to seek the causes, as distinct from legitimation, of violence in the texts or tradition of any religion. The doctrinal situation of each of these religions is clear: they allow of a pacific reading, as of a violent one. At the same time, each major religion and ethical tradition contains provision for discussion of just war, of the conditions under which it is legitimate to use force, and of what kind of force it is legitimate to use. The choice as to which reading is made depends on the political choice of the moment. In the Islamic case there is a concept of legitimate war *al-harb al-mashru'a* or *al-harb al-'adila*. The Quran (9.13 and 22.39–40) gives legitimation for war in self-defence but also enjoins the believer to respect limits in what they do (Quran 2.90).[12] Moreover, the Islamic tradition distinguishes between *jihad*, which is legitimate, and *ghazu*, invasion, or *'adwan*, aggression, which are not. In addition to this set of principles and vocabulary specific to the Muslim world, Muslim states are also committed, as are non-Muslim ones, by the international conventions regulating the conduct of war to which they have subscribed. Under Geneva Protocol II these apply also to non-state groups, rebel forces operating on the territory of these states.

There is, thirdly, in this identification of 'Islam' with 'terrorism' a misuse of the latter term for polemical political purposes: on the one hand, to delegitimate not just the actions but the very programme of political groups – in Palestine above all – who mobilize Muslim peoples, on the other, to confine discussion of terrorism only to Muslim states. The Middle East has seen terrorist actions from above – by states acting in the name of Islam, by Israel, and by secular regimes in Turkey. In his *A Clash of Civilizations* Samuel Huntington argues that 'Islam has bloody frontiers': he does not, however, provide an accurate account of where the responsibility for this bloodiness may lie – in some cases prime responsibility lies with Muslims, in others not. In Bosnia, Kosovo, Palestine, Kashmir, to take but four examples, it does not.

Terror and communal conflict

It is not the terrorism of small groups but two other kinds – 'terrorism from above', or the violent actions of states, and political violence in the context of communal conflict – that in human costs and international consequence are the most serious. In any comparative perspective, the most worrying feature of all 'terrorism from below' in the international context today is not hijacking and bombing and the seizure of embassies: it is the growth of terrorism in communal situations in third world countries, and in confessionally divided countries such as, until recently at least, Ireland. This is where you have violence between Turks and Greeks living adjacently in Cyprus, Protestants and Catholics in Northern Ireland, Hindus and Sikhs in the Punjab, Sunnis and Shi'ites in Pakistan, Arabs and Israelis in the Middle East, the different communities of Lebanon, Muslims and Christians in the Philippines, the Tamils and Sinhalese in Sri Lanka and, more recently, in former Yugoslavia. Here acts of violence by members of one community against another produce a counter-reaction: they produce hatred, they undermine any possibility of a lasting coexistence of the two communities. A spiral of hatred, fear and vengeance takes place. This worldwide phenomenon is killing and maiming thousands of people in the world each year. The focus on involvement of Western citizens as the victims of acts of 'international terrorism' obscures this much larger use of violence in situations of inter-ethnic conflict: long a matter of mainly non-European concern, and occurring only in isolated pockets such as Northern Ireland or the Basque country, it was to become a major preoccupation in the 1990s with the onset of mass inter-ethnic violence in former Yugoslavia.

Such inter-communal terrorism is going on every day and in many places. Those people who do stand independently, such as the Palestinian spokesman Sa'id Hammami, the Social Democratic and Labour Party in Northern Ireland, the non-violent opposition of the Kosovo Democratic League or other comparably courageous people, are cut down by the hatred on both sides; they are spat upon or worse as traitors and moderates. The decomposition of communities where people of different ethnic or religious backgrounds did previously live together in some way with whatever prejudices and grievances is a widespread contemporary phenomenon. It is, arguably, the most worrying aspect in the contemporary world of the misuse of violence by those who are not in power. Here 'terrorism' means terror used against other citizens of the same country, not against international targets and not, to a large extent, against the state.

Some historical conclusions

Some conclusions can be drawn from this history. First of all, there is no general 'theory' of terrorism, a general psychology of terrorism or even a general causation of terrorism. What drives Palestinians or Armenians or drove the Zionists just before they became independent in Palestine is very different from what drove American Weathermen or the Rote Armee Fraktion to use violence. But there are some philosophic preconceptions that are very widespread among terrorists, three of which merit a mention. One is the simple idea that you can shortcut social and political change. In other words, that you do not have to get elected, you do not have to mobilize popular forces, you do not have to create a rebel army, you can just break through the oppression of the state or the social opposition you face by killing a few people or by carrying out a certain dramatic act. The classic example was *Narodnaya Volya*, the People's Will, in Russia during the 1870s, who believed that if you killed fifteen members of the government the whole regime would fall. The same assumption lies behind hijacking and other contemporary actions of terror; it lies equally behind the facile assumption of counter-terror as practised by Israel and the United States in the Middle East which deems that if you kill a few of the other side then the problem will be solved. This fundamental, simplistic assumption that social and political problems can be solved by killing a few people, by terrorizing them, by shortcutting the whole process is the one central and almost universal feature of 'terrorism from below', whether this comes from oppressed groups or from nations. There is a refusal to see that you have to mobilize support, that you have to gain consent. There is also a refusal to see how strong your opponents are. It is a politics born of desperation, not in the sense that people are necessarily destitute or desperate, although some of them certainly are, but in the sense that all other means of change are apparently exhausted.

The second aspect of terrorism, the second fallacy that goes with it, is the idea that 'propaganda of the deed', be it blowing up a Paris restaurant in the 1880s or hijacking a plane or kidnapping an ambassador in the 1980s, will mobilize your own side. This is the simplistic assumption that the scales will fall from people's eyes, that they will rise up and seize power and all will be solved. The fact that you get your picture on the front page of the *New York Times* for a day, or get worldwide diffusion of some communiqué, does not mean you are going to change the world, although too many people have imagined that it does. The fact that you get prime time news coverage will be forgotten tomorrow. Both forms of philosophical simplification remain prevalent: they reflect a refusal to understand what is required for serious political change.

Thirdly, in contexts of terrorism against other ethnic groups and in communal situations, there is a recurrent moral evasion: since terrorism is illegitimate against other human beings, the answer is not to forswear terrorism, but to deny the humanity of the other side. This may range from rage and contempt to the denial that the other side constitutes a legitimate ethnic group with any collective right to self-determination, to a deeper denial of the very entitlement of the other side to basic considerations of dignity and survival. Such attitudes could be found in the rhetoric that characterizes the other community as 'animals', 'vermin', 'insects' and the like. It is reinforced by propaganda promoting hatred and attempting to degrade the other side. In its denial of the entitlement of the other side to humanitarian treatment, something going beyond rage or reprisal, it seeks to square the moral circle, purportedly upholding the principles of humanitarian treatment in the name of which oppression suffered by one's own side is contested whilst oppression of the other side is simply denied. It is a dramatic example of that very rejection of universality that is so central to all nationalisms.

The first step in countering terrorist arguments is, therefore, the assertion of the entitlement of all humans to humane treatment. The second concerns the distinction between combatant and non-combatant: for it is the denial of this difference that provides the other philosophical prop for terrorist actions. Less absolute than the argument about the sub-human character of the opponents, the argument that runs, 'They are all guilty' provides an equally suitable legitimation for indiscriminate violence. Yet this has as little validity as the first: in all societies, industrialized or not, or with whatever degree of political consensus, there is a distinction between combatants and non-combatants, between those who may be objects of legitimate violence and those who may not. Again, universality may provide the answer, for, in the final analysis, none of those who argue that all members of the enemy society are militarily active would for a minute accept the argument as applied to their own society.

This leads to the question of efficacy: does terrorism work? Terroristic actions and counter-terroristic actions may work if they have a very specific goal; for example, to get some prisoners released or to get a very specific government policy changed or a minister removed, to get a ransom paid, to get some dismissed workers taken back. In the history of the American labour movement in the late nineteenth century, certain terroristic actions produced such a positive result. But precisely because it is circumventing political and social change, terrorism cannot achieve major social change on its own. If we look at the history of anarchists and other bombers in the nineteenth century, they got nowhere. The same goes for the urban guerrillas in Latin America and for the Weathermen and the Rote Armee Fraktion.

If, however, we take cases where national liberation movements have used violence and terror, some of them have succeeded. It can be argued, though, that in each case their success is attributable to reasons other than the use of terror. The Zionist movement in Palestine did not achieve statehood primarily because of the use of terror. It was organized, it was funded, it fought, it had a political organization: it was for those reasons that it succeeded. The same goes for the Algerians, as it does for the Irish in the first phase of the independence movement up to 1921. The same would go for Kenya, South Yemen, Cyprus and so forth. Terror was not the central factor in their victories. If we look at cases where nationalist movements have used terror and have not succeeded – the post-1968 IRA, the Basques, the Québecois, the Armenians of the Armenian Secret Army for the Liberation of Armenia (ASALA), the South Moluccans – we can see that their failure to date is attributable to the fact that they lack the necessary social and political strength to enforce their cause. The case of the Palestinians is also instructive in this regard: years of 'terrorism from below', from the mid-1960s to the mid-1980s, produced little response from either Israel or its main supporter, the USA. On the other hand, the proclaimed willingness to have a political dialogue with Israel, announced at the Algiers conference of the PLO in November 1988, combined with the political pressure of the *intifada* which had begun in 1987, did produce a context where substantive negotiation was possible and culminated in the Oslo agreement of 1993.

This does not mean, of course, that terrorism does not have consequences. It does have consequences, and quite serious ones. The most obvious is that terrorism usually renders states more repressive. It leads to various forms of state crackdown including intensified 'terrorism from above'. We saw this in a comparatively minor way in West Germany in the 1970s with the *Berufsverbot*, the attempt to root out of state employment (and that includes primary schools) anybody who had radical left-wing connections. We saw it in a much less polite way with military regimes in Argentina and Uruguay in the 1970s; we saw it in Turkey in 1980 when the military junta came in on a law and order platform. Even the ancient Greek tyrannicides, Harmodias and Aristogeiton, failed in their attempt to overthrow the Athenian tyranny and went on to provoke greater dictatorship. The second consequence that follows from terrorism is retaliation. What the United States and Israel did in Lebanon in the 1980s and 1990s are examples of this retaliation:

they did not achieve their results. With their use of state violence, they suffered from the same moral as well as political deficiencies as their opponents.

The third and by far the most important consequence of terrorism perpetrated with communal motivations is, of course, that it generates hatred. It breeds fear, it makes it much, much more difficult for people to cross the communal lines to try to build family or political or other ties. The result is that in Lebanon and in Northern Ireland you now have generations of young people who have been brought up to hate the other community and to see them only as killers. The piles of martyrs mounted and there are always justifications. I recall the IRA person who said to me, 'Oh, we're not against them because they're Protestants, we're against them because they're fascists. Don't you know the difference?' Some such justifications can for a minute begin to sound quite revolutionary and non-sectarian. But the reality is that communal hatred of this kind is highly sectarian, has no revolutionary character and always intensifies. It is the major consequence of terrorism.

The only adequate response to the challenge of terrorism, from above or below, is to develop a moral and legal position to deal with the conduct of war and to place terrorism in such a framework. As I have already argued, there is sufficient basis in both Islamic and other traditions for moral discussion of the legitimacy of violence by states and by those opposed to them. These elements of guidance are reinforced by the very precise provisions of the Geneva Conventions – the four Conventions of 1949 regulating the conduct of states in war, and the two Protocols of 1977, which regulate not only war between states and opposition groups but also the actions of opposition groups themselves.[13] These enshrine the limits on state power, but equally allow for the right of revolt by those suffering national or social oppression. The Geneva Conventions make possible moral dialogue between conflicting political groups and across supposedly fixed civilizational and religious boundaries.

Following the Geneva Conventions, then, when is it legitimate to use violence at all? This right is termed in contemporary writing as *jus ad bellum*.[14] It is illegitimate to use political violence in societies that are democratic. This would apply in the cases of the IRA and ETA; their use of violence is not legitimate *tout court*. Beyond the question of the right to wage war there is also the question of right in war, *jus in bello*. Here we have to be clear that certain acts constitutive of what is conventionally called terrorism are in any situation unjustifiable: civilians and prisoners of war are to be treated properly; all use of violence is to be proportionate; certain weapons are in themselves illegitimate.

The essential guideline in discussing 'terrorism from below' is proportion. The phenomenon of international terror is a secondary phenomenon. It is not the major threat to international order. It is not a major phenomenon in international relations today. It is very unpleasant for anybody associated with it and for anybody who fears it, and that includes anyone who gets on an aeroplane. It must nevertheless be kept in proportion and not inflated for other political ends.

The crucial moral guideline is that when a group commits acts that could be regarded as terrorism, these must be separated from our judgement of the justice of its cause. People whose causes one dislikes can behave well, and people whose causes and whose grievances one considers to be justified can and do commit acts of terror. The act no more disqualifies the cause than the cause justifies the act. One must recognize that the frequently made attempts to discredit by reference to their tactics the Palestinians, or the Armenians or the Kurds in south-east Turkey, all of whom are people with legitimate national grievances, are fallacious and to be rejected.

Finally, to return to the question of policy, we can say that beyond all other considerations the search for political solutions has to go on. From those places I know a bit about – namely Ireland, Palestine, Sri Lanka and the Punjab – I would argue that terror has made political solutions even more difficult. At the same time, it has made them all the more necessary. The protagonists in this war – the advocates of 'law and order' on one side, the defenders of 'progressive atrocities' on the other – have to yield to dialogue and, ultimately, democracy. It may take some time.

4
Anti-Muslimism: A Short History

Hostility to 'Islam' and the notion that there exists an 'Islamic threat' external to European society have in recent years come to acquire an additional, more inward-looking aspect and to be directed against Muslims living in Western and other non-Muslim societies. Racism in European countries, above all in France, has taken on a more explicitly anti-Muslim character. In the USA, where Muslims are not a noticeable immigrant community, anti-Islamic rhetoric is a significant factor in political discourse; in India it has provided the mainstay of the Hindu chauvinist Right.

The tone of this rhetoric is often alarmist and encompasses racist, xenophobic and stereotyping elements. The term 'anti-Muslimism' is used here to signify such a diffuse ideology, one rarely expressed in purely religious terms, but usually mixed in with other rhetorics and ideologies. Insofar as one can term it thus, anti-Muslimism is a semi-ideology, that is, a body of ideas that, like gender and racial prejudice, is often articulated in conjunction with others that have a greater potential to function independently. It involves not so much hostility to Islam as a religion – indeed, few contemporary anti-Muslimists take issue with the claim of Muhammad to be a prophet or with other theological beliefs – but hostility to *Muslims*, to communities of peoples whose sole or main religion is Islam and whose Islamic character, real or invented, forms one of the objects of prejudice. In this sense anti-Muslimism often overlaps with forms of ethnic prejudice, covering peoples within which there may well be a significant non-Muslim element, such as Albanians, Palestinians or even Caucasians.

At first, it would appear that the prevalence of this rhetoric poses no analytic problems. It is seen by many Muslims purely as a continuation of the enduring hostility of the non-Muslim world to their religion and is often regarded in the West as a continuation of the rivalry with the Islamic world and the threat of Muslim invasion that goes back to the seventh century. Words such as 'embedded', 'ingrained', 'age-old' and 'traditional' come into play, along with such speculation as that recently revised by Samuel Huntington, that conflict repeatedly arises along historically established cultural 'fault-lines'.[1] For some, hostility to Muslims requires no justification because it is itself a legitimate response to the threats and the militant rhetoric that emerge from the Muslim world.

But analysis needs to go further than this. In the first place, invoking history can provide little guidance as to why and how such rhetoric is used now. Unless we argue for the existence of transhistorical ideological formations, Jungian archetypes or Blochian *mentalités* that determine our behaviour, the appeal to history is unilluminating, although it provides (for both sides) a reserve of ideological themes upon which to draw. This search for contingent causes also suggests that even in the present historical period there may be no single reason for the re-emergence of anti-Muslimism. The rhetoric of one country may well influence another – Serbian stress on Muslim 'terrorism' is an obvious case in point – but while there may be elements of common determination, it may also be the case that in each particular instance rhetoric originates from different causes and serves different purposes.

This stress on contingency is directly pertinent to a second explanatory belief, common among many Muslims, that anti-Islamist prejudice is an enduring feature of non-Muslim society. In this perspective the current prevalence of anti-Muslim sentiment requires no particular explanation according to time or place. There is, and has always been, a worldwide anti-Islamic conspiracy, which manifests itself in different forms and is an intrinsic part of the global hostility to Muslims. Thus, long-standing issues such as those

concerning Palestine, Kashmir and the southern Philippines are all
seen as part of some secular hostility going back to the Crusades,
and have now been joined by a new set of products of that
conspiracy – Bosnia, Salman Rushdie, Nagorno-Karabagh, conflicts
over veiling and education in Western Europe. The first thing to
say about this approach is that it is itself ahistorical and essentialist,
though it is of course only one instance of many such approaches
based on transhistorical explanations and is inevitably promoted
by those who claim leadership of 'victim' groups. In nationalist
contexts, too, the world is full of people claiming that their people
are the victims of some timeless and pervasive hostility – the Serbs
and the Greeks are among the more prominent recent cases. Equally
common in contexts of racial and gender conflict are analyses based
on timeless and apparently determinant phenomena (racism and
patriarchy can be represented as such phenomena). The same
applies to the most brutal of all twentieth-century experiences, that
of the Jews. The claim that gentile society is in some way
intrinsically and pervasively anti-Semitic is common to many
writers, and the suggestion that it may not be, that it has an element
of contingency and indeed variety, is often in itself seen as a
concession to the racism identified.

This issue of timeless hostility is reinforced by those who justify
hostility to 'Islam' on the grounds that it is indeed the Muslim world
that is aggressive, has always been so and deserves the opposition
that it has produced. The argument that in some way Muslims 'deserve' or 'provoke' the resentment they encounter rests upon two
potentially reinforcing arguments. The first is psychological: that
the assertion by Muslims of an all-pervasive menacing hostility is
an example of projection – that is, of identification with the 'other',
the non-Muslim world, of something that is in fact a *product* of
the Muslim world. In other words, Islam's recurrent emphasis on
khatar, corruption and the rest reflects the aggressiveness of Muslims, not that of their opponents. The second argument is more
concrete and contemporary, in that it does not take one long to
find, in the statements of Muslim leaders, claims of precisely the
kind of confrontation, rivalry and incompatibility that the anti-
Muslimists assert. Such statements have been found throughout
Muslim history and are the stock in trade of the Islamists. Sayyid
Qutb on the evils of Western *jahiliyya* or Khomeini on the corruption of the West are cases in point. More immediately, many

Islamists have responded to the collapse of communism by arguing that they are the successor challenge to the West, and a more long-lasting and effective one at that. Khomeini made precisely this point in his curious letter to Gorbachev in 1989. In Britain, the leader of the 'Muslim Parliament', Kalim Saddiqi, repeatedly states that the next century will be characterized by the Islamic challenge to the West. We are therefore, in purely ideological terms, faced with a phenomenon that is quite unlike those other stereotypical hostilities, anti-communism and anti-Semitism. In the case of anti-Semitism, Jews did not subscribe to the myths of the anti-Semites; and in the case of anti-communism, there was certainly a communist challenge from 1917 to the mid-1980s but it did not take the form that it was often claimed to take.

Analysis of anti-Muslimism has, therefore, to take account of these complexities. It has to provide an explanation that, while taking account of historical continuities, is contingent and specific; it has to show how the very real cases of anti-Muslimism have causes other than that of timeless *kafir* hostility, and it has to provide alternative explanations for cases that Islamists see as proving their point – Bosnia is an obvious example. It has to accept that Islamist propaganda often compounds anti-Muslimism, but to separate out what are legitimate issues of disagreement or rivalry between Muslims and non-Muslims from the projection of anything defined as 'Islamic' as part of some global and unitary challenge. Analysis of Islamism and Islamist movements that brings out the contingency and variety within them, together with the role of contemporary political and social factors, allows for a separation of myth and reality by the establishment of some elementary facts: that 'Islam' is not one phenomenon but many, that the Islamic states have not posed a strategic threat to the West since the seventeenth century and that the issues underlying current unrest are ones of development and political change.

Equally, an analysis of anti-Muslimism provides the context for developing what can be a discussion between Muslims and non-Muslims over issues that are genuinely in dispute and in which morals, traditions and interpretation vary. The worst that such an analysis could do would be to argue that there were no issues at stake or that all criticism of the Islamic religion, whether doctrine or practice, is itself based on prejudice.

The following analysis is an attempt to clarify the current ori-

gins and character of anti-Muslimism, with the intention of sepa-
rating out those issues that are legitimately in dispute from those
that are not. It considers but makes no prior assumptions about
the extent to which history plays a role in determining these and
the extent to which there are similarities in the emergence of anti-
Muslimism in different countries. This analysis leaves open the
extent to which anti-Muslim discourses are, in cause or content,
wholly or mainly directed against the Islamic religion; and the extent to which the anti-Muslim theme is deployed in contexts where
it is issues of ethnicity and disputes over territory or power that are
at stake and its targets are either not Islamist in political character
(such as Bosnians) or are only partly Muslim (Palestinians,
Eritreans, Albanians). Rather, the aim here is to begin with some
case studies and to deal with four broad questions: first, the history of anti-Muslimism in each particular context, the history being
seen not principally as cause or origin, but as thematic reserve; second, the growth of anti-Muslim rhetoric and movements over the
past decades; third, the particular themes emphasized in this rhetoric; fourth, the apparent functions of this rhetoric within each
country.

The term 'anti-Muslimism' is, therefore, used to cover not only
hostility to the Islamic religion itself, but also to peoples who are,
in whole or significant part, Muslim and who are conventionally
categorized as being part of the Muslim world. Criticisms that are,
on the basis of available evidence, legitimate are not covered by
this term. Thus, critical discussions of Sudan's and Iran's human
rights record, of Quranic verses sanctioning rape in marriage or
patriarchal authority over women, of the practice of clitoridectomy
or of the terrorist acts of Islamist organizations are not subjects of
anti-Muslimism, although Islamists will be quick to say they are.[2]
It is never easy to identify what is and is not the product of prejudice, but we all need such distinctions and must try ourselves to
make them. To say that one Bahai or Jewish or Armenian banker is
corrupt and exploitative may, if the evidence is there, be valid; to
say he is corrupt *because* he is Bahai or Jewish or Armenian, or to
say that because one is, all are, is prejudice, as is the attempt to
deny that peoples other than these are not similarly capable of corruption. Similar distinctions can and should be made with regard
to issues raised in the context of Islam.

Orthodox Christianity: Serbia and Greece

After the rise of Islam in the seventh century, Orthodox Christianity had a moving, often hostile frontier with the Islamic world to which it progressively lost territory, leading to the fall of Constantinople in 1453 and the Ottoman conquest of the Balkans in the fourteenth and fifteenth centuries. As historians have pointed out, the challenge of Islam had important consequences within the Orthodox world. The rise of iconoclasm in the eighth and ninth centuries was, for example, a response to Islamic hostility to images of living beings.[3] But the elements of history that are most pertinent to contemporary anti-Muslimism date from the conquest of the Balkans. From this period certain central themes emerged. These included the image of the Orthodox Christian lands as the barrier or rampart between the Muslim world and Europe; the notion of the Muslims as demographically superior and as able to expand rapidly through high birth rates and settlement; the memory of the destruction of Christian holy places by Muslims; and the sense of the trauma and pathos of conquest despite heroic opposition. In the Serbian case, much mythology and sentiment surrounds the battle of Kosovo in 1389, when the Serbian tsar was defeated by the Ottoman armies. The River Drina, which traverses Serbia, was also invested with special significance because of the battles of that time. In the Greek case, the loss of Constantinople, the preferred capital of Hellenism, plays a similar role.[4] To these themes the Ottoman period added a number of others. The Muslim or Turkish rules (the two terms used interchangeably) were caricatured as cruel and corrupt; the Turks were said to favour particular forms of brutality, including homosexual rape, against Christians;[5] and the image arose of the Muslim populations moving into previously Christian lands. A culture of resentment, paranoia and self-pity was thus generated and codified with the rise of the nationalist movements in the nineteenth century, which led to the independence of Greece in 1830 and of Serbia in 1878. This culture was perhaps all the more bombastic because Ottoman rule had in fact been rather benign: Christian communities had collaborated with the Turkish regime and relations between the three religious communities of the Balkans – Catholic, Orthodox, Muslim – were relatively harmonious. To the shame of defeat at Kosovo was added that of centuries of collusion.[6]

The rise of a new anti-Muslimism in Serbia draws, in the first instance, on the experience of World War II, when significant Muslim support from Bosnia and elsewhere was provided to the Croatian *ustasha* state, with the backing of, among others, Hajj Amin al-Husseini. In post-war Yugoslavia such ideas were suppressed in the name of a new pluralism of nationalities, and in 1974 the Muslims of Yugoslavia, of whom there were around two million, were declared to be a third major nationality of the country, along with Serbs and Croats. Propaganda against Islam and Muslims began to emerge later, and in relation to two issues in particular. The first was the migration of large numbers of Albanians into Kosovo, especially in the post-war period, and the subsequent Serbian charge that this was another case of demographic invasion, which would mean the weakening of Serbian identity. The second issue centred on the trials of groups of Bosnian Muslims accused of being pan-Islamists, of receiving support from Turkey and/or Iran and of simultaneously being in league with an anti-Yugoslav (in other words anti-Serb) exile network based in Vienna. In the 1980s, when Iranian press reports began criticizing Yugoslavia for its treatment of Muslims and for problems relating to the building of mosques, the Yugoslav communist press increased its level of anti-Islamist propaganda.

With the disintegration of the communist regime after the death of Tito, Serbian nationalism became a more explicit part of government policy.[7] Serbian academics, mobilized by the regime, produced a history that denied the legitimacy of the Muslim communities in the Balkans – whether Bosnian, Albanian or Bulgarian – and which sought to portray Muslims as playing a central part in some perennial anti-Serb and anti-European conspiracy. One recurrent theme was the claim that the Bosnian Muslims were really Serbs who had converted to Islam for financial reasons and hence were traitors to the Serbian nation.[8] The function of this writing, directed both at Serbs and at a possibly broader anti-Muslim European public, was to degrade and demonize the Bosnians and other Muslims, and thus to legitimize and reinforce the persecution of these peoples.[9] Above all, it served to deny the right of the Bosnians to self-determination, to their own state. Bosnia, it was claimed, was an invention of the communists in 1945. The issue of Kosovo became central to the tone of Serbian nationalism, and the press was replete with articles on the threat posed by the Albanians. This was linked to the crescendo of nationalist sentiment that accompanied celebrations of the six hundredth anniversary of the battle of Kosovo in 1989. Serbian propaganda also began to report on the takeover and/or destruction of Christian holy places by Albanians. The issue of homosexual rape was given special prominence in two particular cases. In one instance a Serb named Martinovic was allegedly attacked by a group of Muslims on 1 May 1985 and had a bottle shoved up his rectum.[10] Martinovic became a national symbol, with poems lamenting his fate and pictures of him on a cross. The second case was that of the leader of the nationalist Serbs, the politician Vojislav Seselj, who claimed to have been raped seventeen times by Muslim policemen while under arrest in Bosnia. Both cases were embellished with propaganda about Turkey's expansionist aim to reconquer the Balkans, with Serbia now portrayed as the bulwark against the new Islamic threat, and both Serbia and Greece facing encirclement.

The outbreak of fighting in Yugoslavia from 1991 saw the further development of these themes. Here it is important to note that it was not only the Serb leadership of Slobodan Milosevic and his Serbian Socialist Party (the former League of Communists of Serbia) that was responsible. While Milosevic routinely attacked the Albanian presence in Kosovo and denounced forces that he claimed were trying to fragment Yugoslavia/Serbia, his two main opponents, Seselj of the Serbian far-right Radical Party and the otherwise more centrist Vuk Draskovic of the SNO (Srpski Narodna Obnova), went much further than Milosevic in anti-Muslimism. Thus Draskovic made a particular point of spreading alarm about the Islamic threat in his 1990 election campaign and spoke of the rise of what he termed 'the *ustasha* janissary state'. He said he would 'cut off the hand' of anyone raising a Muslim flag. In Croatia, a Catholic country ruled not by the Ottomans but by the Austro-Hungarian empire, Franjo Tudjman was equally vociferous in his anti-Muslimism, in addition to his well-known anti-Semitism (in private, he regularly referred to Bosnian President Izetbegovic as 'the Algerian'). Of course, one of the things Croatian nationalists denounce the Turks for is settling *Serbs* in the Krajina area, four or five centuries ago. What all this would suggest is that the prevalence of anti-Muslimism in this context has at least as much to do with contemporary needs and calculations as with any historical determination.

In Serbo-Croat there is a range of words used to vilify Muslims:

the most common are *turkein*, 'Turk', and *balija*, usually meaning a violent, lazy and stubborn person.[11] A casual reading of Serbian press materials since the start of the war in Bosnia reveals a plethora of anti-Muslimist themes, some drawing on the Serbian past, others obviously drawn from available international themes: Muslims using chemical weapons, Islamist terrorists and fundamentalists pouring into Bosnia, the destruction of Orthodox churches and monasteries, drug-running from Muslim areas, the faking of human rights abuses and of starvation by Muslims, Turkish and Iranian strategic plans, German collusion with Muslims in anti-Serb policy, fundamentalist laws being applied to women in areas under the control of the Sarajevo government.[12] A graphic illustration of this sentiment was given in an interview with the Serbian Bosnian military commander General Ratko Mladic in August 1993.[13] Mladic evoked the importance of the Drina: 'This river, the Drina, is the spine of the Serb state and it will be the mother of Serbia in the future. Some forces in the West did not want the Berlin Wall, but they wanted a border along the Drina. It will never be a borderline again.' Rejecting accusations about his ethnic cleansing, he claimed that the Serbs were the victims: 'Serb mothers watched their children taken away by the *Musulmani* to become sultans' kids to be sold as slaves ... The Islamic world does not have the atomic bomb, but it does have a demographic bomb. Atomic bombs are under some kind of control. Their enormous reproduction is not under any kind of control.' Wherever Muslims go, Mladic stated, 'very swiftly one man with five or six wives creates a village. Then they build a mosque and there you have it! Gorazde is not Istanbul, not Izmir, not Ankara. The Muslims who live there are not of that soil. They were not raised there.' Mladic talked confidently about how he would blockade UN soldiers and Muslims into Bosnian towns: 'When the snow is three metres thick, the UN will beg us to bring them food.' By mid-1994 Mladic's forces had destroyed upwards of 800 of the 2,000 Muslim places of worship in Bosnia.

In the case of Greece, a somewhat different configuration has operated. Since 1821 and in the recurrent crises of World War I and more recent clashes over Cyprus, Greek animosity has been directed in particular against Turkey and, to a lesser extent, Albania, where a Greek Orthodox minority was persecuted under Hoxha's regime. Thus in Greek nationalist rhetoric the threat of Turkey is recurrent

– in Cyprus, in the Aegean and, perhaps most dangerously, in the Greek-held area of western Thrace where a Turkish-speaking minority still exists. In the novels of Nicos Kazantzakis, for example, Turks are referred to as 'dogs'. More recently, Turkish influence in post-Soviet states and the war in Yugoslavia have aroused anti-Turkish and more generally anti-Muslim sentiment in Greece. As Radovan Karadzic, the Bosnian Serb leader, stated when visiting Athens in May 1993, 'Only God and the Greeks are with us.'

Beyond a recurrent nationalist Turcophobia, certain particular themes have contributed to this.[14] First, the issue of western Thrace is very sensitive in Greek politics, and there is a widespread belief that the Turks, through the local minority, will try to get it back. In 1990 anxiety about this reached fever pitch when two Turkish-speaking deputies were elected to the Athens parliament: they have been the subject of nationalist vilification in the press ever since. Second, the end of communism in Albania has created friction with the new government in Tirana and unleashed chauvinism against the estimated 300,000 Albanians who have come to work in Greece, mainly as illegal immigrants. Third, the Greek Orthodox Church has become more alarmed and concerned about its position, in Greece and in other Orthodox countries, not so much as a result of Islam, but as a result of the resurgence of the Catholic and Uniate churches, which claim not only souls but also property and status. As a consequence, the Greek Orthodox Church has become more assertive of its religious and social position and thus, indirectly, more hostile to the Islamic world.

These themes are all reflected in the Greek press with varying degrees of intensity. Thus the right-wing nationalist press regularly carries articles on Albanian and other Muslims as illegal immigrants (*lathrometanastis*), drug-smugglers, agents of a long-standing Turkish conspiracy and so forth. Articles argue that the region of Epirus is under 'Albanian occupation'; headlines read, 'Every day 300 new illegal immigrants arrive',[15] 'Invasion of murderers', 'Illegal immigrants, the scourge', 'Threat to our society'. Many other articles stress the Turkish encirclement, the arc that threatens Greece. Interestingly, increased Turkish influence in Central Asia is often presented not as a welcome diversion from the Balkans but as a sign of Ankara's expansionism, a token of what is to come in Greece.

However, the extent of this anti-Muslimism should not be

overstated. In Greek national mythology the (Orthodox) Bulgarians have often ranked second only to the Turks as enemies: one of the main heroes of Greek national history is *vulgarochthonos*, the killer of Bulgarians. Greece has, traditionally, had good relations with many countries of the Middle East and has projected itself as the *yefira*, the bridge, between Europe and the Arab world. In some Greek nationalist propaganda the Jews are the main enemy, and the Arabs/Muslims even pitied as victims of the Jews. While the Greek political scene is rife with anti-Turkish and now anti-Macedonian propaganda, its coverage of issues around Islamic religion and of immigration varies from the grotesque to the objective. In all of this, hostility to Islam as a religion, derived from Greek Orthodox concerns, is insignificant: indeed it is the Catholic and Uniate threats that are seen as the greatest religious problem, not the Islamic.[16] Once again, it would appear to be secular, contemporary political concerns such as strategic influence and immigration that provide the real occasion for anti-Muslimist ideology, rather than an animosity that is timeless and religiously based.

A third country of historically Orthodox culture, which saw the mobilization of such sentiments, was Bulgaria. Here, in the dying years of the communist regime, and to bolster its falling fortunes from 1985 to 1989, the ruling party fell back on anti-Turkish and anti-Muslim racism, directed at the roughly 10 per cent of the population of Turkish origin who spoke Turkish and at the Pomaks, a group of around 50,000 Bulgarian-speakers in the south-east of the country who had converted to Islam under the Ottomans. The basis for anti-Turkish and anti-Muslim racism already existed in Bulgaria, a legacy of centuries of Ottoman occupation and conflict with Turkey. Indeed, a study of words referring to Turks in Bulgarian found that around 90 per cent of them had negative connotations, and the Ottoman *robtstvo* (enserfment) was the target of much nationalist denunciation. In general, relations between Bulgarians and Turks within Bulgaria had been reasonably good. The Turks had been allowed to use their language, to wear their *shalvar*, or 'baggy' trousers, and to celebrate *bairam* along with Bulgarian national day. However, in the 1970s and 1980s the cultural and religious rights of Muslims had been curtailed, with closures of mosques and restrictions on education. Then in 1984 the Bulgarian Communist Party went a stage further and initiated a campaign to force Turks to acquire 'Bulgarian' names, arguing that all genuine Turks had left the country in 1945 and that all those who remained were in fact Bulgarians, that is, Christians who had been forcibly converted to Islam under the Ottomans.[17] This campaign was accompanied by propaganda about the Turkish threat, about those 'who dance to Ankara's tune' and the linking of Turkish ambitions to NATO encroachment on Bulgaria's sovereignty, about a possible replay of the Turkish invasion and annexation of part of Cyprus in 1974, and about the high birth rate among Turks.[18] In 1989, when political controls were relaxed, the regime allowed and, in many ways, instigated the mass exodus of Turks from Bulgaria to Turkey. In the space of a few months, 350,000 Bulgarian Turks fled the country. If a year later about half of those who had fled returned, the human cost and long-term poisoning of Bulgarian life remained.[19] As in Serbia, the rise of hostility to Muslims, combining religious with nationalist hostility, reflected political instrumentality in a context of decomposition and crisis. The difference was that in Bulgaria, unlike Serbia, the collapse of communism led to a reversal of this policy and to a degree of progress, within the context of political pluralism.

India

The country in the world where anti-Muslimism has made perhaps the greatest impact in recent years, where it is most central to a political and ideological mobilization, is India. Here the right-wing Hindu movement, represented by a cluster of overlapping groups, has made the campaign for a reassertion of the Hindu character of the country, against Muslim influence, its central programme. This has led to rising communal violence and to an increasingly hostile attitude to Muslims.[20] Muslims are abused as *ganda* ('low status', also 'low caste') and as *katwa* (literally, 'half-penis'). Often the Sanskrit world *mleccha*, meaning both 'outsider' and 'impurity', is used. A literature of justification and abuse has been produced by the parties involved in this campaign. The pages of *The Organiser*, the weekly paper of the Rashtriya Swayamsevak Sangh (RSS), are full of predictable themes: Muslim infiltration of Hindu regions, the fate of women in Muslim society, Pakistani support for terror in India, the destruction of Hindu holy places by Muslims.[21]

In one sense, this is not uniquely directed against Muslims: it is in part a campaign to turn India from a secular into a religion-based state. Indeed, many of the anti-secular themes sound similar to those heard in Islamist countries, and all non-Hindus – Christians, Jews, as well as Muslims – are regarded as the potential foe, along with secular-oriented Hindus such as those in the other political parties. It has also been argued, with some justice, that the main line of conflict is not between Hindus and Muslims but between communal and secular Hindus and that the major cause of the rise of the Bharatiya Janata Party (BJP) and its allies is not the Muslim presence but the failure and corruption of the Congress Party.[22] In many ways the history of the Congress Party is parallel to that of other post-independence secular modernizing regimes, most notably the National Liberation Front (FLN) in Algeria. Like the FLN, the Congress Party can be said in part to have encouraged the rise of religious parties, in this case Hindu communalism, by adopting some of its slogans itself. But the Muslims are certainly the major target of this attack: they are by far the largest non-Hindu minority in India (110–120 million out of 950 million, or 12–13 per cent of the total). It is the centuries of Muslim conquest that the Hindus want to avenge and reverse, and the Muslim threat 'within' is linked to the threat from 'without' in the form of Pakistan. Some of the themes found in the Indian case mirror those in the Balkans: resentment at the Muslim conquests of the fifteenth and sixteenth centuries, alarm at Muslim demographic and immigration trends, denunciation of the Islamic threat to the unity of the country, reciprocal policies of ethnic cleansing and, of course, the contest for the control of holy places. On the latter issue, for example, supporters of the destruction of the Ayodhya mosque justified the action by arguing that the Muslim conquerors destroyed all the Hindu temples in northern India. In the words of one Hindu nationalist, 'Not one temple was left standing all over northern India. It was a conscious spell of vandalism. No nation with any self-respect will forgive this. They took over our women. And they imposed the Jazia, the tax. Why should we forget and forgive all that?'[23]

There are, however, important differences between the Indian and the Balkan cases. The particular history of the rise of Hindu chauvinism is linked with that of the emergence of the Muslim League from the 1920s and the creation of Pakistan in 1948. The

BJP and RSS explicitly reject secularism, whereas the Serbian nationalists do not. In the long run, the potential for explosion and loss of human life are even greater in the subcontinent than in the Balkans.

The history of the rise of Hindu anti-Muslimism is linked to the development of Indian politics since World War I. This is not the place to explore the reciprocal process by which an increasingly explicit Hindu Indian nationalism interacted with an increasingly separatist Muslim faction to produce the partition of 1948. Suffice it to say that each fed on the other, but that in the event the main poles of division were between a predominantly secular Indian state and a predominantly Muslim Pakistan. However, there was from the beginning a third force, that of Hindu communalism and chauvinism, which, in its self-justifying history and ideology, mirrored the language and terms of the Muslim League. This was, in particular, expressed in the policies and ideas of the RSS founded in 1923. Its ideology can be gauged from the writings of M. S. Golwalkar, its intellectual inspiration and one of its main organizers until his death in 1964.[24]

Golwalkar begins from the evocation of an ideal Hindu polity, the Hindu *Rashtra*, which his party is committed to restoring. This ideal is influenced by conventional German romantic ideas of the nation, including the reverence for the original language, Sanskrit, and involves the denial of other non-Hindu peoples. When Golwalkar began writing in the 1930s this category denoted Jews, Christians and Muslims, and the Sikhs were excluded as in effect a sub-branch of Hinduism. This Hindu communalist reassertion also involves a gradual reshaping of the Hindu faith, what has been termed the 'Semitization' of Hinduism. Thus, what had hitherto been rather androgynous gods are turned into male warriors and one god, Ram, is given precedence over others; congregational worship is introduced; and what had previously been rather diffuse holy texts and stories are given the status of sacred books.[25]

This project of Hindutva, Hindu revival or, more accurately, assertion of Hinduness, is tied to a justificatory historiography.[26] India is referred to by its Hindu name, Bharat, this being the name of one of the younger brothers of Ram. The fate of Bharat is seen as having been doomed by the Muslim conquests of the fifteenth century, a process that pursued its anti-Hindu dynamic through the period of British rule and up to the creation of Pakistan. Partition, sometimes referred to as 'the vivisection of the motherland', is unacceptable:

> Our Motherland has been partitioned. Some people ask me to forget this fact. But I, for one, can never persuade myself to forget it. I would appeal to you also not to forget this tragic episode. It is an abiding humiliation for us. We have to pledge ourselves resolutely not to rest content until we have wiped out this blot.[27]

Indeed, it is striking, in the writings of Golwalkar, how little the British figure as an enemy at all. Muslims have continued, even after dividing Bharat, to conspire against it, flooding the country with immigrants, planning to extend Pakistan's rule, challenging Hindu domination in Kashmir and so forth. Thus Golwalkar writes:

> Alien traits found today in the life of Muslims and Christians of Bharat may be traced to history. Both these sects were imported into Bharat by foreign rulers, and throve under their patronage, as their instruments. These foreign rulers did not nationally establish the superiority of their faith before propagating it. Instead, they used terror to alienate our nationals from our ancient traditions, and used the converts to prop up their rule. A large number of people embraced these faiths out of fear or greed, and simultaneously they adopted foreign ways of life too. These faiths, therefore, symbolize our slavery.[28]

Golwalkar argues that the Muslims of the twentieth century are planning not to defend their Pakistani state but to restore the Mughal Empire, ruling over all India. Despite his hostility to Christians, Golwalkar has no problem in identifying with Christian resistance to Islamic forces: 'If Charles Martel had not stopped the Muslims at Tours in 732, today the entire Europe would have been under the banner of the Star and the Crescent.'[29]

The RSS remained on the relative margins of Indian politics for the first three decades after independence: it was banned in 1948 after the Congress Party alleged that one of its members had assassinated Gandhi. But in 1969 an associated cultural front, the Vishwa Hindu Parashad (VHP), was founded and in 1980 another party, the BJP, became a militant and increasingly successful advocate of

Hindutva politics. Tied to the RSS, with its mass of disciplined and lightly armed members, or to the Shiv Sena ('army of Shiva'), an even more militant group founded in 1966 on a programme of Maharashtra chauvinism, these forces acquired a major influence in Indian politics both at the electoral level and in mass actions, culminating in the seizure and rededication of the Babri Masjid, the mosque in Ayodhya where it was claimed Ram was born, in December 1992. This event was preceded and followed by clashes with Muslims in a number of Indian cities.[30]

Three themes in particular are central to this current wave of fundamentalism. The first is the call for the reconstitution of a Hindu nation. This nation is to be established on a version of Hindu values: while it is not argued that the non-Hindus should reconvert to Hinduism, it is implied that many of them were converted by force and would therefore revert to Hinduism if they could, and that in some (undefined) way they should accept Hindu cultural values. 'Let Muslims look on Ram as their hero, and the communal problems will be all over,' proclaimed *The Organiser* in 1971. Hence the rejection of secularism, similar to the claim of Islamists and distinct from that of, say, Balkan anti-Muslimists. Secondly, the national territory of the state should be reunited, with the reincorporation of Pakistan. Here there is an evident contradiction with the desired expulsion of Muslims. It goes without saying that all other attempts to break away, such as that of the Sikhs in the Punjab fighting for 'Khalistan' or of the Mizos and Nagas in Tripura, should also be opposed. Thirdly, there is a great emphasis on the dangers of mass Muslim immigration. Golwalkar, discussing 'internal threats' to Bharat, began with the Muslims who, he said, had become an even greater menace with the creation of Pakistan. Golwalkar wrote that the Muslims pursued two strategies – external aggression, from Pakistan, and internal weakening, through migration – and accordingly he saw the settlement of Muslims in areas of Bharat as part of a planned conspiratorial process.[31] A book on West Bengal promoted by the RSS, *Paradise for Infiltrators*, evokes themes familiar in other contexts: 'West Bengal may be part of India but in reality it is like a disposable concubine of Bangladesh.' The ruling Communist Party and the Congress Party are attacked for patronizing this 'infiltration'. For the Muslims, 'everything that man needs for a civilized living is available to them at no extra cost. There are no bars against him. He can purchase land for residential and agricultural purposes, get his children admitted in schools, have ration cards issued to him, have his name entered in the voters' list and yet follow his Islamic way of life. Such are the bounties of Indian secularism.'[32]

This anti-immigrant theme was especially evident in the communal clashes in Bombay in 1992–93 and in the discourse of the Hindu leader, Bal Thackeray, head of the local branch of Shiv Sena. Agitating in a city where 15–20 per cent of the population are Muslims, Thackeray has denounced Muslims as 'anti-nationals' and 'traitors', and referred to their districts of the city as 'mini-Pakistans'. 'My fight is against pro-Pakistan Muslims. The Pakistani extremists, the Bangladeshi Muslims and the Muslims staying in this country for years together, giving shelter to them – all these people must be kicked out. Even if he is a Hindu giving shelter to these kinds of Muslims, he also must be shot dead.' Thackeray also advocated the use of violence against Muslims, in contrast to the less aggressive construction of Hinduism: 'You have to react, you have to retaliate. I believe in constructive violence. I am not Mahatma Gandhi. If Muslims do this mischief again with Hindus, come what may, by whatever means we have, we will spare our lives.'[33] Asked what he would do with illegal immigrants from Pakistan or Bangladesh, he was happy to reply: 'We will compel them to leave. After all, I am not a member of Amnesty International.'[34] When Thackeray and his Shiv Sena associates came to power in the province of Maharashtra in early 1995, one of their first acts was to change the name of the capital from Bombay (derived from the Portuguese for a 'good bay') to Devi Mumbhai, after a Hindu goddess.

If, in India, this anti-Muslim discourse is perhaps more developed than anywhere else in the world, its incidence is one that bears some relation to other movements. Hinduism gave European fascism one potent symbol, the swastika, the symbol of good fortune (*su-asti* in Sanskrit). The very ideology of *Rashtra* that is promoted by the RSS is based on the application of European conceptions of nation and religion to India. It is a modern ideology, with the added element of the supposed common stress on the Aryan ethnic and linguistic heritage of those opposed to Muslim expansion. This original RSS ideology, derived from European racism of the interwar period, has now adopted some of the elements of contemporary anti-Islamism, notably the stress on Islam as the source of terrorism and the pseudo-strategic concept of a Muslim 'arc', in this case stretching from Turkey to Indonesia, within which India is located. The social and political factors that have led to the rise of the RSS, the BJP and others are also familiar from other contexts: the collapse of the power and legitimacy of the secular nationalist regime, growing social tensions in the cities, to which is added the intervention of a determined and well-organized ideological force, with the support of at least some in the state apparatus and among the middle classes.[35]

The West: Europe and the USA

If the visibility of mass anti-Muslim sentiment in the Balkans and in the Indian subcontinent appeared as a relatively recent phenomenon, a feature of the latter half of the 1980s, the same could hardly be said of the developed Western world, both European and American. Here a range of anti-Muslim sentiments had prevailed for far longer, so much so that it was easy for commentators to write in terms of some underlying but enduring religious and cultural antipathy in Western Christianity, going back not just to the imperial period ('orientalism') but to the earlier confrontations of the Ottoman assault of the seventeenth century, the Crusades and the initial repulsion of the Arab invasions in the eighth century.[36] In one of the most famous polemics against Islam, the French linguist and 'orientalist' Ernest Renan declared in 1883 that it was essential for the rational, scientific 'Aryan' spirit to conquer the irrational 'Semitic' mind of Islam.[37] For Muslims and non-Muslims alike it seemed that this confrontation was 'ingrained' in the Western world, its most recent manifestations but the latest chapters in a long-running and apparently continuous story.

The elements of this continuity are not hard to find. The wars with the Islamic world, from the eighth to the seventeenth centuries, were a major preoccupation of Christian Europe. The Crusades, launched in the late eleventh century by Pope Urban II, were a major defining point in mediaeval Europe. In the Iberian Peninsula, the very state and its identity were forged in the battle to expel the Muslims, and once this was completed in 1492 the ideology of militarized and religious offensive was transferred to the conquest of the Americas. The conquistadors saw themselves as crusaders, as did those who brought Christianity to the Baltic states in the twelfth and thirteenth centuries. Later, with the Ottoman advances of the fifteenth and sixteenth centuries, a further chapter of anti-Muslimism was written: one can, indeed, suggest that it was this experience above all that shaped European attitudes, just as it was the rise of the Mughal empire that formed Hindu sensibilities. As Norman Daniel has pointed out, this period saw the earlier image of the Muslim as 'Saracen'[38] replaced by its new all-purpose variant, 'Turk'. One famous example of this was to be found in the 'War Sermon' of Martin Luther, who in 1529 saw the Turks as realizing biblical warnings of divine punishment, such as those relating to the Flood and to Sodom and Gomorrah.[39] One of the best-selling works of the period was that of Bartholomew Georgevich of Croatia, *Tribulations of the Christians Held in Tribute and Slavery by the Turks* (1544).[40] In Austria, the racist Right has used as its hero Count Ernst Rüdiger von Starhemberg, commander of Vienna during the 1683 siege.[41]

The relics of these campaigns are readily visible in modern European culture – in the abusive use of the term '*turk*' (meaning stupid) in Dutch, in the Italian warning to children who do not behave, '*Mama, i turchi!*' and in the abusive term *marroquino*, in the celebration of the defeat of the Muslims in the French *croissant* or the Viennese *Kipfel*,[42] in the names of English pubs ('The Turk's Head') and, indeed, in the national symbol of one of the emergent European regions, Corsica, which has taken the eighteenth-century flag of the Moor's head, itself borrowed from the Crusades, as its symbol.[43] Certainly these themes are available for current usage, as are those, of equal historical importance, that express Muslim concern about Christian hostility. But to identify these relics and revivals is not to prove a continuity of culture or politics, let alone to prove that contemporary anti-Muslimism can be explained in terms of this past. Several considerations, beyond a general scepticism about the automatic transmission of culture and the effectivity of an archetypal substratum, would suggest otherwise.

In the first place, if we survey stereotypes of Muslims and Arabs we find that they are, like many such stereotypes, contradictory. Thus Islam, today associated with austerity and the denial of the material, was long seen as a religion of hedonism, sensuality and male pleasure – as expressed in images of the *harem*, the *odalisque* and the *seraglio*. Equally, the concept of the Arab or Muslim as militant, aggressive and active goes together with that of the Muslim as quintessentially passive, accepting and submissive before God. Strikingly, Primo Levi records that in the concentration camps the inmates whose spirit was broken were known as the 'Muslims'.[44] Secondly, it is not possible to generalize about the experience of Western states, particularly if this involves the USA. For reasons above all of geographical location, but also of different imperial experience, the role of anti-Muslim sentiment varies from country to country. The states of the northern Mediterranean were, for centuries, far more exposed to Muslim attack than those of northern Europe. Thus, not only the initial Arab attacks and occupation but also the later experience of Italy with Arab naval attacks (condensed in the term 'Saracen') were not replicated in the north. (The one other place where this image of Arabs and Muslims as pirates was found was, surprisingly, in North America. The clash between US ships and 'Barbary', i.e. North African, ships in the early nineteenth century was to form the basis for much later imagery, not least with regard to Qaddafi.) That these threats and the identities of those so threatening were confused is evident from the widespread use of the term 'Moor', a pre-Islamic, Roman term that also gives us 'Morocco' but came to combine, as in the case of Othello, Muslim identity with African origin. To these earlier differences must be added those of colonial experience. For France the encounter with Arab and Muslim North Africa was a formative experience, culminating in the traumatic Algerian war of 1954–62. Italy had a less violent but none the less important experience in Libya. Spain too had a major confrontation with the Arab world, in the conflicts over Ifni, the Western Sahara and, to this day, Ceuta and Melilla. These were, however, but one aspect of several colonial confrontations – notably with Vietnam, (Christian) Ethiopia and Latin America respectively.

In the British case, the confrontation with the Islamic world was far less important: true, there was the occupation of Egypt and the death of General Gordon at the hands of the 'fanatical' Mahdists in the Sudan in 1885. Probably the most influential British encounter with Muslim society was that brought about by the presence of hundreds of thousands of British soldiers in Egypt during World War II, out of which much contemporary anti-Arab racism emerges. But the Muslim encounter was far less important for Britain than for France. French has many Arabic words derived from the North African experience, while nearly all 'Muslim' words in English come from the Anglo-Indian vocabulary derived from a predominantly Hindu experience, within which the Persian vocabulary of Hindustani played an important part. For much of the British imperial period other foes were more prominent: Irish Catholic nationalists, Hindu mutineers in India, Zionists in Palestine, Greek Orthodox guerrillas in Cyprus, Christian and pagan Mau-Mau opponents in Kenya, Chinese communists in Malaya. In several of these contexts – India in the 1850s, Palestine in the 1940s, Malaya and Cyprus in the 1950s – the Muslims were not only not the main enemy but were to a greater or lesser extent allies of, or at least partial collaborators with, the British. The result is that, both in popular stereotype and in more recent racist manifestations, hostility to Muslims as such plays a relatively smaller role. It is true that one of the main terms of abuse of South Asians is that of 'Paki', short for 'Pakistani' (the insult is, however, lost on speakers of Urdu, the language of many Pakistanis, in which *paki* means 'pure'), but this is almost wholly a racial epithet, referring to skin colour and clothing, and is applied indiscriminately to South Asians of any religion, be they Muslim, Hindu, Christian, Buddhist, Sikh or Jain. In the American case almost the only images of Muslims available until the 1960s were in films – Valentino as the Sheikh of Araby, Palestinian terrorists in *Exodus*.[45] Once a set of conflicts began, however, a new abusive vocabulary developed: 'rag-' or 'towel-heads', 'camel-jockeys' (a euphemism for people who have sexual relations with camels) and so on.[46]

To this must be added, as a partial corrective, the actual history of Western–Muslim relations over the past century. This is not one of concerted or unremitting hostility. The Dutch, for example, had a long history of alliance with the Moroccans against their common foe, Catholic Spain. In Poland, too, there was, prior to the disappearance of the state in the 1790s, a tradition of alliance with the Ottomans against the common enemy, the Habsburg empire. Christian hostility to Muslims is usually proved by reference to the Spanish *reconquista*, which culminated in the fall of Granada in 1492. But this degree of hostility was particular to the imperial regime of that period and contrasted with an earlier period of greater tolerance within Christian Spain. The history of European relations with the Ottoman empire in the nineteenth century was one of both conflict and accommodation, the latter often involving alliances between various European powers and Istanbul against other 'Christian' powers – Napoleonic France in the 1800s, Britain in the 1830s and 1850s and later Germany. In both world wars the Western antagonists devoted considerable energy to winning over Islamic sentiment, not least because in three cases – Britain, France, Holland – Muslims comprised a considerable proportion of their subject peoples. In World War I, for example, Kaiser Wilhelm presented himself as the champion of the Muslim world. The British, ensconced in Egypt and the Arabian Peninsula, made much of their being 'friends of the Arabs', be it in the World War I alliance against the Turks or in the arms sales deals of the 1960s and later. In the whole period since 1945 the record has been mixed: in the 1950s and 1960s, the West supported monarchical 'Islamic' polities such as Saudi Arabia against the much greater threat of socialist, nationalist and communist movements in the third world, a policy that was to reach its culmination in the substantial CIA backing for the Afghan *mujahidin* in the 1980s. Indeed the whole picture of a 'West' unremittingly hostile to the Islamic world is rather contradicted by what occurred in Afghanistan after 1979.

These correctives may support an analysis of the growth of contemporary anti-Muslim sentiment that is rather more contingent, in terms of country and time. In terms of the past one or two decades, one may indeed distinguish between two strands of anti-Muslimism that may be termed 'strategic' and 'populist'. One is related to issues of security – nuclear weapons, oil supplies, terrorism – while the other is concerned with the presence of Muslims within Western society – immigration, assimilation, race, veiling and so forth. The two may be linked, in one generic and timeless 'threat', but the elements are rather different. Strategic anti-Muslimism dates from the early 1970s and is above all a result of the 1973 OPEC price rises: even though these were not the result of a uniquely Muslim coalition (OPEC includes Venezuela), the 1973 rises provoked a reaction that included anti-Muslim and associated racist hostility to Arabs and Iranians. This was particularly so in the USA where, for the first time, what had hitherto been experienced as an independent economic system was exposed to a form of foreign pressure, conceived of as blackmail or threat. Then came the Iranian revolution and, for the USA in particular, the hostages crisis, which confirmed the image of the Islamic fanatic and terrorist: this rhetoric did not distinguish Persians from Arabs. Side by side with this alarm, related to oil and the hostages, was the diffusion of a set of anti-Arab prejudices emanating from the Arab–Israeli dispute. These had been identifiable since the 1940s, but became more evident from the 1960s onwards, partly as a result of the 1967 war and then as a result of the rise of a terrorist faction within the Palestinian movement. These stereotypes were played up in the press, but were reinforced by novels such as Leon Uris's *Exodus* and *The Hajj*, and by films. In the USA in particular the composite Arab-Persian-Muslim-terrorist was established through the intersection of these influences. With the end of the cold war another chapter was written: numerous politicians were heard to proclaim that the USA was now facing the threat of Islamic militancy, and this received partial confirmation from the Gulf conflict of 1990–91. In 1990 Vice-President Dan Quayle, in an address to cadets at the Annapolis naval academy, linked Islamic fundamentalism to Nazism and communism. The right-wing Republican candidate in the 1992 presidential campaign, Pat Buchanan, declared: 'For a millennium, the struggle for mankind's destiny was between Christianity and Islam; in the twenty-first century it may be so again. For, as the Shi'ites humiliate us, their co-religionists are filling up the countries of the West.'[47]

Press analysis played up the sense both of a transhistorical force and of a concerted worldwide campaign: from the 1979 Iranian seizure of US diplomatic personnel, through the holding of Americans as hostages in Lebanon to the bombing of the World Trade Center in New York in 1993, the threat seemed to be getting closer. A television documentary, aired in December 1994 and titled *Jihad in America*, presented a dramatic picture of Islamism hitting directly at the USA.[48] Such was the strength of this anxiety that when, on 19 April 1995, a bomb exploded outside a government building in Oklahoma City, killing hundreds, the immediate response of many media commentators and of the police was that it was the work of Middle Eastern terrorists. Men of Middle Eastern complexion were sought; terrorism 'experts' pontificated on television; there were calls for pre-emptive strikes on Middle Eastern states; a wave of public attacks on Arabs and Muslims occurred.[49] The culprits were, on this occasion, home-grown American crazies.

The culture of anti-Muslimism in the USA was distinguished in several respects from that of Europe. On the one hand, it was not to any significant extent concerned with the issue of immigration or with an internal or demographic threat to US society. This was partly because of the more variant and multicultural character of the USA and partly because while in Europe the 'immigrant threat' was represented by Muslims (among others), in the USA (Catholic) Hispanic migrants took that role. In the USA the focus fell on what was seen as the set of security threats – restrictions to the supply of oil, hostage taking, terrorism – that had emerged from Middle Eastern society in the 1970s and 1980s. In Europe these issues, although present, were a less prominent focus of concern. For Europe, 1973 marked a shock, but not the one it represented in the USA, since Europe had always been dependent upon foreign imports. The hostage crisis had, for obvious national reasons, less impact in Europe. Terrorism did arouse concern, but the relatively less dominant position of pro-Israeli sentiment meant that there was not the obsession with terrorism that prevailed in the USA. Moreover, European countries had themselves had recent experiences of terrorism that had nothing to do with any Muslim force: the British with the IRA, the Spanish with ETA, the Germans with the Baader-Meinhof group, the Italians with the Brigate Rosse and the fascist counterparts, the French with the OAS.

Strategic anti-Muslimism was certainly present in Europe, both because of the proximity of European countries to the Muslim world and because, as in so many strategic fashions, Europe copied the USA. Thus in an article published in 1993 under the title 'Islam's New Drive into Europe', Sir Alfred Sherman, a former personal adviser to Margaret Thatcher, wrote:

> There is a Moslem threat to Christian Europe. It is developing slowly and could still be checked. But the policies of the Western powers have done almost everything possible to help it grow. The factors that created the threat were: 1. Totally irresponsible immigration policies in western and central Europe, which have rapidly created an increasingly militant minority of 15 million Moslems there. 2. The alienation of Turkey by the European community, which rejected Turkey's sincere efforts to join the EEC, virtually compelling it to seek identification with a Moslem world it was trying to escape from. 3. Germany's aggressive policy in the Balkans, calculated to break up Yugoslavia and Czechoslovakia, suppress Serbia and achieve hegemony in the region with Hungarian help. 4. Vatican support for this policy and the Pope's persistent court of Arab states regardless of the interests of their Christian minorities ... The gradual Moslem

colonization of western and central Europe owes much to social and spiritual disorientation there ... Another factor was the decline of Christian and Western values caused by the unlearning of Western history, including the threat from Islam. In essence pro-Islamism – like pro-third worldism and (until recently) pro-Sovietism – are symptoms of the collapse of belief in their own values among the west's intellectuals and politicians.[50]

In similar vein Clare Hollingworth, a veteran British defence correspondent, under the title 'Another Despotic Creed Seeks to Infiltrate the West' wrote:

Muslim fundamentalism is fast becoming the chief threat to global peace and security as well as a cause of national and local disturbance through terrorism. It is akin to the menace posed by Nazism and fascism in the 1930s and then by communism in the '50s.[51]

A quite different element was introduced from the mid-1980s onwards with the rise of anti-Muslim sentiment as part of the anti-migrant and more generally racist sentiments in many western European countries, tied to alarmist speculation at the end of the cold war about the new 'Islamic' threat.[52] Thus in Europe strategic anti-Muslimism combined with popular anti-Muslimism from the mid-1980s onwards. A number of particular issues involving Muslim immigrants fuelled this: these included the dispute that broke out in France in 1989, and which was repeated again in 1994, over the veiling of Muslim girls going to school ('*l'affaire foulard*'),[53] the campaigns by Muslim organizations in Britain in protest at Salman Rushdie's *The Satanic Verses*, and the prominence of Turks as targets of racism in Germany. The most extreme case of hostility to Muslims was undoubtedly that of France, where the right-wing Front National headed by Jean-Marie Le Pen openly called for the repatriation of up to three million North African immigrants and stimulated a general climate of permitted anti-Arab racism.[54] During the French presidential elections of 1995, for example, in which Le Pen won 15 per cent of the vote, Le Pen sympathizers openly voiced anti-Arab views. 'My father told me that Arabs are worse than mice,' one 31-year-old woman told a reporter. Another attacked the way in which those of North African origin claimed

social security: 'They are French when they get their unemployment benefit, Arab when they misbehave.'[55] During one of Le Pen's
election rallies in Paris a 29-year-old Moroccan, Brahim Bouarram,
was thrown into the river by skinheads, and drowned. Le Pen refused to apologize, saying it was the kind of 'incident' that happened
in any big city and indeed that it might have been triggered by a
provocation against the Front National.[56] Such was the hostility to
Arabs that right-wing demonstrators denounced the main conservative candidate, Jacques Chirac, with the slogan '*Chirac à la Mecque*'
('Chirac to Mecca').[57]

It was striking too that in other European countries the racist
Right made anti-Muslimism particularly central. In Belgium the
Flemish right-wing Vlaams Blok blamed the country's budget deficit on Walloons and on the welfare costs of supporting Moroccans
with large numbers of children. In Sweden the leader of the New
Democratic Party, Ian Wachtmeister, declared in 1993, 'I must con-
fess that in my Sweden there will not be many mosques', a statement
that was followed within two days by an arson attack on a mosque.
Another right-wing politician, Viviane Franzen, asked at the same
time: 'How long will it be before Swedish children are bowing to
Mecca?' In Austria, the recently founded Freedom Party (FPO), in
particular its leader, Jochen Haider, highlighted the dangers of mass
immigration and the loss of Austrian identity. In his New Year's
message for 1993 he warned that Austrian schoolchildren were losing their culture, since in some classes in Vienna, where there was
an above-average percentage of Muslim children, crucifixes were
being removed.

Anti-Muslimist sentiments of this kind can be quoted from
several European countries, where they express the new racist and
anti-immigrant politics that has emerged. The causes of this lie in
the first place in two issues separate from Islam or Muslims – the
pervasive social unease arising from the economic recession and
the rise of an anti-foreign and anti-'coloured' resentment that
focuses, in many cases, on Muslims. But even here it is hard to
disentangle the different elements in the prejudice. In Britain Muslim
immigrants have encountered hostility ever since the first Muslims,
Yemenis and Somalis, began arriving around the time of World
War I. In 1919 there were widespread anti-Arab riots in several
British ports: but the terms used to describe these Arab sailors –
Bolsheviks, Fenians, negroes – had no special religious character,

and the most specific term used of them, *lascar*, was a generic Anglo-Indian word for an Asian sailor.[58] With the large-scale migration of Muslims from India, Pakistan and Bangladesh, the term 'Paki' acquired widespread usage in Britain, but it was again not necessarily religious in connotation. It was indeed only in the late 1980s, more particularly with the *Satanic Verses* affair and the Gulf war, that an identifiable anti-Muslimist trend emerged at the mass level in Britain. In sum, anti-Muslimism emerged throughout Western Europe in a context of broader xenophobia and economic recession: it was linked to the particular contexts of political competition in each country, yet it also had certain limits. In some cases this was due to the fact that for European far-right groups the main object of hostility remained the Jews, and in this context Muslims were, if anything, regarded as victims of a supervening Zionist conspiracy.

Israel

No relationship is more controversial or complex than that between the Islamic and the Jewish worlds, above all because of what has occurred since the mass migration of Jews to Israel in the late nineteenth century and the establishment of the state of Israel in 1948. The massacre of twenty-nine Muslims at prayer in the mosque at Hebron by the Israeli terrorist settler Baruch Goldstein in February 1994 appeared to be but the culmination of this antagonism. Here, above all, images of an eternal, transhistorical hostility prevail on both sides. For Muslims, the story seems clear enough: the Quran itself states that the Jews are the enemies of Islam,[59] and this has been vindicated by the establishment of the state of Israel and the occupation not only of Muslim lands in general but of cities and places of worship central to the Muslim faith. No wonder, it might appear, that Islamists and indeed Muslims have for the several decades past seen 'Zionism' as a central element of the anti-Islamic conspiracy and Israel as an entity created for the purpose of dispossessing and oppressing Muslims. For their part, Israeli politicians, particularly but not exclusively those of the nationalist Right (Gush Emunim), stress the danger posed to Israel and to Jews in general by Islam, and recast the Arabs as the ancient foes of Israel, the gentiles and, more specifically, the Amalekites of the

Bible. The Bible[60] commands that these Amalekites be exterminated, just as, in a verse frequently used by nationalist settlers on the West Bank, the gentiles should be struck down.

The relationship of Jews and Judaism to Islam has, however, been more complex than this would suggest, and remains so. First, while claims of complete tolerance by Muslim states of Jews are exaggerated, the history of relations between Jews and Muslims prior to the 1890s was not all antagonistic. The record of Islamic states towards Jews was, on the whole, much better than that of Christian states, and this was most evident in the acceptance of large numbers of Sephardic Jews who were expelled from Spain. On their side, Jewish writers tended not to express great hostility to Islam. With the emergence of Jewish mysticism or *kabbalism*, a strain of hostility to the Islamic religion did emerge,[61] as is evident in the writings of the thirteenth-century writer Nachmonides. The Andalucian writer Maimonides wrote critically of Jews who studied Islam, but he distinguished between Christianity, which was a form of idolatry, and Islam, which was not. He himself quoted from Muslim texts with respect, and served as personal physician to Saladin, the Islamic Kurdish leader who drove the Crusaders out of Jerusalem.[62] It can, however, be argued that until the emergence of Zionism, Jewish writers were far more concerned with Christianity than with Islam.[63] Even after the Zionist movement began, the main preoccupation of Zionists was not with the Muslim world but, given the rise of fascism, with the European states. It was only after 1948 that the Arab world became the object of clear confrontation in Jewish eyes, and then it was seen as hostile not so much because it was Muslim as because it was gentile. Arab states such as Nasser's Egypt were, in Israeli rhetoric, compared with Hitler's Germany and regarded as another political force bent on destroying the Jews.

There were certainly elements of anti-Arab and, by implication, anti-Muslim racism and prejudice in Israel prior to 1948. From the 1890s people referred to the local population in disparaging terms, as 'donkeys' and so forth.[64] The very project of the Zionist movement explicitly involved the displacement of the local Arab (and partly Christian) population from their lands and thus contained, at least implicitly, a racist denial of their rights and common humanity. The goal of a 'land without people, for a people without land' was, therefore, anti-Palestinian. The early Zionist poet Ben Yahuda wrote, 'How beautiful is Israel without Arabs.' But Zionist ideology was not as yet specifically or mainly anti-*Muslim*: the main ideological orientation of the European settlers who came to Israel was that they were, in addition to being representatives of the Jewish people, also in the vanguard of European civilization, against the barbarians and natives whom they found in Palestine. In this their attitude was not markedly different from that of other white European settlers in the third world. And this 'civilizational' arrogance also meant considerable prejudice not just against Arabs but also against Oriental Jews, who were considered uncivilized and little better than the Arabs. One account of Ashkenazi hostility to Oriental Jews illustrates this graphically:

> A whole vocabulary of racial slurs referring to the Oriental Jews became commonplace: 'Khomeinists', rabble (*asafsuf*), hooligans (*biryonim*), masses (*amkha*), Moroccan cutthroats (*Morocco sakin*), cave-dwellers (*shluhim*), pagans (*ovdai elilim*), fanatics (*babe salee*). Mordechai Gur, a Labour candidate and former Chief of Staff, warned a heckling group of Oriental Jews, Likud supporters, in a development town, 'We'll screw you like we screwed the Arabs in the Six Day war'.[65]

The term *avoda aravit*, literally 'Arab work', was used to refer to sloppy or substandard work. Nothing could be more indicative of this than the use of the term *aravit* (Arab) to refer to Oriental Jews. The term *shluhim*, 'cave-dwellers', came into common usage in the 1950s as an Ashkenazi term of abuse for Moroccan Jewish immigrants who had, allegedly, been cave-dwellers in their land of origin. Conversely, the early Zionists used to refer to Arabs by the most common term of abuse of all in Hebrew: *frenk*, the Yiddish word for anyone in European dress. Since the Jews wore their black dress, *kapota*, and the Arab educated classes wore western European clothing of the period, the Arabs were assimilated to Christian gentile society.[66]

Hostility to Arabs and Muslims was therefore mixed up with a wider rhetoric of racism and hostility to gentiles in general and to people who had originated in Arab society, be they Muslims, Christians or Jews. The more specific anti-Arab/Muslim hostility was to develop only later, in the aftermath of the 1967 war and, even more so, in the aftermath of the Iranian revolution. After 1967, with the Israeli occupation of the West Bank and Gaza, there emerged a much stronger current of militant and nationalistic irredentism, epitomized in the settlers and the newly influential Gush Emunim ('the bloc of the faithful'). It was in this context that orthodox rabbis began providing a religious justification – deploying elements available in the Judaic tradition – for occupation of the West Bank and the violent displacement of Arabs. In 1968 Samuel Derlich, head chaplain for the Israeli army, wrote to soldiers that it was a *mitzvah* (religious duty), recorded in the Bible, 'to destroy Amalek'. When some army officers protested, forty other rabbis wrote to defend Derlich and to certify that his statement was consistent with *halakhah*, Jewish legal tradition.[67] At the same time, particularly from the mid-1970s onwards, the parties of the religious Right, the *haredim*, were to play an important role in Israeli politics, and to propagate a more assertive and prejudicial attitude towards non-Jews as a whole, including Muslims.[68] This internal shift in Israeli politics was compounded by external events – the triumph of the Iranian revolution in 1979, with its clear hostility to the very existence of Israel, the emergence of a pro-Iranian Shi'ite movement in Lebanon from 1982 onwards and the rise among Palestinians of the Islamic Resistance Movement (*Harakat al-Moqawama al-Islamiyya*, or Hamas). By the late 1980s and early 1990s it did, therefore, appear as if Israel was locked into an overarching battle with the Islamic world, a view that many Islamists, intoxicated with their visions of a worldwide Zionist and Jewish hostility to Islam, were quick to confirm.

The most extreme anti-Arab trend was, however, represented by the movement of Rabbi Meir Kahane and his Kach movement, which occupied a militant, violent place in Israeli politics from the early 1970s until Kahane's assassination in 1990. Kahane proffered a militant reading of the Talmud and the Halakha, according to which Jews were enjoined to fight non-Jews and indeed those corrupted, 'gentilized' and 'Hellenized' Jews who did not agree with him.[69] Central to his message was the call for all Arabs to be forcibly deported from Israel.[70] Kahane wanted a law to be introduced making it illegal for any Jew to have sexual relations with a non-Jew and for all non-Jews to be denied citizenship in Israel. 'Give me the power to take care of them [the Arabs] once and for all,' he declared to a rally of supporters in Jerusalem in 1989, after a Palestinian attack on a bus in which sixteen people died. His supporters were reported as replying, 'Death to the Arabs and their [Jewish] leftist friends.'[71] Kahane's rhetoric was clear, hateful and threatening:

> The Arabs are cancer, cancer, cancer in the midst of us. But there is not a single man who is willing to stand up and say it ... I am telling you what each of you thinks deep in his heart: there is only one solution, no other, no partial solution: the Arabs out! Out! ... Do not ask me how ... Let me become defence minister for two months and you will not have a single cockroach around here! I promise you a *clean* Eretz Israel! Give me the power to take care of them![72]

In this context, the incidence of overtly anti-Arab and anti-Muslim rhetoric has become much greater in Israel, especially among West Bank settlers and the parties of the nationalist and religious Right. One of the texts most frequently cited by settlers is verses 5–9 of Psalm 149, which form part of the Jewish morning prayer. This includes the lines, 'Let the praises of the Lord be in their mouth and a two-edged sword in their hand. To execute vengeance upon the gentiles and punishments upon the nations. To bind their kings with chains and their nobles with fetters of iron.' These words are widely interpreted as legitimating attacks by settlers upon local Arabs, and find their more vernacular expression in slogans scrawled on walls: 'Only a sucker doesn't kill an Arab', 'Death to the Arabs', 'To make mincemeat of the Arabs', etc.[73] At the funeral of Baruch Goldstein, one rabbi declared, 'One million Arabs are not worth a Jewish fingernail.'[74] Such attitudes among militant settlers find their parallels in the religious establishment, especially among the sections of the rabbinate who act as chaplains to the army and in association with settler organizations and parties. Thus in July 1993 the head of the Public Committee for the Defence of Human Dignity, Rabbi Mordechai Yedidya Weiner, called on the government to allow the organs of Arabs killed during the *intifada* to be used for organ transplants, in order to dispense with the need to extract organs from the bodies of Jews, since such extractions are deemed to be forbidden under orthodox Jewish law.[75] Earlier in the year Ovadia Yoseph, a rabbi who heads the religious party Shas, had expressed his view clearly in a sermon when he said that 'Arabs are worse than the wildest animals'. Such attitudes, while not characteristic of the statements of most Israeli politicians, are, however, those of an important minority within Israel who evidently feel that they can utter and disseminate such views without fear of contradiction, legal or political.

Those who propound anti-Muslimism within contemporary Israel and in related sections of the Diaspora are themselves quick to resort to arguments about some enduring, eternal conflict between the Muslim and Jewish worlds. In doing this, they can easily find themes and symbols from the biblical past and from subsequent history to bolster their argument. From their perspective, as we have seen, Palestinians, Arabs as a whole and indeed many in the whole Muslim world consider Jews to be the enemies of Islam. Yet this obscures the manner in which the current usage of anti-Muslim rhetoric has developed and distorts the longer and more varied history of Jewish–Muslim relations. The contemporary form of Jewish hostility to the Arab and Islamic worlds and the reciprocal anti-Jewish and in many cases anti-Semitic rhetorics of the Arab and Muslim worlds reflect above all a recent and contemporary history, not the resurgence of some archaeological conflict. Thus in the rhetoric of right-wing Israelis, Palestinians are attacked as 'Hitlerites' or as modern versions of the Ukrainian peasants led by Chmielnicki who killed Jews in the seventeenth century, more than as part of some eternal Muslim threat.[76] The origins of the most extreme anti-Arab racism, that of Kahane, lie more in the polarized racial politics of New York, in a fusion of anti-Nazi and anti-black confrontational themes, than in any specific engagement with the Arab or Muslim world. In Kahane's rhetoric the Arabs are but the latest bearers of the title 'enemy of Jews'. The Middle Eastern sources of this confrontation lie in modern history, in the actions of Weizmann and Ben Gurion, Balfour and Peel, Nasser and Khomeini, rather than in the resurgence of the Amalekites or of some Talmudic ideological essence. As elsewhere, anti-Muslimism in Israel is a modern, contingent and instrumental ideology.

Conclusion

This introductory survey, necessarily schematic and incomplete, allows of no easy analysis of the genesis, content or impact of anti-Muslimism, any more than it permits of complacency about the pervasiveness and manifold uses of this contemporary ideology. In one sense the debate over ideological genesis and form is irrelevant to the most pressing political and human issue, namely the incidence of this prejudice, linked to others of race, faction and party, in so many countries. No one surveying this phenomenon and the ease with which it is reproduced and embroidered throughout the press, in political discourse ranging from the most vulgar to the most 'serious', can fail to feel concern and shame.

Yet as part of any response to it and analysis of its relation to other forms of racism it may be pertinent to suggest some analytic conclusions. First, while historical legacies certainly play a role – in the Balkans, in India, in Western society and in Israel – these cannot explain the incidence of anti-Muslimism today. Like all cultural residues and themes, it is their revival, reformulation and redeployment in contemporary contexts that has to be explained.

Secondly, it is certainly possible to identify a set of core anti-Muslim themes that are found in different contexts. Terrorism, demographic expansion, strategic encirclement, the oppression of women and dirtiness are the common preoccupations. But this does not prove the existence of a single anti-Muslimism; rather it suggests how, in addition to themes generated within a specific context, others available from the international media are deployed.

Thirdly, without conceding to the claim that hostility to Muslims is justified by what some/all Muslims have done, it is pertinent to identify the ways in which some in the Muslim world have contributed to this phenomenon. Islamists have made claims about the homogeneity of Islam and the challenge that it represents. Such claims can seem to accord with the charges made by opponents of Islam. Equally, those opposed to Islamist movements of the present or Islamic imperial forces of the past have tended to reproduce and internalize the rhetoric of their foes. To reformulate a phrase of Régis Debray's, 'Islam has Islamicized anti-Islam'. Both the iconoclasm of the Byzantine empire and the evolution of a Christian doctrine of Holy War were instances of this mechanism, which is working today in the transformation of Hinduism, the myth of Islam as a replacement for communism in threatening the West, and the hypostatization of 'Islam' in Western discourses.

Fourthly, in none of these cases is anti-Muslimism the defining feature of the ideology or conflict in which it is deployed. It is linked to other issues – of ethnicity, colour, intra-communal conflict, administrative corruption and inter-state conflict – and depends to a considerable degree on the progression of these other processes and disputes. Such an analysis of anti-Muslimism as a 'semi-ideology' may provide little comfort to those who are the objects of such prejudice. It may, however, contribute to the formulation of a response to it, as well as to an understanding of the broader issues of prejudice, racism and ethnicity in the contemporary world. In a reformulation of the infamous question of Mao Zedong, 'Where do correct ideas come from?', one may ask, 'Where do incorrect ideas come from?' In this case the answer would seem to be that they do not come from an immutable, recurrent, historical archetype, nor from any essence of Western or Christian or non-Muslim society, but from a set of contemporaneous national conjunctures, in which politicians and their associate ideologues draw on themes present in history or in the discourses of other states for their own current and specific purposes. It is those purposes, not the prevalence of a world anti-Muslim conspiracy, that need addressing.

5
Confusing the Issue: 'Islamophobia' Reconsidered

An anxiety of our times: 'Islam' versus the 'West'

No subject in contemporary public discussion has attracted more confused discussion than that of relations between 'Islam' and the West. Whether it be the discussion of relations between Muslim states and non-Muslim countries, or that of the relations between non-Muslims and Muslims within Western countries, the tendency has *on both sides* been, with some exceptions, towards alarmism and simplification. Alarmism has concerned the 'threat', which, from one side, 'Islam' poses to the non-Muslim world and which, on the other, 'the West' poses to Muslims. Non-Muslim simplification involves many obvious issues: terrorism – as if most Muslims are terrorists or most terrorists are Muslims; the degree of aggressiveness found in the Muslim world and the responsibility of Muslims for this; the willingness of Muslims to allow for diversity, debate, respect for human rights. It is not only the sensationalist media, but also writers with an eye to current anxieties of the reading public, such as V. S. Naipaul who, in 1994, endorsed the destruction of the Ayodhya mosque, and Samuel Huntington, who reinforce such misrepresentation. Muslim simplification is itself two-sided: on the one hand, a stereotyping of the 'West', on the other, the assertion of a unitary identity for all Muslims and of a unitary interpretation of text and culture.

The core simplification involves these very terms themselves: 'the West' is not a valid aggregation of the modern world, and lends itself far too easily to monist, conspiratorial presentations of political and social interaction; but nor is the term 'Islam' a valid shorthand for summarizing how a billion Muslims, divided into over fifty states and into myriad ethnicities and social groups, relate to the contemporary world, each other or the non-Muslim world. To get away from such simplifications is, however, virtually impossible, since both those opposed to 'Islam' and those invoking it adhere to such labels. Moreover, as much of this literature shows, those who are most intent on critiquing standard Western prejudices about the Muslim world themselves fall back on another set of simplifications. Instead of fearing or hating anti-Muslim stereotypes, we are now invited to respect, understand, study 'Islam'.

Islamophobia, Eurocentrism, stereotyping

The literature under review here ranges across several aspects of this question.[1] The Runnymede and Wilton Park reports identify misinterpretations, above all in the West, of the Muslim world and advocate a more tolerant, informed relation to the Muslim world. They reflect an approach derived, on the one hand, from race relations and, on the other, from inter-faith dialogue. They both set current frictions in the context of the long historical relations between Muslims and the Christian world, both identify the role of the media in reinforcing stereotypes, both advocate greater discussion between communities. Most significantly, perhaps, they accept the term 'Islam' as a denomination of the primary identity of those who are Muslims; they avoid discussion of the diversities within Muslim societies, in terms of ethnicity or the interpretation of the Muslim tradition and its application to the contemporary world.

The volume by Bobby Said, a sociologist writing in a Nietzschean–Foucauldian vein, strikes a less emollient note. Said seeks to provide a critical 'conceptual narrative' relating how the Western world has come to identify an Islamic threat. The category 'fundamentalism' he sees not primarily in terms of the social or political factors that occasion it within specific Muslim societies, but rather as a Eurocentric response by the West as its hitherto undisputed domination of the Muslim world is challenged. Eurocentrism, the bane of so much analysis of the region, is, he argues, not so much a product of a historical Western hegemony, but a response to the threat that the decentring of the West now poses to that hegemony: it is a sign of decline, not of enduring power.

Islamism is, in this context, something to be welcomed: the return of the repressed, a rejection by Muslims of Western domination. Said excoriates those in the Muslim world – be they liberal modernizers of the eighteenth and nineteenth centuries or the Kemalists of the twentieth – who have tried to learn from the West and so modernize their societies. Said also denies the argument that Islamism contains another variant of radical Western discourse, seeing this as another form of hegemonic denial: those who have argued this – Aziz al-Azmeh, Sami Zubeida, myself – come in for spirited attack. Islamism is a discursive construct that rejects the West, a form of modernity that is non-Western.

In contrast to these three works, which treat 'Islam', for the purposes of their argument at least, as a unitary object, and Muslims as a single community, the other three works stress the diversity of Muslim societies and of non-Muslim responses to them. The two works edited by Kai Hafez, a scholar at the Orient Institute in Hamburg, examine the different historical and modernist interpretations of Islam and the different interactions of Muslims with the West. *Der Islam und der Westen* covers political thought, the status of women, terrorism and economics, together with the foreign policies of specific Muslim countries and peoples – Iran, Algeria, Turkey, Bosnia, the Palestinians, Central Asia and Pakistan. *Islam and the West in the Mass Media* provides a subtle and disaggregated account of the coverage of the Muslim world, relating it to different strategic priorities (e.g. the enormous disproportion in regional coverage), to the distortions contained within the media of the Muslim world and to the broader changes of globalization. It includes an informative chapter by Elizabeth Poole on British press coverage of Muslims.

The study of Turkey by Hugh and Nicole Pope is a study of an actually existing Muslim society. Turkey exemplifies many of the general issues in this debate, illustrating as it does the tensions of modernity, not least those between a secular state and an Islamist opposition and between the Turkish state and the equally Muslim but politically secular Kurdish opposition. Their assessment of the contemporary Turkish scene has drawn strong attack from those who associate them with a trend known as 'the second republic': by this is meant those who wish to lessen the hostility of the state to Kurdish and Islamist opposition, by, for example, permitting the wearing of the headscarf or *turban* in universities, and granting an element of autonomy to the Kurdish regions.

To read a concrete study is a breath of fresh air: here Islam ceases to be a monist abstraction and becomes something specific and diverse – belief, history, culture, literature, symbol, political and economic force. Thus, in marked contrast to Iran, the Turkish Islamists try to invoke the monarchical, Ottoman past in their favour. On the other hand, the Alevi Shi'ite minority is staunchly secular – for fear of the Sunni Islamist majority. The Kurdish parties have shunned Islamism – the PKK is as secular as you can be – yet many Kurds vote for the Islamists. As elsewhere, all is also not as it appears: in Turkey of the 1980s, as in Algeria, Pakistan, Egypt and the Israeli-occupied Palestinian lands, the state indulged in promoting Islamism as a means of isolating the Left, only to find its client had slipped the leash. Turkey matters not only because it is the symbol of the secular–religious conflict in the Muslim world but also because it shows how, in a variety of ways, other forms of interest and identity interact with religion. The analysis of the Popes, like that in the two volumes edited by Hafez, enables us to get away from the stereotypes of confrontation and piety that too often afflict this subject.

Modernism and variety

To identify conflicts between Muslims and non-Muslims is, however, not sufficient for explaining such tensions or for identifying how to resolve them. It is here that some of the conciliatory coverage, exemplified in the Runnymede and Wilton Park reports, may be open to question. Too often political and humanist good intentions seem to have got the better of sociological analysis. In the first place, there is the question of historical context. It is tempting, but misleading, to link contemporary hostility to Muslims to the long history of conflict between 'Islam' and the West. Bobby Said does this – 'the return of the repressed' – without evidence. Even more so is it mistaken, as so many commentators seem to think they are clever by doing, to ascribe contemporary hostility to

'Islam' to the end of the cold war: this presupposes something for which there is little evidence, namely that modern society, 'the West', needs an enemy.[2] One has to apply to this prejudice, and indeed to the study of prejudice in general, the same sociological critique that is applied to other ideologies: the perennialists *will* argue that such ideologies are permanent, be they Islamophobia or anti-Semitism. But a modernist reading is also possible and more plausible.

The past provides a reserve of reference and symbol for the present; it does not explain it. The Ottoman siege of Vienna in 1683 or the Crusades do not explain current politics; they are used by them. A modernist interpretation, with regard to this prejudice as with regard to others, also offers more hope, the possibility of change. If negative attitudes to Muslims are more contingent, rather than embedded in the collective psyche or national character of Western society, then it is more likely something can be done. Here the analysis in the Runnymede Report of the media runs the risk of overstating its case: for if in the *national* British press there is still much that is distorting, this is less so in the local and regional press. Coverage of Muslims in, say, Birmingham or Cardiff has changed over the years, in response to education and political protest: the situation is not as fixed as might appear, and for modernist reasons.

To this historicization can be added the pertinence of national differences on both sides. On the European side, as the Hafez volumes bring out, there are significant differences of emphasis, prejudice and engagement depending on the colonial histories, the geographical location and the composition of the immigrant community. The issues of conflict within Western societies vary: Rushdie in the UK, the headscarf in France, Turkish–Kurdish rivalry in Germany, anti-Arab racism in the USA. Equally, the relation of different Muslim societies to the Western world is distinct. Secular nationalism and communism have provided as much resistance as has Islamism. Alliance and cooperation have been as prevalent as conflict: the Kaiser sought to lead Muslims in World War I, the Soviet Union backed *jihad* and national liberation from the 1920s to the 1970s, the CIA funded the Afghan *mujahidin* in the 1980s.

To the diversities of history can be added that of identity. All those who are Muslims certainly consider Islam as part of their identity. They respect the five injunctions of Islam, they practise the rituals of life in an Islamic way, they celebrate Muslim festivals, they call their children by Muslim names. Equally importantly, and central to this issue, they experience a degree of common identity with Muslims who are oppressed elsewhere – be they in Palestine, Bosnia or Kashmir. Yet these commonalities of faith, practice and solidarity are not the whole story. Islam may, in some contexts, be the prime form of political and social identity, but it is never the sole form and is often not the primary one. Within Muslim societies divisions of ethnicity matter much, often more than a shared religious identity; this is equally so in emigration. There is no lack of difference between genders and classes, between those with power and wealth and those without. No one can understand the politics of, say, Turkey, Pakistan or Indonesia on the basis of Islam alone. Despite rhetoric, Islam explains little of what happens in these societies.

The claim of a shared Muslim identity is, therefore, a distortion if this is meant to imply the primacy of such an identity. It is equally a distortion if it implies a common or given interpretation of that tradition. Perhaps the greatest disservice that invocations of 'Islam', of community and of tradition – indeed of the whole communitarian and identity rhetoric of today – do to understanding is to distort the degree to which what is presented as 'Islam' or any other religion is itself diverse and changing. The claim of fundamentalists, indeed of all religious or nationalist elites who claim to be interpreters of the perennial, is that they are representatives of a given: therein lies authority. But such is never the case. This is what is well explained in the essays in *Der Islam under der Westen*, and which is the core of the modernist account of Islamism and Islamic thought. Bobby Said vigorously rejects a monist interpretation of Islam, but he offers no specific, researched analysis of what Muslim thinkers have said or of their concepts. Indeed, his very rejection of reformers such as al-Afghani and Abduh would seem to imply the aspiration for a similar essentialist and unchanging view of Islam.

What this implies for the study of Muslim societies and for the study of Muslims in Western Europe is an analysis of 'Islam' much less general and less absolute than has often been the case, as claimed by representatives, often patriarchal, sectarian and self-appointed, of Muslim societies. On the one hand, what is presented as 'Islam' may well be one, but by no means the only possible interpretation. Aziz al-Azmeh has shown well, for example, in 'Islam and Modernities' how the apparently given symbol of Islamism, Shari'a law, is itself a modern creation and liable to many contingent interpretations: there is no one Shari'a that Islamists can invoke. The Taliban interpretation of the place of women in society or of the ban on images of the human figure is one, but very much a minority view. Similarly, views by fundamentalists about the impropriety of Muslim women in the West training to be doctors or engineers represent another minority interpretation.

The mistake of those opposed to anti-Muslim prejudice has been to accept, *as the one true Muslim answer*, particular and often conservative versions of that tradition.[3] Even more so, the identification of Muslims with supporters of terrorism or fundamentalist groups is a distortion. A work like that of the otherwise judicious Gilles Kepel, *Allah in the West*, misrepresents the Muslims of the UK, France and the USA as if they are in large measure adherents of the Bradford Council of Mosques or of the Black Muslims. In more extreme vein, Sheikh Omar Bakri Mohammad of *al-Mohajirun* was to claim in January 1999, during the controversy over British subjects being arrested in Yemen, that in every mosque in Britain and the Middle East young men were receiving military training.[4] Allah *is* in the West, but in different forms.

Most challenging from an analytic point of view is the analysis of the intersection of identities. It is easy to visit a Muslim country or study an immigrant community and present all in terms of religion. But this is to miss the other identities – of work, location, ethnicity – and, not least, the ways in which different Muslims relate to each other. Anyone with the slightest acquaintance with the inner life of the Arabs in Britain or of the Pakistani and Bengali communities will know that there is as much difference as commonality.[5] The repeated feuds over sites of worship – common to Muslims, Hindus, Sikhs, Jews – testify to the intrusion of other, secular factors and to different interpretations of the tradition. The analytic challenge is to identify how the tradition and religion are shaped, how the modern is presented as the traditional and how other factors of ethnicity, class and sect play a role.

There may, therefore, be occasions on which 'Islam' is the main or sole identity, not least when people are attacked on that basis, but such occasions are rare. To take the most divisive international issue of the 1990s: if there can be an Islamic solidarity with Saddam Hussein, there can also be one with countries Iraq has attacked, Iran and Kuwait, just as there is a strong Islamic opposition by Iraqis to Saddam's regime.

Islamophobia or anti-Muslimism

Such historicization and disaggregation are relevant to the issue of defining prejudice against Muslims.[6] That there is such as a thing as 'Islamophobia' is undoubtedly true. Recent examples in the British press are not hard to find.[7] Elsewhere we can see similar trends: in Denmark the People's Party has made such hostility central to its programme;[8] in 1998 Hollywood produced an alarmist film, 'The Siege', focusing on Islamic terrorism – in marked contrast, be it said, to its indulgent treatment of Irish republicanism. Nor is this specific to the Christian or Jewish worlds. Perhaps the most striking instance of hostility to Muslims today is to be found in India. The BJP ran for re-election in 1997 on three anti-Muslim issues: rebuilding the temple at Ayodhya, removing separate legal codes for Muslims and ending the special status of Kashmir. Other policies – renaming Bombay after a Hindu goddess, rewriting history books – follow a similar logic.

The positing of a continuous, historic past of confrontation may not only be historically inaccurate but may ascribe cause to religion, an eternal factor, where other, more contingent and contemporary causes may be at work. It also misses the point about what it is that is being attacked: 'Islam' as a religion *was* the enemy in the past – in the Crusades or the *reconquista*. It is not the enemy now: Islam is not threatening to win large segments of Western European society to its faith, as communism did, nor is the polemic, in press, media or political statement, against the Islamic faith. There are no books coming out questioning the claims of Muhammad or the Quran. The attack now is against not Islam as a faith but against Muslims as people, including, indeed especially immigrants. Equally, the 'Islamophobic' attack is against states that may be among the most secular in the world, as Saddam Hussein's is. If we take the study as one of negative stereotyping, of what in German is called the *Feindbild*, the 'enemy image', then the enemy is not a faith or a culture but a people. Hence the more accurate term is not 'Islamophobia' but 'anti-Muslimism'.

Use of the term 'Islamophobia' may also convey two other, misleading associations. One is that the term reproduces the distortion, already discussed, that there is one Islam. 'Islamophobia' indulges conformism and authority within Muslim communities: one cannot avoid the sense, in regard to work such as the Runnymede

Report, that the race relations world has yielded, for reasons of political convenience, on this term.

Use of 'Islamophobia' also challenges the possibility of dialogue based on universal principles. It suggests, as the Runnymede and Wilton Park reports do, that the solution lies in greater dialogue, bridge-building, respect for the other community: but this inevitably runs the risk of denying the right or possibility of criticisms of the practices of those with whom one is having the dialogue. Not only those who, on universal human rights grounds, object to elements in Islamic tradition and current rhetoric, but also those who challenge conservative readings from within can more easily be classed as Islamophobes.[9] The advocacy of a dialogue, one that presupposes given, homogeneous communities, places the emphasis on understanding the 'other', rather than on engaging with the ways in which communities, national and religious, violate universal rights. The danger in these reports is that they are defined, if not monopolized, by representatives of religious bodies and of community organisations, who apply to them the conventions of inter-faith dialogue.[10] The churches have a role in educating their own people about their own faith, but also about the everyday lives and political grievances of other faiths, Muslims included. This cannot and should not be at the expense of a critical examination of the way in which these religions treat their members.

'Islamophobia' may also have confusing practical results. The grievances voiced by Muslims in any society may relate directly to religious matters – connected with school curriculum, dress, diet, observance of ceremonial days. But much of what is presented as the Islamic critique of the West has little or nothing to do with religion: it is secular, often nationalist protest and none the less valid for that. Support for Palestine, denunciations of Western hegemony in the oil market, solidarity with Iraq, denunciations of cultural imperialism, protests at double standards on human rights – these are all part of the 'Muslim' indictment of the West, but are not necessarily religious in content or specific to the Muslim world. The Chinese denunciation of Western human rights interference, on grounds that it violates sovereignty, is the same as the Iranian. It has little to do with belief and a lot to do with political power in the contemporary world. Similarly, within Western society, issues of immigration, housing, employment, racial prejudice and anti-immigrant violence are not specifically religious: the British term

'Paki' can, in a racist attack by white youth, as easily denote a Hindu, a Sikh or a Christian from Tamil Nadu as a Muslim.

Nor should the international implications of all this be overlooked, not least because they so directly affect the level of dialogue within Western societies: the violation of human rights, in the name of religion or secular power, is found in many Muslim societies. The analysis within the West of attitudes to Islam and of renderings of Islamic tradition cannot be divorced from what is going on *within Muslim societies themselves*: here horrendous violations of human rights are being committed against Muslims, in the name of religion. The fight against fundamentalism is not, as Bobby Said presents it, between the West and the Muslim world, but within the Muslim world itself: the briefest acquaintance with the recent history of Iran, Afghanistan, Pakistan, Egypt or Algeria would bear this out. Those who protest the loudest about such violations are inhabitants of these countries, i.e. Muslims themselves: their protests are framed in universal terms and demand a universal response.[11] This is as true for political prisoners, trade unionists, journalists, women, as it is for representatives of ethnic groups within Muslim countries who are denied recognition and group rights. There are, as in any discussion of human rights, difficult issues here – relating to accuracy of information, approach, impartiality. But to deny their right to make these protests, on the grounds that there can be only one Muslim voice or that their invocation of universal principles violates tradition, is a paradoxical conclusion for those who begin by protesting at non-Muslim discrimination against Muslims. 'Islamophobia', like its predecessor 'imperialism', can too easily be used to silence critics of national states and elites.

A return to universalism

Underlying much of this discussion and of policy debates is the question of how far we are able to apply universal categories of analysis and ethics to different religious and political communities. Current fashion has it that this is no longer possible or desirable: Huntington, on the Right, and Bobby Said, on the Left, would, in their own ways, agree. So too would Islamists and their anti-Muslim opponents in the West. Yet it may be that all is not quite so relative as it appears. In the first place, much of the political language of protest and difference is itself part of a universal vocabulary: this is as true for the universal invocation of rights as it is for the universal and very modern principles of sovereignty and national independence. Contrary to Bobby Said, I would sustain the modernist argument that much of Khomeini's rhetoric, like that of Islamists elsewhere, is derived from a modern and Western populist and revolutionary vocabulary. For all that Islamists reject aspects of the modern world, they are grappling with similar problems and use similar instruments, of which the modern state and the resources of the modern economy are central. One of the most striking and original assertions of this universalism has come from the President of Iran, Mohammad Khatami: he argues from a shared reason and a shared cultural and intellectual interaction for the possibility of common values.

Nowhere is this modern context more important than in regard to the fissure that, perhaps more than any other, separates most Muslims from their non-Muslim fellow-citizens or Muslim states from the West, namely the inequality of rich and poor in the contemporary world. Islamism is a form of protest – political and discursive – against external domination, just as Islamist movements within these societies are protests against social and political power that excludes them from power. It is important, however, and a point post-modernist friends of resistance too easily forget, to note that the Islamists are far from being the first to contest the inequalities of modernity: nationalism, on the one hand, and socialist, populist and communist movements, on the other, have long contested Western hegemony. The twentieth century was one of relentless denial of Western hegemony, long before Khomeini and the FIS appeared on the scene.

The problems are, however, not only whether such a challenge can succeed, but also whether, in posing such a challenge, other violations of rights may not occur. Power relations and distortions of truth and history occur within protest movements as much as in relations between these movements and their oppressors. Hence the false salvation offered by those who, out of well-intentioned ecumenism or partisan engagement, seek to remove the possibilities of critical dialogue with regard to those who invoke religious discourse. The alternative to the clash of civilizations need not be the mutual indulgence of communities.

6
Oslo 1993: A Possible Peace

London, March 1999

Anyone concerned about the Middle East will have been affected by the Palestinian–Israeli agreement of September 1993. Of course this agreement is a dangerous one and leaves many questions unanswered. It may well go wrong. It has been made by two quite precarious national leaderships. It is, in historical perspective, greatly unjust to the Palestinians, who will end up with, at best, around a quarter of what was once their territory, and for whom there is not yet a guarantee of a sovereign state. Within both Palestinian and Israeli societies it has aroused anxieties. None the less, it is a welcome event, of potentially great significance: it arouses some hope; it sets a marker for future advance. The principle of mutual recognition by Palestinians and Israelis has been established, with the assent of much of the outside world, and the possibility of two states is now there. That, at least, provides a basis, and one to go back to, even if things break down in the months and years to come.

Can the agreement work? The international context suggests some optimism. The agreement is one of several that have been reached in the past few years, some of them in conflicts that have involved much greater loss of life than the Arab–Israeli conflict. Some of these agreements have failed (Afghanistan, Angola), others are stymied (Sahara, Cyprus) or in a state of uncertainty (Cambodia,

Mozambique, South Africa). But others have, more or less, worked: El Salvador, Nicaragua, Namibia, Eritrea. The odds are that the Palestinian–Israeli agreement will be, for some time, in the middle category, but this comparative listing suggests that surprising things may happen.

What are the reasons – beyond mutual exhaustion and the workings of years of secret contacts – that led Arafat and Rabin to agree to this compromise? Here again the international context is important. The end of the cold war lessened the sense of both sides that they had an unconditional external patron. The Gulf war, in the form of Saddam's missiles, highlighted Israel's vulnerability and undermined the self-confidence of the PLO. Perhaps most importantly, the rise of Islamic fundamentalism promises to present many dangers to both Arafat and Rabin in the years to come. They will be the better able to face these threats if they have worked out some deal between them. Whatever happens in Jericho or Jerusalem, these are enduring and major trends that are pushing the two sides and the other secular Arab regimes around them (particularly Egypt) to the table. They are battening down the hatches before the storm breaks.

The agreement signals a shift in attitudes by the protagonists, and forces a comparable shift amongst those following Middle Eastern affairs from the outside. This is particularly true in regard to the legitimacy of the Palestinian case. Outsiders found it easy to criticize the Palestinians for not accepting the reality and legitimacy of an Israeli state. The Palestinians 'should' in some abstract sense, have accepted the legitimacy of an Israeli state in 1947, when the partition plan was first mooted; the idea of the two peoples living in one state, 'secular democratic' or whatever, already seemed naïve. All sorts of explanations, in terms of the particularly unrealistic or intransigent or anti-Jewish propensities of the Palestinians, were invoked. But these arguments were unrealistic: no people in the world could easily accept that, in the space of two or three generations, the majority of their national territory had been taken by a settler population. The Palestinians resisted with whatever means were at their disposal; some, but by no means most, were reprehensible. One can only wonder what the response would have been on American or British or French territory if a comparable demographic and territorial shift had occurred.

For Palestinians and Israelis the agreement opens up at least the possibility of a better future – one in which over time the two peoples could free themselves from the fear of war, from the agonies of the past. But it is not just for those directly involved that the agreement may offer some emancipation. Throughout this conflict, the discussion outside the Middle East has been polarized and embittered, repetitive and selective. Everyone knows the arguments on the Jewish side and on the Arab side: you can read them all in the correspondence columns of the press to this day. The Left, until 1967, denied the rights of the Palestinians to their own state because of the quite separate issue of the genocide of Jews in Europe. Even after 1967 many continued to take this position. The most perceptive and enduring commentary on the whole issue from the Left was produced in separate studies in the aftermath of that war by two Jewish Marxists, Isaac Deutscher and Maxime Rodinson, each of whom took issue with the nationalist myths of both sides and the misuse of the genocide.

On their side, supporters of the Palestinians denied the legitimacy of an Israeli state on all sorts of grounds, many of them spurious. The zenith of this aberrant solidarity was the 1970s debate on 'Zionism as racism'. If this is taken to mean that Israeli nationalism contains prejudices against Arabs, then of course it has an element of truth to it; but according to this argument all nationalisms are racist. There is a difference between identifying racist elements in a nationalism and denying the legitimacy of that nationalism entirely. Or 'Zionism is racism' could be interpreted as meaning that the ideology of building a Jewish state in Palestine denied the rights of the Palestinians: this is also certainly true. But there was another message mixed up in all this, itself a racist one, namely that the Jews in Palestine had no right to their own state and, for that reason, the whole campaign was pernicious and in the end backfired.

Much of this debate invoked history. For outsiders the richness of the biblical and classical resonances invested the conflict with a special significance as well as special difficulty. But one may wonder whether all this history did anyone much good and indeed whether the sense of historical uniqueness, the aura of tragedy and doom, is justified. Perhaps the Arab-Israelis and the Palestinians behaved and will continue to behave in much the same way as other people in the world. This is because of something neither side will admit: namely that they are essentially creatures of contingency, products of an arbitrary and recent history, which has created two nations in a matter of a few decades. Reconciliation rests not on arbitrating their ancestral claims but rather on denying the relevance of history at all.

The Jews invoke their biblical claims, the Palestinians see themselves as the heirs of centuries of occupations and as descendants of the Canaanites before them. But here, as in so many other parts of the world, these invocations of history are spurious. Nationalism – the division into nations each claiming a separate state on the basis of distinct identities – is a recent phenomenon, a product of political change in the past century. The Palestinian nation emerged from this process and was forged in the conflict with the Zionist project itself, i.e. since the 1920s. Although the Jewish people has existed for millennia, there is no Jewish 'nation' in the modern political sense. The basis of the historic claim to the land of Israel is one that few people not directly involved could accept: the argument that a particular piece of land was 'given by God' hardly allows for rational assessment, while a claim based on historical occupation fares little better, given that the historic kingdom of Solomon and David lasted for only around 80 years. Any argument for the legitimacy of an Israeli state has to rest on contemporary, and generalizable, criteria: although most Jews did not and do not live in Israel, out of a part of the Jewish people an Israeli nation, Hebrew-speaking and resident in the Middle East, has emerged. Its opponents deny its legitimacy on the grounds that it was created through immigration and settlement, but this would, if generalized, be true of many other nations the world over.

Nationalists refuse to acknowledge the modernity, the contingency, of their claims. They insist on harking back into history. Long history there is, and of course one can track down the peoples and traditions that are the ancestors of today's nations. But the map of nations as we see it today is not the result of ancient patterns. Rather, it is a result of a series of accidents, many of them recent. History cannot predict which nations would in fact emerge in the modern era, nor can it give us answers to questions of legitimacy.

In the chaos of the post-communist world, all sorts of nationalisms have arisen. What is striking about so many of them is how, in feverish invocation of the past, they ignore the lessons of other conflicts and reproduce the origin myths of other nationalisms. It is one of the paradoxes of nationalism that while each one claims to be original they are, in their essentials, all the same. Croats denounce Serbs who, it is said, were brought by the Ottomans in the sixteenth century. Both Armenians and Azeris talk nonsense about the claim to Nagorno-Karabagh. In Northern Ireland nationalists deny the rights of Protestants on the grounds that the latter were colonizers – in the sixteenth century. The search is on for 'pure' members of nations, and this is linked to the maximum claim on territory. Traditions, some genuine, many not, are cobbled together to create new nationalisms.

The common ground of Israelis and Palestinians, shared with many other nations in conflict in the world, is the very contingency and the very arbitrary nature of the entities they now claim to represent. This does not mean they have no right to states of their own or that, in the name of some higher cosmopolitan or binational ideal, they should live together. Obviously, given the animosities and fears that now exist, they cannot live together in one state. They are, in this as in other respects, normal nations. The Arab–Israeli dispute was not, and is not, some conflict of 'another' kind.

The solution does not depend on the reconciliation of ancient or traditional antagonisms, but rather on the acceptance that Israelis and Palestinians are entitled to what other peoples have, neither more nor less. The outside world, too, would then be freed from the mire of historical retrospection and association.

7

A Decade After the Invasion:
The Unease of Kuwait

Kuwait, 2000

Some ten years after a sudden, brutal occupation by Iraq, Kuwait gives, at first sight, the appearance of having returned to normal. Virtually all the damage done by the Iraqis to buildings has been repaired, the oilfields are functioning, the state has normal diplomatic relations even with states such as Jordan, Yemen and Sudan with which it was at odds in 1990–91. The trio of Al Sabah rulers who have held office since the late 1970s – Amir Jabir, Sheikh Saad, the prime minister and crown prince, and Sheikh Sabah, the foreign minister – remain in office and in power. There are even some positive consequences of the occupation. The parliament, dissolved by the Amir in 1986, was restored immediately after liberation. The hundreds of *diwanias*, or social and political discussion groups, to which Kuwaiti men and, separately, women throng every night of the week are in full swing. The press is notable for the extent of its freedom, the greatest in the Gulf region. The conflict between Sunnis and Shi'ites within the population, exacerbated by the Iran–Iraq war of 1980–88 and a number of terrorist incidents within Kuwait, has abated. Even the environment has enjoyed positive side-effects from the conflict: the impact of sandstorms has been greatly reduced by the debris of the oil fires that Saddam Hussein ignited as he departed. Oil prices are up, businessmen and the envoys of every Middle Eastern state throng the lobbies and anterooms.

Yet beneath the surface of this city, the centre of which resembles a form of modern US city without the alcohol, the trauma of 1990–91 remains, and is in some ways more intense. The shock of a sudden invasion, even one that came when over a third of the population was out of the country at the height of the summer heat, hit everyone: thousands lost their lives, offices, official buildings and private houses were despoiled. At the Kuwait Research and Studies Centre they produce a wealth of literature on the occupation based on the half million documents left behind as Saddam's forces fled: testimonies of Kuwaiti resistance demonstrated in the documents of Iraqi intelligence officers, maps of the eastern parts of Saudi Arabia for apparent use in a possible thrust down the coast, plans for the destruction of the oilfields, lists of goods to be looted and taken back to Iraq. Those who sacked the National Museum knew what they were looking for. They also took the animals from the zoo. Billions of dollars' worth of planes were also taken, some to be destroyed on the ground in Iraq, some flown to Iran and then returned, after protracted negotiations, by Tehran.

Everyone knows it could all happen again. It is as if a Czech or a Pole had felt, in 1955, that Hitler was still there, looming next door with an unknown armoury and gradually raising his oil revenues. Thousands of US and British servicemen are based outside Kuwait city, the majority allowed to visit it, the pilots kept away for fear of retaliation. Security precautions at Western embassies leave no doubt that the threat of Iraqi actions is constant.

I have dinner at the house of a leading opposition politician. In the 1970s he used to visit Saddam as a private envoy of the Amir, in the hope of finding a compromise on the border. After an incident in 1973, when Iraqi forces made a limited riposte to Kuwaiti forces along the frontier, Saddam berated them for their restraint. 'When a cat annoys you, you don't pull its tail, you cut off its head.' After 1979, when Saddam murdered many of his close associates and set out on the path of aggression that was to lead first to the war with Iran and then to that with Kuwait, all contact was broken. He shows me how the Iraqi soldiers set fire to part of his house as they cooked in his living room. A friend who has organized a committee to defend freedom of speech in Kuwait against fundamentalists, tells me, as we drive home, of his experiences as a prisoner in Iraq: thousands cramped into a rotting barracks, with no sanitation, nothing to sleep on, people urinating on each other, a friend dying of diabetes because there was no medicine, the horror of air bombing during the air war, the near-fatal encounter with a roadblock of anti-Saddam rebels in the days of the March uprising that followed the war. A lifelong opponent of Western domination in the region, he along with all his companions broke into cries of 'Long Live America' when they met the first Western roadblocks on their way home.

A deep, enduring insecurity remains. Saddam has not changed one jot, everyone knows it, and he could try to start the whole thing again tomorrow morning. Throughout the city signs point people to the nearest air-raid shelter. Manoeuvres at the UN to negotiate a partial lifting of sanctions unsettle diplomats. Above all, there is the gnawing issue of the missing: thousands returned, but over 600 remain, their names listed, their faces on posters. There is, ten years on, no news at all about them: the Iraqis refuse to confirm or deny that they are alive. Even the leaders of the Kuwaiti Ba'th party, who refused to endorse the invasion, are missing. The hope that some may be alive is sustained by the conditions in which they were rounded up near the end of the war, and by the recent revelation that Iraq, unbeknown to anyone, had for years been holding Iranians after their war with Iran. Every family is touched directly or by near kinship. I visit a senior official in the foreign office. He expresses concern about Iraq. Only when I leave does someone tell me he has two sons still missing.

Returning after 28 years I am, however, struck by other changes that accompany and predate the Iraqi invasion. From the 1930s to the 1970s the main axis of conflict in Kuwait was between the Al Sabah ruling family, beneficiaries after 1946 of oil revenues, and the merchants of Kuwait city. Some supported the Al Sabah, others were Arab nationalists who pressed for great freedom and greater control of the country's finances. In 1975 and again in 1986 the Amir dissolved the elected parliament rather than face continued criticism. Above all, it was pressure for accountability, after a stockmarket crash, that seems to have been the spur for the 1986 dissolution. But from the 1960s onwards the state began to draw into the political system the more tribal Bedouin and Sunni parts of the population. This was accentuated by the Iran–Iraq war of 1980–88: in that war Kuwait supported Iraq – 'We had no choice,' said one official – and relations with the 25 per cent or so of the Kuwait population who are Shi'ites deteriorated. There was an attempt on the life of the Amir in 1985 and other incidents. The Shi'ites lost influence in the armed forces and the administration, in favour of the tribal elements. Although in 1990 the Shi'ite population, mindful of the fate of their counterparts in Iraq, were prominent in the resistance, the invasion, by placing greater strain on the society, pushed this process of conservatism further. The result was what one sociologist calls the *tashir*, or 'desertification', of Kuwait society.

The Shi'ites were not an oppressed minority: their position is better than in any other Sunni Arab state. A recent reform of the legal system has given them their own court of appeal. They have their own MPs. The improvement of relations with Iran after 1990 has also helped: the Iranian ambassador is reported to have recently told Shi'ite prayer leaders he did not want any trouble from them. Iran needed good political and financial relations with Kuwait. But the rise of a Sunni fundamentalism, backed to a greater or lesser extent by Saudi Arabia, worries the Shi'ites as it does the liberals. The more cautious Muslim Brotherhood, organized in *al-Haraka al-dastouriya al-islamiya*, the Islamic Constitutional Movement, claim to have broken since 1990 with their Sunni associates elsewhere (who supported Iraq). The more militant *salafis* have links to Saudi Arabia and publish a monthly called *al-Minbar* (The Tribune). The prime minister recently called for the closure of the *sanadiq khairiya*, or charity boxes, which the fundamentalists position around the country. The response of one Islamist leader was to say that if that was done, he would call for the closure of all unlicensed churches and Shi'ite gathering places, or *husseiniyas*, in the country. When the government introduced a measure to ban women wearing the face cover from driving, there were calls for a violent response. Inexorably, an extra-parliamentary Islamist opposition is growing. There is much denunciation of *al-ghazu al-thaqafi*, 'cultural aggression', and of *taghrib*, literally 'Westernization', but the term also embraces any approximation (even to Shi'ites).

The issue around which this now-triangular conflict has crystallized is that of women's suffrage. Since independence in 1961 only Kuwaiti males have had the right to vote and stand in elections. During the Iraqi occupation the Amir promised that women, who were part of the national resistance movement, would be given the vote after liberation. The political class prevaricated, so, after dissolving parliament and calling new elections, the Amir issued a decree, one of 60, concerning the participation of women in the next election in 2003. The opponents of women's suffrage, joined by others who said they were in favour but did not want to be instructed by the Amir on political reform, voted the measured down. Last Tuesday it came to the vote again: as women massed in the upper galleries of the dramatic white parliament building, many of them wearing orange T-shirts saying, 'Yes to Rights in 2003', the all-male deputies below went through their set pieces. Applause from the galleries greeted the argument by Dr Hassan Jawhar Hayat, a political scientist, that there was nothing in the constitution banning women from voting. But in the end prevarication, stupidity and patriarchy prevailed again: the vote went 32 to 30 against women's suffrage. A political scientist who toured the *diwanias* of opposition MPs after the vote found a mood of jubilation amongst the men gathered there.

One Islamist MP told the story of a woman he knew who had been nursing her ailing father in hospital: if she had been an MP she would not have been able to do that. Others cited various texts of the Quran and Hadith. Universal patriarchal themes, packaged in local and communitarian form, were widespread. Some people blamed the US ambassador for publicly supporting the suffrage campaign. In Kuwait, as elsewhere, e.g. Egypt, the unholy alliance of Islamist and ex-leftist anti-imperialists digs in on social issues. Abdullah al-Nafisi, once a leader of the independent camp, has become a darling of the Islamists. The parliamentary vote was in fact much worse than a 30–32 defeat since the 'yes' camp included around a dozen members of the cabinet, nominated to parliament by the Amir. The anger on the part of the mobilized women was evident. At the university a professor long committed to this cause gave the thumbs down sign to signal the outcome as she passed a class sitting an examination. One of my LSE students asked me, the day before I left, 'Why did we fight to defend them if they won't give women the vote?' Next day CNN arrived to cover the story. A bad day – for Kuwait and its friends, the reputation of the Arab world and Islam.

The other issue on which the power of Islamism has shown itself is censorship. Kuwait has long had and still has among the freest media in the Arab world. But over the past two years the annual book fair, to which publishers from all over the Arab world come, has been subject to pressure from Islamists. A censorship committee vets all books – in 1998 around forty books were banned, in 1999 the number went up to 200. These include works on the history of Islam, writings by Mohammad Arkoun and others. My own *Islam and the Myth of Confrontation*, published in Arabic by Saqi Books, is among them. All books that refer to Islam go to a committee in the Ministry of Awqaf. When I met the Minister, Dr Adel Khalid al-Sebeih, he promised to find out why the book had been banned and to write to me. Maybe there had been a mistake in the translation, he said. I may never know, as a few days afterwards Dr al-Sebeih was relieved of his post.

At the book fair, the Saqi publishing house stand had plenty of literature, but dozens of its books were not there. Its journal *Abwab* was on sale but some of its issues were also banned. Issues that might well have aroused concern did not do so: one publisher displayed a set of translations of books by Che Guevara. The Bahraini poet Qasim Haddad, a long-time opponent of the government in that island and the victim of political arrests, addressed a packed meeting. I had not seen him since we met in half-secrecy in Bahrain in 1971. Among those in the audience was the Kuwaiti writer Leila al-Othman, who, along with another writer, was the object of a trial relating to stories she had written ten years before. Leila al-Othman's stories tell of a passionate, tense, changing inner world of Kuwaiti women. Betrayal by kin and neighbours stalks her pages. *Zahra Enters the Neighbourhood* relates how the newly wealthy buy up previously tightly knit areas. *The Walls are Being Torn Down* is a bitter tale by a woman now imprisoned for having an illegitimate child, who was seduced by her brother-in-law while caring for her sister's children. Hidden tensions, the sea, sudden reversals of fortune permeate her pages. For prurient Islamists there is, no doubt, much to preoccupy them here. Recently two other writers, political scientists, had been objects of judicial proceedings: one Ali Baghdadi, chairman of the university department, had been released after two of four weeks of a prison sentence by the Amir. The other, Dr Shamlan al-Essa, had left the country for Washington DC for a year, in protest. One woman who has campaigned

long against a conservative interpretation of religion remains defi-
ant: 'We must wring the necks of these holy texts to get the best out
of them,' she tells me.

The failure to get the women's suffrage measure through parliament and the general climate of harassment of free speech highlights
what is an underlying sense in the country of political drift, or, as it
is put in Arabic, *rukud*, 'stagnation'. The government was in favour of women's suffrage and of a social security bill, which the
Islamists also killed on the grounds that it was 'un-Islamic', but
did not act decisively enough to mobilize support. With the same
leaders in place for more than two decades, there is a widespread
feeling of inaction at the top. Three examples will serve. The new
National Museum has not been reopened after 1990, reportedly
because of quarrelling within the royal family, male and female. A
decision on building an aluminium smelter has been stalled for
years, because of lack of authorization of terms and uncertainty
about the reliability of supply (in midsummer when Kuwaiti citizens all have their air-conditioners on) and the price of electricity.
And negotiations with foreign oil companies about opening up new
oilfields in the north are marooned for lack of agreement on concession terms. There are rumours that the prime minister, Sheikh
Saad, ailing and reticent, will retire. The weekly *al-Zaman*, owned
by Sheikh Nasir, one of the sons of the foreign minister, Sheikh
Sabah, voices concern at the lack of movement, but so far to little
effect.

Those who do speak out may encounter discrimination and,
where not, a process of labelling, *tasnih*, which puts critics into
neat boxes. There has been no violence on a par with the assassination of one left-wing critical MP soon after liberation, but less
abrupt forms of pressure, as much from below as from above, per-
sist. In ministries and academic institutions, frustration with the
lack of change is noticeable. A classic case of paralysis is the English-language Kuwait TV news: this is a parody of official Arabic
broadcasting, as endless wooden and padded statements about the
actions of the rulers are read out in deadpan American English by
announcers in *dishdashas*. One person who taught in an English
literature department told me that they could not work on writers
from America or Australia because this was not recognized as 'English'. And throughout the society this inaction from the top is unable
to match the activity from below. The result is that the list of books

and poems that teachers are allowed to give their students to read is narrowing, as more and more comes under a vague, unofficial but inexorable Islamist ban. No Iris Murdoch, because she favours gays and lesbians. No John Donne or Byron, because they tell of love. A safe canon remains – Chaucer, Herbert, Joseph Conrad, Joyce's *Portrait of the Artist as a Young Man*.

The air of control and the tensions it produces are reinforced by the ban on alcohol. Unlike Bahrain, Dubai and Oman, which allow drinking, at least in hotels, Kuwait does not: the result is, first of all, that Western businessmen choose not to live here, let alone hold conferences here. 'We would be Dubai if we only allowed alcohol,' one Kuwaiti told me. The press reports the case of a trader – name and nationality unstated – who was caught smuggling 800 cases of alcohol, valued at £1 million, into the country by sea, disguised as soap and washing powder. The paper reports that the arrest has been warmly greeted by the Kuwaiti population. Of course, the reality is very different: vast quantities of whisky – 'black apples' for Johnny Walker Black Label and 'red apples' for Johnny Walker Red label – are brought in, through safe supply networks patronized by unseen senior Kuwaitis. The great night for drinking is Wednesday evening, the start of the weekend. The price per bottle is around KD45, rising to KD100 at festival time. 'We have more alcohol in Kuwait than in Bahrain,' one person boasts to me. Western diplomats bemoan the fact that they cannot get businessmen and other dignitaries to come here. They also suggest that some of the envoys from poorer countries finance their embassies by selling supplies.

Kuwait has, however, in marked contrast to Saudi Arabia, a climate of extensive religious tolerance. There are no Sunni mosques in Tehran, no Shi'ite places of worship in Saudi Arabia. The latter allows no signs of public Christian worship. In Kuwait, by contrast, not only do the two Islamic sects live side by side, but there is also open practising of Christianity. At the cluster of churches near the Sheraton Hotel, mass is said in English, Arabic (Latin and Maronite rites) and the tongues of the Asian south – Tamil, Tagalog, Konkani, Mayalalam. At al-Ahmadi, in the south, worshippers visit 'Our Lady of Arabia'.

Where this tolerance ends, however, is in relation to non-Kuwaitis in the economy and social life. The oil boom has, over the decades, brought in a large army of immigrants, who perform most of the work. Prior to 1990 many of these were Arabs, but the great majority were then expelled – the Palestinian community has gone down from around 350,000 to an estimated 35,000 today. In the weeks after the liberation there was widespread maltreatment. Today there are tens of thousands of Egyptians, many living as single men in barrack-like conditions. In a recent riot in the suburb of Khaitan, a result of a quarrel with an Asian shopkeeper, several Egyptians were killed. This is a topic that promotes unease. A senior minister recently compared the status of foreign workers, Bengali office boys on KD17 a month, to slavery. A visiting Arab intellectual, who put his reputation on the line by defending the Kuwaitis in 1990, finds an air of racism and touchiness. Foreign nationals speak warmly of life in Kuwait, the friendliness and security they encounter. The bureaucratic delays they meet are blamed on Egyptians. 'But,' they add quietly, 'you should see the way Kuwaitis treat their servants'.

Relations with the outside world are now largely proper but, given the neighbourhood, tense. The Kuwait Fund for Arab Economic Development, which distributed money widely before 1990 only to see many of its major recipients support Iraq, still declines to give aid to Jordan, Yemen, Sudan. Instead aid now goes to Bosnia and Albania. But this very week the Yemeni and Sudanese ambassadors finally arrived and presented their credentials to the Amir. Kuwait adds its voice to the Palestinian cause, and its press publishes archaic attacks on 'Zionism', even as attitudes to Palestinians remain harsh. Relations with Britain and America are close, but there is nervousness about the intentions of future US presidential candidates and the fickleness of Western public opinion. Saudi Arabia is not universally regarded as a friend either: few forget that it was the Saudi forces who in 1920 annexed two thirds of Kuwaiti territory, a forcible action ratified by Britain in the Treaty of Uqair of 1920. Above all looms the brooding monster to the north: many a conversation returns – after touring globalization, Blair, Chechnya and much else – to speculation, unresolved as ever, about what Iraq might do and what might happen if 'he' goes. Kuwaitis ask me what they can do to improve relations with Iraq and with Iraqis. I regret to have little positive to tell them.

An hour's drive north of Kuwait, through a landscape sanitised of the more evident signs of recent war, the reality of this paralysed confrontation looms into view. At the gate of Camp Khor, the UN post just inside Kuwait, the personnel of the Bangladeshi Battalion, or BANBAT, are polite but firm: no authorisation, no entry. We sip soft drinks in a guard's house where orders in Bengali and English are pinned to the wall. A notice orders all night-time patrols to ensure that their UN flags are lit up. Conversation with the BANBAT personnel turns to international relations, 'what is the role of peacekeeping in a unipolar world?' one officer asks me. Here, under the hot sun of Arabia is the reality of that peacekeeping we teach in our seminars. 'The peace of the world rests on our shoulders', I am told, and I believe it.

A briefing officer arrives. We are taken to a press room replete with maps. The House of Commons Defense Committee had just been out and it had not escaped notice that one of its four members, nursing the after-effects of a binge in Bahrain the night before, had failed to show up. UNIKOM monitors the Demilitarized Zone (DMZ) which runs five kilometres into Kuwait and ten into Iraq. It runs for 200 kilometres on land, down to where the Kuwait–Iraq borders meets Saudi Arabia, and 60 kilometres out to sea. Within that zone, the Kuwaiti and Iraqi personnel can only be policemen, and can carry only side weapons.

UNIKOM, currently commanded by an Irish general, consists of 195 observers from 32 countries, the 750 men of BANBAT, a German medical team, and an Argentinian civilian logistics and engineering unit. The permanent five members of the UN Security Council each have observers, but since Desert Fox, in December 1998, British and US personnel are not permitted to patrol inside Iraqi territory as Baghdad has said that it cannot guarantee their safety. The mission's mandate, first laid out in UN Security Resolution 687 of 1991 is threefold: to monitor the DMZ on land and sea; to deter violation of the DMZ; to observe and report violations of the Zone by anyone, including western aircrafts. Since the border delimitation of 1993 the mandate also empowers UNIKOM to 'prevent and redress' violations without recourse to the Security Council, and to observe Iraqi military installations on what became the Kuwaiti side of the border. Apart from its two main bases – Camp Khor and Umm Qasr – and many observation posts within the DMZ, it also has liaison offices in Kuwait and Baghdad.

Over the past two years there have been three significant violations: a drive-by shooting in late 1997 of a UNIKOM patrol base in which a Ghanaian observer was wounded; a hijacking in May 1999

by armed Iraqi civilians of a UN vehicle – the occupants were released by the side of the road on the way to Baghdad; an incident in
September 1999 in which two Kuwaiti policemen were shot in as
yet unexplained circumstances. The greatest activity takes place at
night and involves smuggling: container trucks of a certain Scot-
tish export arrive in Umm Qasr and their contents make their way
towards crossing points on the frontier. Under cover of darkness
smugglers transport these cases to trucks waiting on the Kuwaiti
side. It is well organised and officials can only speculate at where
the labour force to ferry the crates from one side of the frontier to
the other can be found.

The Kuwaiti side of the DMZ is most wholly deserted, but the
Iraqi is most certainly not: tens of thousands of people live in Umm
Qasr, Abdali and Safwan and move freely between the DMZ and
Iraq. The greatest security threat to these Iraqis comes from land
mines – the Kuwaitis have cleared their side. At the border post at
Abdali, BANBAT are on one side, the Iraqis on the other. In the
distance we can see the cranes of Umm Qasr, Iraq's only deep-sea
port. The berm or earthern wall, rises up on the Kuwaiti side, a
deep ditch and electrified fence run along the frontier. A few yards
inside Iraqi children play in delapidated houses. Iraqi personnel in
their characteristic dark green uniforms peer at us with intent.

A couple of hundred yards away, in a converted Iraqi naval hospital, is the main UNIKOM base. This is also the site of the
UNIKOM bar. Some months ago, a couple of American civilians
made a dash for the Iraqi side to get a drink: they found themselves
detained for some weeks at the pleasure of the Iraqi authorities.
Not, it seems, a wise border across which to stage an unauthorised
crossing.

The trauma of the 1990–91 war has, if anything, intensified
rather than clarified the tendency to geopolitical fantasy that is
hard to avoid in these and other parts. Many a claim is made about
the US role prior to the invasion in August 1990 and the encouragement given to Saddam. Britain is also held to account for reports,
allegedly found in released Foreign Office documents, about a willingness by then Foreign Secretary Selwyn Lloyd to allow Iraq to
take over in the late 1950s. Most people hold, in some way or another, that the 'West' is keeping Saddam in power – otherwise they
would get rid of him, surely. There is speculation about the role of
the US ambassador – the *mandub sami*, or 'High Commissioner',

as he is called in a harking back to colonial times. He has, I am told, been instructed to stay for an additional year, because something is being hatched for Iraq. Jordanian Prince Hassan is mentioned as a possible future king of Iraq, restoring the Hashemite dynasty ousted in 1958. Both Britain and the USA are, needless to say, preparing their own candidates for succession within the royal family. For its part the Islamist opposition rails against globalization, designed to corrupt Arab and Islamic morals, and against the free trade being enjoined by the World Trade Organization (WTO).

Kuwait lives an intense, often inward-looking life. 'If you were here for a month you would think this country was as large and important as Argentina,' one Arab journalist tells me. The state itself rests on a definite but in some ways precarious prosperity, the beneficiary of oil revenues of around $7 billion and of an at least comparable return on its investments over the past fifty years. All three of the main forms of earning in Kuwait – state employment, which covers over 90 per cent of the workforce, commissions and allowances for members of the royal family – derive from rent. There are over 2,100 princes entitled to a substantial allowance, and in all areas of life patronage and connections are central. There has been no enthusiasm to lessen the controls of the state on the economy or to broaden the government's economic base. World Bank suggestions to take areas of the economy or raise utility prices are resisted.

Oil has, if anything, strengthened the power of the ruling family. The Al Sabah maintains its privileged access to oil income and to other levers of power, but it has opened debate and cultivated a culture of tolerance unknown elsewhere in the Gulf. A welfare state that pays people not to work, where telephones are free, where there are no taxes, where much of the country leaves when it becomes too hot, where a million South Asian and other workers keep things running is a rare island of stability and civility. Yet this is the hottest and, in some ways, physically most inhospitable city on earth. In the end, say in 200 or 300 years when the oil has all run out, the ferocious heat and environment may reclaim the glass tower blocks and boulevards. The carefully nurtured gardens may wither. The fate of all city states will befall it. In the meantime, the entire Kuwaiti population and most of those of good sense elsewhere have an interest in its survival, against regressive bigots from within and the brutal aspirations of one man and his associates across the border.

8

Iran: The Islamic Republic at the Crossroads

Tehran, September 2000

An air of uncertainty and anxiety hangs over Tehran, now a smog-laden city of 12 million. No one, Iranian or foreigner, is confident about how the next few months will turn out, about whether the reformist current that has swept the country since 1997 will continue or will founder or be overturned in the face of determined and possibly violent conservative opposition. The presidential elections of 1997, in which Mohammad Khatami triumphed as a reform candidate, and the *Majlis* (parliamentary) elections of February 2000, appeared to confirm that a strong majority for reform exists. But these messages from below are met by a ruling elite that is divided and part of which is alarmed by the calls for change. The next testing point will be the presidential elections scheduled for June 2001: nothing, not even President Khatami's commitment to running for a second term, is as yet certain. A revolution that in 1979 swept all before it now faces difficult choices, abroad and at home.

The pressures for political and social change in Iran are accompanied by a widespread debate about the direction of the country, about the further development of the revolution, about Islam and the modern world. Nothing could be more inaccurate in regard to the discussion in Iran and its relation to the outside world than a simple contrasting of 'Iranian' or 'Islamic' values and ideas with 'Western' ones: there is as much diversity within Iran and within Islamic discussion, including within the clergy, as there is in the international East–West dimension. For those of a secular orientation, the influence of Marxism, prevalent two decades ago, has now yielded to an interest in liberal thinking: Popper and Mill, not to mention theories of 'civil society' and a 'third way', have replaced Lenin and Mao. There are those in Iran who want to keep the system established by Ayatollah Khomeini in the revolution and the eight-year war with Iraq. There are many who believe it should change, and some who wish it could remain the same but realize and fear that if it does not change it will be swept aside. The fates of the Shah and of Gorbachev are very much in the minds of the Iranian political elite.

The dramatic elections of recent years have none the less altered the political climate in Iran. There is a strong movement for change, named after the Persian date on which Khatami was elected, the *dovvom-i khordad*, 2 Khordad or 17 May 1997. Part of this protest comes from above and is expressed by Khatami in his call for the rule of law and civil society, but more importantly it comes from below.

Against this background the issue that has provoked most controversy in recent years has been that of freedom of expression and of the press. The Ministry of Islamic Guidance administers censorship but book publishing is relatively free in Iran, provided core issues pertaining to religion and the state are not touched. You can buy books on a range of modern Iranian history. John Gray's *Men are From Mars, Women are From Venus* has been a bestseller, *Angela's Ashes* has sold well in Persian translation, a success not unrelated to its portrayal of the clergy. By contrast, no secular publisher would print Edward Said's *Orientalism*. The press is another matter. After 1997 an explosion of critical newspapers and weeklies took place, allowing for discussion of many social and political issues. These included not only debates on feminism, democracy and liberalism and on different interpretations of Islamic history and culture, but also more direct, sensitive, questions: the foreign bank accounts of senior clerics or the behaviour of the intelligence services.

This press captures a widespread dissatisfaction. At a meeting in Tehran university in early August to welcome the release from jail of a cleric, Mohsen Kadivar, sentenced to 18 months for 'disturbing public opinion', a university professor, Hashem Aghajaeri, was direct: 'Religion has performed badly when it has gone along with power ...Those who believe Islamic jurisprudence is a kind of divinity on earth, that it cannot be criticized or judged by the law, must enter debates with Islamic thinkers and let voters choose. Governments that suppress thinking in the name of religion are neither religious governments nor even humane governments. It is time for the institution of religion to become separated from the institution of government'. His audience of 1,000 students were reported to have applauded vigorously (*International Herald Tribune*, 5–6 August 2000).

However, those opposed to change have fought back. Some independent writers were charged by clerical courts with opposing Islam or the revolution and in 1998 a spate of assassinations of writers was blamed on rogue elements within the security forces who were later brought to trial. In 1999 there were clashes between students and the security forces. In 2000 the clamp-down became much stronger. After a conference on Iran held in Berlin in April, under the auspices of the Heinrich Böll Institute, several of the participants were arrested and tried when they returned to Tehran. They included two supporters of women's rights, Mehrangiz Kar and Shahla Lahiji, a leader of the student organization Daftar-i Tahkim-i Vahdat (The Office for the Strengthening of Unity), Hojjatislam Hasan Eshkevari, a reformist cleric, and the editors of three newspapers later banned – Reza Jalaipour of *Asr-i Azadegan* (Age of the Free), Ezzatollah Sahabi of *Iran-i Farda* (Tomorrow's Iran) and Alireza Alavitabar of *Subh-i Emruz* (This Morning). The most prominent of all those who were arrested after Berlin was Akbar Ganji, a journalist who had written about the involvement of high officials in the killing of intellectuals. He was sentenced to ten years' imprisonment and five subsequent years of exile to a remote village.

As in other authoritarian systems, external threat has been used to justify internal repression, but here too some relaxation is evident. The changes in regard to external relations are in some respects more consolidated. In September 2000 as the country marked the twentieth anniversary of the outbreak of the war with Iraq, Tehran was dominated by giant posters celebrating the 'holy defence' of the country against attack. There were, by comparison, few images of the revolution itself. Posters and paintings commemorated the soldiers who died in the eight-year war, as well as a group of Iranian diplomats killed by the Afghan Taliban in 1998. This commemoration of the war was, however, not only a way of remembering the past and mobilizing support for the state. It also served to mark out a possible future line for Iranian foreign policy. There is a tangible sense of nationalism in the political atmosphere and of the need to identify what is in Iran's 'national interest'. This turn to nationalism has implications both for Iran's support for broader 'Islamic' causes and for the tenor of debate internally.

The Islamic revolution of Iran replicates in its rhetoric and action many of the tensions that beset other revolutions: internationalist militancy and defence of the state, appeals to other oppressed peoples and exaltation of their own people. The French revolution proclaimed *la grande nation*. Two centuries later posters in Tehran recall the words of Ayatollah Khomeini, who referred to Iran as *in mellat-i bozorg*, 'this great nation'. The Iranian revolution also replicated in its cultural policy some of what China had gone through: Iranian intellectuals sardonically remark, in regard to the current climate of arresting and prosecuting critical writers, that their country did the reverse of China. It had its '100 flowers' campaign after its 'cultural revolution'. In China the former occurred in 1957 and took the form of a persecution of those earlier allowed or even encouraged to speak freely. This was followed by an all-out onslaught in the cultural revolution that began in 1965. The Iranian cultural revolution, launched as an attack on the universities in 1980, served, however, like its Chinese and Russian precursors, not only to attack 'foreign' ideas and influences, its stated purpose, but also to destroy a diversity of tradition and culture *within* that country itself. In Iran this involved an assault on the more hedonistic trends in Persian poetry, a ban on women singing and even, for a short time, a ban on chess.

As befell earlier revolutionary regimes, the Iranian state is now aware that in the early years of power it paid a high price for its repression at home as well as for its export of revolution to other states. In private officials recognize two large mistakes in particular: the seizure and occupation of the US embassy in November 1979 and the failure to make peace on favourable terms with Iraq in July 1982. The US embassy compound in the city centre is still used by the revolutionary guards, its wall covered with anti-imperialist posters. Yet henceforward, it is implied, interest rather than ideology will prevail. One result of this new approach is a desire to improve relations with the Arab world (Khomeini refused to use the term 'Saudi Arabia', referring to it as 'the so-called Kingdom of Najd and Hijaz') but there has been a significant improvement in relations with Riyadh and diplomatic ties with Egypt and Algeria, hitherto denounced as secularist oppressors, have been renewed.

One Arab country with which Iran has not improved relations is Iraq. The twin objects of US dual containment always judged it wiser to try to portray the other as the real enemy of international stability rather than to band together, and both continue to support opposition groups committed to the overthrow of the other's regimes. Iranian pilgrims and traders now visit Baghdad and Shi'ite shrines in Iraq, but the rhetorical war continues. Saddam has, in recent months, stepped up propaganda about Iran as the enemy of Iraq. Iran knows that, in the longer run, a revived Iraq may turn on it again, as it did in 1980.

The rethinking of foreign policy is, therefore, part of the even broader debate within Iran about the future of the Islamic Republic itself. Here there is much talk of democratization and of *jame-yi madani*, 'civil society'. On three earlier occasions in modern history Iranian society has erupted in protest and civil action from below: in the Constitutional Revolution of 1906, when up to 15,000 protesters took refuge in the spacious 40-acre grounds of the British embassy; in the period of nationalist prime minister Mosadeq (1951–53); and in the months preceding and following the fall of the Shah (1978–79). Each of these earlier experiments in civil society was crushed – the first two with active foreign involvement. The question is whether this will happen again. The Iranian debate involves much speculation on the preconditions for democracy itself and familiar obstacles are produced. Decades ago these were 'imperialism' or 'oriental despotism'; the current 'favourite' obstacle is that Iran is, by dint of its oil, a 'rentier' society, or, for the more secular, it is the very undemocratic nature of the clergy.

Equally important for today's debates is the legacy that this earlier history left in the field of literature and social criticism. Iran has, throughout modern times, had a vibrant literary culture, one that draws on the writings of the Persian past, but has also interacted with much of Western literature. In the 1950s and 1960s there was a vigorous translation of Western writings, limited only by censorship of those works, such as *Macbeth* or *Hamlet*, that portrayed the slaying of a monarch. Much, but not all, of this writing was influenced by Marxism of an orthodox communist kind: Gorky, Sartre and Jack London were favourite authors. Many of these writers were critical of both forms of conservatism afflicting the country, that of the Shah's regime and that of the Islamic clergy. Yet this engagement with modernism from abroad was accompanied by an effervescence within the clerical world that found its expression in the revolution of 1979.

Opponents of change accuse the reformist writers of being 'against Islam'. Ayatollah Khamene'i declared, in his letter of last August to the *Majlis* calling for controls on the media, 'If the enemies infiltrate the press, this will be a big danger to the country's security and the people's religious beliefs'. Others speak of the 'silent aggression' and 'cultural aggression' coming from abroad, in league with those within. Yet what is not at stake is the Islamic character of the state itself, in the sense of broad respect for Islamic values and history and for the nationalism that the revolution articulated. In the south of the city a huge complex is being built around the tomb of Khomeini, who died in 1989, and people there talk of turning it into one of the great pilgrimage sites of Islam, along with Mecca, Jerusalem and the Shi'ite shrines. Over it hangs the red flag of Imam Hussein, grandson of the Prophet Muhammad and the founder of Shi'ite Islam, who died in 680. Crowds, many from Central Asia, throng the approaches. One man I spoke to, a 28-year-old driver for a ministry, expressed his criticism of the current elite through his praise for Khomeini: 'The Imam was a straightforward man (*sade*), he did not lie. He was not like the others,' he said.

Twenty years of economic mismanagement and political repression and a growing contempt for the corruption associated with many of the clergy have led a shift of opinion within the country. How far this will go no one can tell. Some restrictions – on women's dress code – have been eased, but the country is still far from allowing the kind of mixture of Islamic and Western clothing that is common in other Muslim states, such as Egypt. The protest movement is influenced by economic aspiration and by a Western world seen through videos and magazines and familiar from the large post-revolutionary diaspora.

It is unclear, however, what people want and how far even

Khatami is prepared to go. Certainly, more than two decades after the revolution, the old slogans no longer work. The economy is not delivering and there is widespread unemployment. Many of those who supported the revolution and fought Iraq are now disillusioned. Younger people are resisting the social restrictions imposed by the state. There is a huge hunger for political freedom and free speech. Reports suggest that this feeling, far from being confined to Tehran, is even stronger outside Tehran. In early August riots broke out in the southern city of Khorramshahr, scene of some of the heaviest fighting in the Iran–Iraq war: elements of the *pasdaran*, or revolutionary guards, attacked a reformist meeting.

This is not, therefore, a conventional situation of social protest challenging a state: the division runs within each. The movement from below faces a state that is divided within itself. Against the reformist movement is ranged a coalition of clerical power, associated with the spiritual leader or *faqih*, 'jurisconsult', Ayatollah Khamene'i, and some elements in the military, and backed by conservative militia forces. The position of the *faqih* has become the most controversial in Iran: reformers want the position curtailed and subject to election; conservatives shout the slogan, 'Death to the those who are against the *faqih*'. The clergy are divided, as they were in the revolution. Some favour social and political reform. Some even blame the revolution for discrediting Islam in the eyes of the population.

One of the most militant critics of the regime, Abdullah Nuri, was imprisoned after a trial in which he openly questioned the clerical hold on power and denounced the corruption and abuse of office of his fellow mullahs. Others are deeply entrenched in the regime and have acquired wealth and power through it: thanks to a system of foundations, or *bonyad*, which acquire money from the state for social and economic activities, they are now a financial as well as a cultural force, and they do not wish to lose this power or privilege. One of the leading clerics, Ayatollah Jannati, has been clear enough, observing, 'You cannot save Islam with liberalism and tolerance'. True to ideological type, Jannati went on to question whether, in an Islamic republic, there was a need for novels.

As president, Khatami himself has wished so far to maintain a coalition with Khamene'i. Many of his followers do not want this to continue. In August 2000, when Khamene'i intervened in parliament to stop a liberal press law from being passed, he caused great anger within the reformist camp. If Khatami does not press ahead with his reform, then he runs the risk of losing his support and facing increasing criticism. If he breaks with Khamene'i, then there is a risk of a confrontation with the clerical–security complex that opposed him. The followers of Khatami do not want violence, but those opposed to reform are prepared to use it, as they have shown in the past. It is believed that the reformers have the upper hand in the armed forces and the ministry of intelligence, and that a majority of the revolutionary guards voted for reformist candidates in the *Majlis* elections: but the judiciary and some of the security forces remain opposed to change.

At the moment there is a certain pause in the competition of reformers and conservatives. The great popular expectations that accompanied the *Majlis* elections of February have faded. Several of the leading figures of the *dovvom-i khordad* reform movement, clergy and other intellectuals, are in prison, even while their books are on sale across Tehran. There is uncertainty about the economy and about Khatami's ability to push through economic reform: this is all the more difficult because some of those who favour the liberalization of social and political life are opposed to liberalization of the economy, as they are to any examination of past human rights abuses. One particular issue of contention is foreign investment. Iran is not offering international oil and gas firms the production-sharing agreements that other producer states do, and there is little sign of sufficient political support for this at the moment.

More importantly, however, Khatami may not be able to keep the support of those who have up to now supported him. The next few months may be decisive for the future direction of Iran and for the fate of the revolutionary regime. Whatever happens, Iran's writers and journalists will have plenty to say about the on-going developments and who is responsible for them: what is not clear is whether these words will find their way into print.

9
Saudi Arabia:
A Family Business in Trouble

Riyadh, 1997

It does not take one long when travelling to Saudi Arabia to realise that one is entering a domain of sanctioned religiosity. At Jeddah airport, the customs officer searching for alcohol and other prohibited imports enquires when the arriving passenger is going to convert to Islam: prefiguring the claim of a lecturer who told me that he taught traffic regulations by reference to the words of God, the customs official notices I can read Arabic and tells me that the answers to all the world's problems are to be found in the Quran. 'Next time you come through, you should have converted,' he cheerfully opines.

Nonetheless, on the occasion of the National Festival for Culture and Heritage, universally known as 'al-Jinadiria' after the suburb of Riyadh that houses an annual handicrafts exhibition, a certain ecumenical spirit seems on offer. The Jinadiria is one of the few occasions when Saudis can express themselves more freely in public: a fare of camel-racing in the day and metaphysics at night throws a curious light on the society and its concerns. A favourite royal visitor from Britain, referred to in Arabic as the Emir of Wales, lectures on the shared values of Islam and Christianity. Perhaps more is read into this than is warranted: in the Gulf the position of crown prince is usually associated with political office – prime minister in Kuwait, deputy prime minister in the Saudi Kingdom. His enthusiastic participation in the *arda*, or Saudi tribal dance, backed by a cast of over two hundred from a beduin operetta, and cheered by the all-male crowd who burst onto the stage, seems to delight his royal hosts.

Officialdom seems less well pleased with Helmut Schafer, the German foreign office minister, whose speech to the Jinadiria criticizing the denial of human rights in Europe *and* the Islamic world is only selectively reported in the press. The Emir of Wales is introduced as coming from *shaqiq* Britain – a term implying close family links normally reserved for Arab states. Germany is merely *sadiq* – friendly, but not too much so.

This is not a country where it is easy to come by reliable information. There are no firm statistics on the most important economic indicators, oil output or revenue. Few independent observers believe the official population statistics of around 15 million. No-one seems to know how many Saudi princes there are, each entitled to a *khususia* or allowance of hundreds of thousands of dollars, and to perks including free air travel. Much depends on the atmosphere and in this, the year 1417 by the Islamic calendar, the rulers and owners of the Kingdom of Saudi Arabia give the sense of having some short-term reasons for feeling a little more at ease.[1]

The price of oil (which costs domestic consumers 50p a gallon) has risen by 35 per cent, adding an estimated $9 billion to an income of around $42 billion. In the tense context of the Gulf, the two main sources of unease, Iraq and Iran, both appear temporarily to be in defensive mood. Within the country, the wave of opposition known as the *salafiyyin*, the conservative and in some ways fundamentalist critics of the regime, have been less in evidence, as repression, exile and money take their toll.

But in other respects unease continues. On Riyadh's 'Thirty Street', so called because of its width in metres, a thoroughfare better known as a place where men can thrust their visiting cards through the windows of passing women in cars, the empty site where a bomb went off in November 1995 destroying a US-Saudi military training centre still stand empty. A later bomb, in Dhahran, killing 17 Americans and wounding over 300 remains unexplained. There are rumours that those involved in the first, for which four men were executed after a secret trial, were associated with the *mutawwa'in*, the Islamic vigilantes attached to the Ministry of the Interior who tour the city in brown jeeps, harassing inadequately covered women and those who do not observe the hours of prayer. Investigations on the second bomb remain even more obscure: there have been many arrests in areas suspected of fundamentalist influence, Sunni and Shia, above all in the al-Thuqba district of Jubail, known for *salafi* influence. But some Saudis suggest that there is a high-up connection, possibly some prince or military commander, whose disclosure would embarrass the regime.

It is not such bombs that pose, however, the biggest problems for the Saudi state. These reside in longer-term problems for which no easy or rapid solutions appear available. The first is paralysis at the top: in Riyadh there is more than a hint of late-Brezhnevite Moscow, of an Islamic tribal variant of 'stagnation'. The three key people in the country are King Fahd, Crown Prince Abdullah Commander of the National Guard, and Sultan, the minister of defence. The king is 74, in poor health, and has assumed power again after a temporary regency by Abdullah. The other leading princes, all sons of the founder of the regime, Abd al-Aziz ibn Saud, who died in 1953, defer to him: there is much talk of 'paralysis' at the top, as major policy issues, not least economic change and the crab-like pace of constitutional reform, remain unsettled. Abdullah is believed to be more sympathetic to Arab nationalism, and to want a stronger control on princely corruption.

The second problem is jobs: whatever the precise population figures, Saudi Arabia is becoming a more 'normal' country. Over the past decade per capita income has fallen by up to two thirds, to around $6,000 a year, and more and more young people are looking for employment: attempts to Saudianize the economy meet with resistance not just from foreign but from Saudi employers. Graduates of the Islamic universities set up by King Feisal, who ruled from 1962 to 1975, in an attempt channel Islamist sentiment, are particularly unemployable. This discontent over jobs and money is accentuated by something never far below the surface in the kingdom, namely regional differences: in the more cosmopolitan, Western region, the Hijaz, there is resentment by Hijazis of the beduin tribesmen who overran them in the 1920s and take a disproportionate part of the oil revenue; prominent Hijazis, close to the top of the regime, will openly scorn the claim that their country is not ready for a more democratic system. 'We had newspapers and elections, before the Saudis conquered us,' one told me. In the eastern Shia regions, site of the oil fields, a partial relaxation in the early 1990s has now gone into reverse and the teachers at the Islamic universities openly denounce the Shia as un-Islamic.

The third problem is the state's reliance on the USA. Saddam's invasion came as a big shock to Saudi Arabia, showing that there were real threats to the country, and also exposing the hollowness of the warrior ethos upon which the Saudi ruling family had hitherto based its legitimacy. Attempts by concerned princes to promote the record of their troops in the conflict do not seem to have convinced anybody. Yet, in what others might see as inconsistency, many Saudis resent the US military presence in the country, phrasing this in terms of non-Muslim troops despoiling sacred territory – a fatuous argument for opponents of the Saudi regime to make, since it is only the Saudi state that claims the sacredness of the whole territory, even beyond Mecca and Medina. Resentment against the USA is particularly strong at a time when Washington, through blocking Security Council condemnation of Netanyahu's policies, is seen as being too partial to Israel. The regime is, however, caught: it has moved US forces out of the cities, after the bomb blasts, but they are very much not out of mind.

There is a growing nationalism in Saudi Arabia against the West, as well as against other money-requesting Arabs, but it is a nationalism laced with views of international conspiracy. There is a vogue for books on *istishraq*, 'orientalism', understood as the study of the Arab world seen as part of an imperialist plot. In the opulent bookshops the section on 'orientalism' is next to that on espionage and Western or Zionist conspiracies. Many Saudis believe that the articles in the *Wall Street Journal* and other US papers over the past two years questioning Saudi financial reserves are officially inspired.

Saudi Arabia is a country obsessed with control, most obviously political: no parties or independent publications are allowed. The most striking building in Riyadh, visible on the arterial King Fahd flyover, is the Ministry of the Interior, an inverted pyramid, which claimed the lives of 63 Korean workers when being built with wooden scaffolding. Yet this very obsession, as in other strict Muslim countries like Iran or in communist states, only rebounds. Whisky (for years imported in a weekly flight from Manchester by a now deceased elder brother of the king) abounds at closed social gatherings, even if some at least of the imbibers break off for prayer. While hi-fi shops are illegal, as supposedly violating Islamic precepts, videos, cassettes and journals of all kinds circulate underground. Conversation switches easily from the exalted to the most direct of anatomical issues – Saudi males of an older generation seem especially interested in the facilities offered in London for reinvigorating their genitals: jokes about transplants abound.

This growing social unease on the part of males is mirrored in two striking respects. One is the growing pressure from women: women are almost entirely absent from the public space in Saudi Arabia, fleetingly glimpsed in black cloaks at shopping malls, or being driven by male drivers and relatives around town. At universities women students have to follow lectures over video linkups and conduct tutorials by telephone. Yet levels of education amongst Saudi women are high, in many cases higher than amongst males: 65 per cent of the graduates from Riyadh University last year were believed to be women. Certain sections of economic activity, notably banks, have divisions that are entirely female-staffed. There is a large network of social organizations, under the umbrella of 'charity', in which women are active. Many Saudi women have travelled abroad, and have access to media images and information from abroad on a daily basis. Now that neighbouring Qatar has lifted its ban, Saudi Arabia is now the only country in the world that does not allow women to drive. Literature on gender relations abounds, from assertions of the orthodox Islamic position to studies of women and discourse, replete with quotes from Julia Kristeva, Marilyn French and Laura Mulvey.

Another area of tension is in regard to the law. Officially Saudi Arabia is governed by *shari'a*, or, more precisely, the Hanbali version of legal commentary upon the holy texts. As such it does not need lawyers, and none are indeed trained. Religious judges, or *qadi*, are produced by the Islamic universities and training institutes. The lack of Saudi specialists in law, accountancy and management remains dire. Yet, in response to economic pressure, a code of commercial law, based on the Geneva convention, has been taken over wholesale: to avoid offending the orthodox, it does not fall under the aegis of the Ministry of Justice but is administered by a committee under the Central Bank.

The conflicts involved in this obsessive and increasingly threatened control are visible. One of the subtler forms of media control is evident from the grades of representation of the human form. The ban on portrayals of living images, often associated with the Quran, is in fact a later accretion, borrowed from Judaism and Christianity and without Quranic authority. But in Saudi Arabia and, in an even more extreme form, in Afghanistan it has become part of public morality. Thus on the advertising billboards around Riyadh no human faces are visible: an advertisement for car seat belts shows a headless midriff, one for a four-wheel drive shows a male, his head covered in a headdress. In government offices, however, or on postage stamps portraits of the Saudi kings and princes are everywhere. Gradations of revelation operate in the press: in the Arabic-language Saudi press printed in the kingdom no photographs of females are allowed on the front pages, and only those of pre-adolescent girls inside; in the English-language press women, suitably covered, are printed; in the Saudi-funded Arabic press printed outside, but freely available in the kingdom, unveiled, adult, women abound. On television sitcoms and soap operas with unveiled women are broadcast – but they are licit because their storylines take place in domestic settings and no males are filmed as present.

Another striking index of these undercurrents is to be found in literature: perhaps the greatest surprise for the visitor to Saudi Arabia is the scale of the bookshops. The pre-Islamic poetry of Arabia is the original source of Arabic, and traditional Saudi literature took the form of poetry. No official gathering seems complete without the delivery, in staccato beduin tones, of words in praise of the ruling family and their great works. Poetry remains an important source of inspiration: the work of the exiled Hasan al-Qurashi mixes lyrical and political themes. But poetry is now matched by the novel and the short story. The exiled Abd al-Rahman Munif, in his novel, *Cities of Salt*, portrays the corruption of dynastic rule in a thinly disguised Saudi Arabia. Ghazi Algosaibi, although a former minister and now ambassador to London, has seen two of his novels, *Apartment of Freedom* and *The Madhouse,* banned in the country: they provide a fascinating insight into the world of the nationalist intelligentsia, the former set in Cairo of the 1950s, exploring radical nationalist politics and sexual experience, the latter following the trail of an Arab who goes to America, falls in love with a woman who is Jewish, and ends up in a Lebanese mental asylum. One book by Algosaibi advocating secularism was denounced by the religious establishment for 'apostasy'.[2]

There is now a body of short stories which focus on Saudi women's experience of a stifling society, and the conflicts which they face. These encompass the themes of alcoholism, coercive arranged marriages, male privilege in all its forms, and the denial of individual freedom by family, society and state alike.[3]

Caught by these social pressures and by such dramatic developments as the Gulf war of 1991, the Saudi regime has tried to accommodate change without ceding its privileges. Thus a consultative assembly, and a set of provincial assemblies, were set up in 1993. The regime has also tried to refashion its ideology: although in the past presented as an alliance of the tribal elite – the Al Saud, and its religious counterpart, the Al Shaikh – there is now almost no mention in official statements or in the naming of public buildings of the religious origins of the regime in the eighteenth century revivalism of Abd al-Wahhab. Although some of his descendants, the Al Shaikh, retain positions of influence (as ministers and ambassadors) this is more by virtue of their personal qualities than by descent. Saudi Arabia has sought to give itself a new, more conventional national identity: thus in 1986 the king took the title of 'Servant of the Two Holy Places,' that is, Mecca and Medina.

As demonstrated by the Jinadiria, the state now promotes a sense of national heritage including, to a limited extent, recognition of the architecture and artefacts of pre-Islamic times. The problem with attempts to reclaim this archeological heritage is that overzealous Wahhabis, who come across statues and paintings by chance, too easily proceed to hack out the faces in accordance with their beliefs. Concern about conservative religious response is believed to explain the long delay in opening a planned national archeological museum in Riyadh, as it has similarly blocked the opening of a lavish cultural centre completed some years ago.

But there are clear limits to this process. Neither the king nor any possible successor look as if they are really able to tackle the abuse of financial and other power by the princes of the royal family: US embassy officials resignedly talk of the $14 billion or so of revenue, about a third of the total, that is 'off budget', or unaccounted for. Stories abound of the commissions, (nisbat), allocated tanker cargoes and arbitrary land seizures obtained by princes. One has cornered the market in courier services, another in a branch of car sales, others declare themselves owners of a piece of land where construction is about to begin. As social and economic pressures mount, this issue of unaccounted funds will become pressing: it has already become the number one bone of contention in neighbouring Kuwait where parliament can ask, without much success, for an account of state finances.

At the same time, any process of liberalization will have to encounter two-fold opposition: resistance comes both from the *malaki*, the royal elite at the top, and from the *ahli*, the popular constituency below. '70 per cent of the people in this country are not living in the twentieth century,' one exasperated long-term Arab resident commented to me. Those who have attended the almost weekly carnivals associated with public executions in the centre of Riyadh report no lack of public enthusiasm for them elsewhere. Opposition to increased freedom for women comes as much from males threatened by more competent and less controllable women as it does from the princes at the top.

In this world of uncertainty, rumour, amazing oligarchic wealth and ostentation, it is easy to foresee dramatic futures. There are certainly those, ranging from the militant *salafiyyin* within, to Saddam, or some in the Iranian regime without, who would like to see such a turn of events. An estimated 15,000 Saudis went, with official and US blessing, to fight in Afghanistan: now they form a discontented and experienced nucleus, represented in extreme form by Osama bin Ladin, member of a wealthy family who is threatening terrorist actions from a hideout near Jalalabad. It is less than two decades since a group of armed tribesmen seized and held for two weeks the holy mosque in Mecca.

Yet there could also be another path, one in which the power and greed of the princely caste is gradually but firmly brought under control, and a greater degree of cooperation between the princes and the rest of society, male and female, promoted. There are certainly assets on which to build – enormous wealth in the ground, an increasingly educated society, a substantial public service sector, and an at least significant, if not large, liberal middle class. The Saudi family business cannot go on for ever, and if it does not change it will court ruin. It could, however, as others have done, become a public company, shedding some of its pietistic pretensions and royal privileges. That might well be the best outcome both for the inhabitants of this curious state itself and for the rest of the world that, for better or worse, will continue to rely on its oil for many a decade to come.

10
The Other Stereotype: America and its Critics

London, August 1991

One of the most widely held, and universally unchallenged, tenets of the Left over the past four decades or more has been its hostility to the USA: not just to the imperialist dimension of US foreign policy in its economic and military relations with the third world, most evident in the war in Vietnam, but also the US political and cultural system as a whole. 'Anti-Americanism' is a term often used by defenders of US policy to discredit any criticism of what Washington is doing: but, stripped of this smear character, it does quite accurately characterise an attitude, prevalent on much of the European Left, towards all that America stands for, or is supposed to stand for.

Three things about this attitude are immediately obvious. First, while often phrased in Left terms, it is by no means specific to the Left. Broad conservative and snobbish hostility to the USA, its culture and politics, is a stock in trade of much of the European Right, especially in France. Secondly, while widely held on the Left, it accords with a remarkable and pervasive ignorance of, and lack of interest in, US politics and society: anyone organising a socialist conference or speakers' programme will know that it is much easier to get an expert on Nicaragua, or Palestine, or South Africa than to get someone who can talk informatively about the politics of the USA, domestic or foreign. It is as if, since we all know how terrible the place is, and how uniquely pernicious its influence, there is no need to probe further. Whatever else, this attitude greatly overstates the degree of homogeneity within the USA, and ignores the very diverse political, as well as cultural, forces operating within it.

The third, and most significant, problem with this broad 'anti-Americanism' is that, precisely because it ignores how diverse US political life and influence are, in certain key respects it misrepresents the recent impact of the USA on Western Europe and on the development of the Left in Europe. The formation of the European left in the early part of this century owes little to the USA, although it is worth remembering that the day celebrating the struggles of the working class, 1 May, is of US origin. In the post-1945 context, however, for all the talk of the influence of the second, communist, world, and of the third world, the greatest source of radical ideas in Europe has been the USA: the civil rights movement and its later, anti-racist, variants; the student movement; the anti-war movement; women's liberation; gay liberation. Current campaigns for a bill of rights, freedom of information, greater power for regions all derive support from the US example, as do demands that the head of state pay taxes, and that primary and secondary schooling be free of charge.

There are many aspects of US society that are, compared to Western Europe, pernicious – the absence of welfare programmes, the incidence of crime and drugs, the prevalence of fundamentalist religious bodies, to name but three. But the complacent attitude held by Left and Right in Europe alike, that in all respects US society is more backward than that of the old world, simply does not hold up. The USA, not least in the aftermath of the Gulf war, exhibits a strong vein of cultural and great power arrogance, but it is hardly for the British, the French, the Germans, or even the Spaniards, to claim superiority in that domain. The Vietnam War Memorial in Washington is dignified and restrained, in marked contrast to the bellicose adornments of many European states, Waterloo Station and Gare d'Austerlitz among them. The USA, like Germany, has a lot to teach this country, and others, about decentralisation and regional rights. The attitude of the state to information and the rights of citizens is far superior to that of the closed, arrogant, states of Western Europe. Attitudes to gender are far more advanced.

On an issue that is looming as perhaps the major controversy of the 1990s, immigration, the USA has a wholly different, and more positive, historical experience: there is little talk in the USA about the dangers of 'dilution' and up to one third of all the people now living in the USA were born outside it. On the racial front the great failure of US society has been the treatment of Afro-Americans, a consequence of history and the failure to resolve its legacy which Americans, quick to scorn others for their obsession with the past, would do well to bear in mind. But, in other respects, the USA is a far more successful and vibrant multi-racial society and offers greater opportunity for integration than does any society in the stuffy world of Europe. The Hong Kong Chinese who declined to come to Britain and chose instead to get to the USA knew what they were doing.

European cultural hostility to the USA tends to rest on a curious inconsistency. Great stress is laid on the 'vulgarity' of much US culture, and its pernicious influence on television, language, music and the like. Much of this critique is valid: more rubbish is produced in the USA, and sold around the world, than by any other society. But the cultural impact of the USA has also been of immense positive value: the impact of jazz, of pop music, of quality Hollywood, of US literature, theatre and art have made as great a contribution to the culture of the world as any other nation in the twentieth century. In Britain, there is particular sensitivity about the impact on the English language: here again, it is arguable that the enrichment of the spoken language over recent years is as much as anything a result of American influence, mediating as it does Yiddish, West Indian, Latin American and other elements as well as changes within spoken English in the USA itself. It would be curious indeed if the Left ended up defending the inviolability and unchangeability of language.

When it comes to judgement of the USA's international role, similar problems, of establishing a position critical of US policy and craven Atlanticism, but distinct from a dogmatic anti-Americanism, arise. Again, the choice is not just between critique and acceptance, but between a critique that is simplistic and one that is informed and measured. There is considerable, legitimate hostility to the US influence in Europe but the failure to produce anything but the platitudes of anti-Americanism has been one of the factors contributing to the continued US presence in Europe, in the form of NATO and the Atlantic alliance. Lest anyone underestimate the strength of attachment to this form of US link, they should remember how, even at the height of the peace movement in the early 1980s, a much smaller percentage were prepared to break with NATO: CND, for this reason, ducked the issue. The opportunity now presents itself, with the end of the cold war, for a renewed challenge to this link, not in the name of anti-Americanism, but in the name of establishing a more balanced, equal relationship between both sides of the Atlantic.

The challenge of producing a more measured critical assessment of the USA is posed most sharply with regard to the third world, and it is here above all that the irresponsibility of Left orthodoxy becomes most obvious. That the USA has behaved as an imperial power, in economic and military terms, towards the third world since 1945 is evident. But a critique that simply makes this point avoids at least three others that are of relevance, if not to people in the first world, then to those in the third.

The first is that in this respect too the US polity is not a monolith, with all its policies pre-determined: there is some room for political movement within the USA, by working with those opposed to what prevailing policy may be. For many movements and parties fighting for democracy and independence in the third world some positive engagement with the USA is essential, be this Congress, the press, the State Department or whatever. Simply to say that these are all imperialists and enemies is to miss the point. One has only to look at what, over many years, a range of third world movements actually did – the ANC, which got the US Congress to impose the decisive sanctions legislation in 1986, the PLO, which has tried to sustain a dialogue with the USA, the Eritreans who have built up a working relationship with the USA over the past few years, which served, in part, to secure their recent attainment of de facto independence. The political priority for these and many others is not only to criticize US policy, which they do, but to find a way of engaging positively with it.

Secondly, there is the issue, most sharply posed by the Gulf war, of US intervention. In the face of a series of illegal and imperialistic interventions by US forces over past decades, there has been a tendency for the liberal and left opposition, in Europe and the USA, to oppose intervention as such, in all its forms. But this position is questionable, both historically and politically. First of all, there are in this century some striking cases in which the USA, imperialist and self-interested as it was, has played a positive role in world politics: Woodrow Wilson's support for national self-determination after World War I helped bring independence to a range of countries in Europe; the US role in World War II was of a positive kind. Secondly, there are a number of cases today where more, not less, intervention, in the form of economic and military pressure, is welcomed by the peoples of the countries themselves. Here the Gulf war pointed out the fatal short-sightedness of the Left consensus on both sides of the Atlantic: opposition to the war was based on hostility to 'US interventionism', as if this were a self-sufficient position: it was valid to question whether opposition to Iraqi occupation of another country made war inevitable, but not to argue that because US motives were self-interested, as they certainly were, no international action against Saddam was justified. The issue was posed even more sharply in the aftermath of the war when it became clear that what the peoples of Iraq wanted, and were asking for, was more not less US action, to overthrow the Ba'thist regime and enable them to come to power.

A third issue, and one of special responsibility for the metropolitan Left, is that of the quality of analysis of US society and politics itself. Faced with the monolithic consensus of the mainstream media and academic output, the opposition has too often tended to resort to conspiracy theory, scandal and moral denunciation. Conspiracy and scandal there certainly are, but in themselves they do not constitute an adequate alternative analysis. What has too often happened is that these facile critiques from the European and US Lefts have fed into the conspiracy theories generated in the third world itself: instead of providing analysis that is informed, and which enables action, it too often misleads and disables. To say that the USA is irrevocably opposed to such and such a people – Palestinians, Greeks or whatever – or to 'Islam', or that all US economic influence impoverishes those it affects, is to do no service to peoples in the Third World. They need a guide not to how unremittingly evil the US is, but to how to deal with it, and get the best out of these deals, be they political or economic.

In this context, a strong measure of blame lies with the US Left itself. Beleaguered, courageous and dogged as it is, it has none the less too easily fallen into the mirror-image platitudes, taking what it does not like in the morning's issue of *The New York Times* as the basis for its political position. Some critics of US policy make clear that what they are concerned with is not what is happening in third world countries, for which they are not responsible, but rather the lies and manipulation practised by the US state itself. This is very much the position that underlies Chomsky's sustained and compelling critiques of US foreign policy. But this approach, apparently consistent and defensible, runs a number of dangers.

Firstly, it too easily encourages the view that the whole of world politics is in some way or another a product of US action. It is, in this way, merely nationalism inverted: it does not try to locate the actions of the US government in a broader international context. During the anti-war movement of the early 1980s many of the best critiques of the arms race were produced in the US: but too many wrote as if US arms policy was a product entirely of domestic factors, as in the USSR, and international political processes, did not exist. Similarly, in the critique of US policy in the Gulf, there was too often a tendency to suggest that in some way or another the USA was responsible for the whole thing anyway – by having armed Saddam in the past, by having tricked him into invading Kuwait, or by refusing to let him get out when he really wanted to. Other forces did not count: all was the work, and the fault, of the USA.

Secondly, a focus solely on the workings and misworkings of US policy can too easily be seen as avoiding the issue of politically evaluating what forces within third world countries may be doing themselves and of how outside forces can relate to them. If there is torture, oppression, invasion in third world states, this cannot be dealt with merely by saying that US policy in this context is dishonest. The problem of policy towards Cambodia during the Khmer Rouge period, or of Saddam's invasion of Kuwait, is not merely, or indeed mainly, one of US misrepresentation and moral inconsistency, but rather of what these regimes were themselves doing and of how outsiders, including the USA, could help the peoples so affected to resist them. To be concerned only with the critique of your own government is a form of inverted patriotism and moral solipsism: it was, as ever, well summarised by a remark of Gore Vidal's during the Gulf war that he was not overly concerned about Saddam since he was no worse than the Los Angeles police department. The LAPD had just been videoed beating up a black suspect; Saddam has murdered tens of thousands of his compatriots.

The need for a more measured political assessment of the USA is a matter of great urgency the world over, for two evident reasons. First, the collapse of communism has meant that more and more people the world over look to the USA as a model society and as a source of benevolent influence: to counter this delusion involves first recognising the fact that this is the case, something of no little political significance in itself, but also counterposing to it not the platitudes of anti-Americanism but something more informed. If the Left is going to come up with a coherent and plausible assessment of the US, it has to recognise that masses of the world want to go and live there. There is little point in telling the people of Albania, or China, or Mexico, that they are victims of false consciousness. Secondly, the USA has today grater diplomatic and strategic power than at any time since World War II. It is easy to overstate this, but wrong to ignore it: the question posed for people inside the USA and those who have to deal with it from without is in what ways, small or large, that influence can be put to better rather than worse use, be this in North–South economic relations, in the field of human rights, in that of intervention or of a new potentially non-hegemonic security system in Europe.

Those in Europe, and the US, who have long sustained a critique of US society and of US foreign policy would be well advised to break their often too comfortable and absolute denunciations, and take the opportunities which now present themselves. We may miss the opportunity. The forces within the USA and outside which want to enhance the more oppressive and hierarchical character of the world will certainly not.

11
Global Inequality and Global Rancour

Introduction: The challenges of the 1990s

Globalization, at once an opportunity and a danger, is a topic central to much contemporary discussion of international relations and, equally, of several other branches of the social sciences, among them sociology, geography and economics. 'Globalization' is a term that has come into common currency only in the past decade and encompasses, within many varied and often imprecise meanings, the breaking down of barriers between societies, economies and political systems and the greatly increased volume of exchanges they enjoy, be they in terms of trade, finance, people or ideas. It poses a double challenge for all of us, that of trying to analyse and understand these processes and their longer-run implications, but also that of seeing how we may respond to them: globalization therefore poses normative choices, as much as it defies analytic comprehension.

In regard to both challenges, the analytic and the normative, it is advantageous for us to step back from the apparently overwhelming rush of the immediate. One of the greatest temptations in contemporary discussion of these issues is that of denying historic depth, be it that of the process involved or that of the normative discussion of issues raised by them. In this regard, and in keeping with the Enlightenment origins of this very Academy, it is appropriate to start with one of the classics of international relations itself.

The subject I teach, international relations, aspires to reflect on relations between states and nations in three broad perspectives: relations between states themselves, what has, since the term was coined by Jeremy Bentham in 1780, been termed the 'international'; relations between societies and peoples, in cultural and social as well as economic terms – what has, much more recently, come to be termed the 'transnational'; and what is, from a variety of theoretical starting points, termed the 'structural', that is, the set of contexts, political, economic and otherwise, that constrain the actions of individual states and other actors. It is a subject as important as any other for the understanding of human behaviour and the human condition, but also one that, for a variety of reasons, encourages a high degree of speculation and assertion.

The finest works of theory are often the briefest, and there can be no finer exemplar of this than Immanuel Kant's essay written in 1784, a year before the founding of this Royal Irish Academy: 'Idea for a Universal History' is thirteen pages long and makes an argument that is as relevant now as it was when it was written, arguably more so. Kant advocates a view of history, of possible progress and of the development of relations between states that can lead, through increased cooperation between states, to a form of world government. His aspiration is 'that after many reformative revolutions, a universal cosmopolitan condition, which Nature has as her ultimate purpose, will come into being as the womb wherein all the original capacities of the human race can develop'.[1] A contemporary rendering of this argument, not entirely at variance with what he wrote, is that, as their internal orders become more constitutional and democratic, conflict between states will decline, and that the states of the world can, over time, advance towards a unified, global political community.

This was then an optimistic and remote possibility, and remains so now. Those who have believed, over the ensuing two centuries, that war had already disappeared from international relations, above all as a result of industrialization and trade, have been cruelly disappointed. Equally, the aspiration to world government wins fewer friends today than in the past, partly because of the attachment of peoples to their own democratic state governments, partly because any project of world government as advocated by some may appear as a case for world domination by others. The connection that Kant suggests, however, between domestic political order, international cooperation and the increased common goals of such states, one to which he was to return in his other classic of brevity and insight, written in 1796, is very much with us today.

In historical perspective, globalization represents the economic and social culmination of five centuries of integration of the world into a single world economy, pioneered by the strongest. The political issues it now raises are shaped by the challenges that globalization poses to established systems of political power, most obviously to any project of national self-determination, to 'national', that is, state control over the economy and, in general, to the powers of the sovereign state. But these challenges and the global liberalization of economies have developed in a world of substantially distinct kind, marked by the end of the cold war and with it, for the time being at least, of a world dominated by competing strategic and economic blocs. It is important to understand that change, not only for assessing how the contemporary international situation was shaped, but also in recognizing those ways in which, despite the shift in world politics, that past still remains influential. It is in this momentous change of the late 1980s and early 1990s, a process separate from but interrelated with socio-economic globalization, that an understanding of the contemporary world may begin.

The aftermath of cold war

The end of the cold war, in 1989–91, was the third great punctuation mark of twentieth-century history: it marked as dramatic a shift in world affairs as the ends of World War I and II. Several processes were collapsed into this rapid, unexpected and largely peaceful transition: the end of the strategic nuclear arms race, which had cast its shadow over all of humanity – its most dramatic moment having been in the Caribbean, in October 1962; the end of the great power conflict that had dominated the world for forty years; the end of an ideological conflict in which, for all the rhetoric and opportunism involved, two rival social systems sought hegemony in the world and which was fought out, in the Far East, southern

Africa and Latin America, in acute social conflicts that costs the lives of millions of people; and the emergence of twenty new countries resulting from the break-up of multinational states attendant upon the crisis of communist power.

The causes of this communist collapse and the broader lessons to be learnt from the greatest experiment in purposive, utopian transformation of society will long be debated. The collapse was, in part, a result of globalization itself – of the pressure of a comparatively more successful developed capitalist model on authoritarian socialist societies that were stagnant, intellectually, culturally and economically. But the correlation of communist collapse with globalization is only partial: social change within communist states, in part a result of the very success of communism in education and social progress, and a gradual loss of political will on the part of the Soviet leadership were equally important.[2]

The consequences of the collapse of communism for international relations fall into at least four broad categories. First, international security. The security of the large arsenal of nuclear materials and of chemical and biological materials in the former Soviet Union is unclear. Current international and national controls are inadequate. A small lapse in security with regard to these materials could have very serious international consequences. The ending of the nuclear arms race between the USA and Russia has also been followed by the development of nuclear competition elsewhere: in May 1998, in the most irresponsible international act of the 1990s, India and Pakistan exploded nuclear weapons. States in the Middle East will have taken note, not least of the weak-willed, evasive international response. In the Far East, as Russian and US military power recedes, there is a danger of growing rivalry between China and Japan, with other powerful states, Korea and Taiwan, participating. Let us not forget that the first shots in the international wars of the twentieth century were fired in the Far East, in the Sino-Japanese war of 1894. We can only hope, but cannot be sure, that the equivalent in the 1990s is not the Indo–Pakistani nuclear breakout of 1998.

While strategic, great-power military competition has receded for the foreseeable future, more limited, regional conflicts have continued. In the Middle East, the largest importer of weapons of any developing region, and with the highest expenditures on weapons per capita of any region – at over 6 per cent of GDP three times that of Latin America – a set of overlapping, dangerous rivalries continues. Iraq remains at odds with the international community: it has already invaded two of its neighbours, Iran in 1980, killing one million people, and Kuwait in 1990. We can all hope to see Iraq, a country with great human and economic potential, return to normal relations with its neighbours and the world: but equivocation on the part of European or Latin American states on the dangers currently posed by Iraq does not serve the interests of international peace or justice. In Africa, where optimism about political and economic development grew in the early 1990s, several wars rage, of an increasingly regionalized kind. In the Horn of Africa, two revolutionary states, Ethiopia and Eritrea, have been engaged in another full-scale, war, despite the best efforts of the international community to reconcile and restrain them. In the Balkans, a precarious peace reigns in Bosnia and Kosovo: a frozen settlement may prevail in the former, even as it is evacuated of all meaningful compromise; few believe that peace will hold in the latter. The incidence of arms race, civil war and regionalized international war is accompanied by another consequence of the end of the cold war, the flooding of the world market with small weapons that no state controls and that seriously inflame existing conflicts. The issue of international peace and security, the most classical question in international relations, is therefore far from obsolete.

A second consequence of the end of communism was the redrawing of the international map. During the forty years of cold war the world map had been relatively stable: countries became independent of colonial rule but, with the single exception of Bangladesh, revisions of the state map did not occur. The most obvious consequence of the end of communism has been the fragmentation of four countries – the USSR, Yugoslavia, Czechoslovakia, Ethiopia. For some, not least in Europe but even in some areas of Latin America, this appeared to presage a further revision of state boundaries. Some have talked of a coming postmodern 'amoebization' of states – into hundreds or thousands of entities. So far, however, it has not happened: only where communist power has been in terminal crisis have states fragmented. In Catalonia, Quebec, Tibet, Rio Grande do Sul, the state map has held. So if we are, in the future, going to face a crisis of existing states it will not be a result of the changes of the end of the cold war but of new forms of politics, economic management, associated with globalization and subsidiarity. I myself doubt it, but we can keep an open mind. We need also to recognize our normative weakness on this issue: despite a debate and reflection for over a hundred years on the rights of secession, we are no nearer an agreed set of legal and political principles. Peaceful secession *has* been possible during this time – Norway and Slovakia are cases in point. Ireland negotiated, but fought and voted first. Overall, however, the actual process is pragmatic, ad hoc and usually violent. It may also be suggested that, on the basis of historical evidence, fragmentation into further states should be a last resort.

A focus on secession may, however, be misleading. Far more important than the fragmentation of states has been another dimension of the redrawing of maps, the *fusion* of states: Germany and Yemen, where this has already happened, China and Korea where it is beginning to and is, sooner or later, inevitable. Not only does such unification create strong economies, but it also brings about a revision of regional balances of power. In the weight of history the independence of Georgia, Uzbekistan, Macedonia and Eritrea will, with no disrespect, count for much less than the tectonic shifts accompanying the unification of states divided by communism. Germany is now the dominant economic power in Europe. It will sooner or later come to play a consonant security role. China, with a recent growth rate of 8 per cent per annum and a quarter of the world's population can dominate East Asia.

These processes of redrawing of the map draw attention, however, to another, potentially explosive consequence of the end of communism and one with enormous implications for models of economic management, namely the tensions of the transition. In those countries where communist power has been broken – the former Soviet Union, Eastern Europe – the transition to free market systems has been accompanied by enormous social and economic dislocations. On balance, the more advanced Eastern European states appear likely to be able to manage this, although, even in the former East Germany, this may be accompanied by de-industrialization, unemployment and rising social anger. In the former Soviet Union and some Eastern European countries the transition has been an unmitigated disaster, resulting in a collapse of economic and social standards greater and more prolonged than those of war: a fall on average of 40 per cent in per capital, accompanied by rising crime, collapsing welfare, widespread corruption and criminalization, and topped off by a failure across the board of the post-communist political elites. Of all the former European and Soviet states only *one* – Poland – now has a GDP higher than in 1989. According to the European Bank for Reconstruction and Development, the economies of the former Soviet Union will have declined by a further 5.5 per cent by the end of 1999.[3]

In addition to the human misery involved, a result of precipitate and irresponsible reform and of corrupt political elites, this economic and social degeneration threatens to have longer-term international consequences, in the rise of an angry nationalism linked to economic decline and political instability. The consequences of this lack of political responsibility and good governance affect not only the suffering people of Russia: the $22 billion bailout of Russia in July 1998 did not solve the country's debt problem, because nearly $5 billion of the first tranche rapidly disappeared. This does not, of course, apply in those countries where the political transition has been delayed: China, Korea, Vietnam and, with great consequences for Latin America and Latin American–US relations, Cuba. In all of these countries, however, the strains of economic transition are already evident: Cuba and North Korea are enduring declines in their social and economic levels, and enormous regional and urban–rural tensions are growing in China. At some point in the future a *political* crisis will occur: these one-party states cannot go on for ever. The implications for policy and for the management of international relations are disturbing. When China does enter its political crisis, as it must, the whole world will know about it. For Latin America there is and must remain enormous concern about Cuba, where the US embargo, combined with political paralysis in Havana, has forced deprivation on the Cuban people. We may hope that, in Cuba, a transition will be peaceful and rapid and will conserve the gains of the Cuban revolution, in independence, national dignity and socio-economic provision. The lessons from other transitions do not lend encouragement to this expectation.

This brings me to the last of the consequences of the collapse of communism, its intellectual impact: the discrediting of the be-lief in an alternative, revolutionary, planned, post-capitalist society. Political commentators have had much to say about this: Jorge

Castañeda for Latin America; François Furet, writing of the end of the communist illusion, that Western politics are no longer an alibi for the future; Francis Fukuyama reformulating Hegel in his 'end of history'.[4] There is a serious argument here, which facile critics of these writers too easily dismiss. Communism and all the cognate utopian projects of autarchic socialism, populist revolution, Islamic golden ages,[5] peasant republics and the like were, for all their differences, parasitic on the Bolshevik model and, like it, rested on a fundamental misreading of modern history – that capitalism was indeed preparing its own replacement, its own grave-digger, and that an alternative, post-capitalist order could be built. The limits of reason, linked to a collective political project, have never been more dramatically demonstrated, and at a very high human cost. Fukuyama is right to say that in the contemporary world there is no grand alternative idea to that of liberal democratic society, even if he is wrong to see this as necessarily continuing, or to imply that the whole world, or even most of the world's societies, can attain and sustain such a political system.

Yet it would equally be mistaken to treat the communist experiment, which covered over a third of humanity, as simply a mistake or an aberration: millions of people rebelled, fought, worked, died to construct an alternative order because they found the existing order intolerable. It was the actually existing capitalism of modernity – warlike, oppressive, unequal, manipulative – that produced communism, as an idea and as a challenge. Unless capitalism too can learn from that failure, and in particular address the inequalities it produces on a world scale and which are now far greater than fifty or one hundred years ago, it will face other challenges, moreover costly and ultimately failed ones, in the future. In this sense it is essential to reiterate the lesson of the complacency of the *belle époque*: none of the demons of twentieth-century history – war, mass starvation, ethnic purging, revolution – has been permanently banished from the contemporary world. All may, unless policies sufficiently intelligent and resolute are devised and implemented, return to play a leading role in the course of the third millennium.[6]

Globalization

Globalization has become, over the past few years, the catchword of international economic and political analysis.[7] Clearly something significant and novel is happening. Trade liberalization has been accompanied by a rise in volumes of world trade as a ratio of output; the volume of money traded on the international currency markets has risen from $190 billion per day in 1987 to near $1.2 trillion in 1995; foreign direct investment in emerging economies has gone from $50 billion in 1990 to $150 billion in 1998; more and more of the world has been incorporated into, some would say subjugated to, the vagaries of the market. In the field of technology we have seen the amazing spread, on the one hand, of forms of satellite communication, on the other, of the Internet. In political terms, we are seeing the greater integration of trading blocs, in the European Union and Mercosur, and the creation of new institutions of global economic management, notably the World Trade Organization. All of this is being accompanied by something central to change in international relations, namely a shift in the powers of the state: whatever else globalization entails, it would appear to involve a significant reduction in some traditional powers of states to control flows of finance and goods, to regulate interest and exchange rates, to form a national culture, to limit the flow of goods, not least narcotics and small arms and, above all, people, across their frontiers. Globalization is in this sense often associated with forms of political ungovernability.

A particularly astute analysis of this impact of global change can be found in the work of my late colleague, the international political economist, Susan Strange:[8] her argument is that power is increasingly structural, not unit-based, i.e. not focused on states. She identifies four power structures in the contemporary world – security, production, finance, knowledge. Only the first, security, and that to a decreasing extent, is monopolized by states. The other three are impersonal structures that affect states, multinational companies and individuals in ways that human agency, states included, finds it hard to control.

There is, however, a need for some caution here, starting with two questions about this process, of a perhaps quintessentially British quality: first, what do we mean by it? secondly, how new is it really? Globalization invites exaggeration, dramatic statements about change, what is sometimes termed 'globaloney'. Globalization can in economic terms mean several things: measures to encourage trade liberalization, rising percentages of trade relative to GDP, rising foreign direct investment as a percentage of GDP, rising foreign direct investment as a percentage of total investment within a country. These are distinct processes.

These processes also need to be put into historical and comparative perspective. As already noted, the creation of a unified but increasingly unequal world economy by the most powerful states, and I stress *states*, began around 1500. The transmission of religious, cultural and political ideas across frontiers goes back even further. One of the hallmarks of globalization, the ability to transmit information and financial instructions simultaneously between continents, has been available since the laying of transatlantic cables in the 1860s: it is politics, not technology, that has limited flows. The growth of a global, continuous market, open twenty-four hours a day and able to move large quantities of money, is a product of the breakdown of the Bretton Woods system in the early 1970s, perhaps the time from which to date the globalization of today. Yet trade liberalization today in the developed countries has only in the last decade passed the levels of the pre-1914 period. Most trade is domestic trade and, if not, then with other developed countries. For OECD states FDI runs at around 6 per cent of domestic investment, not a token of a globalized economy.

The role of the state in economies remains very strong: the state share is running at very high levels, on average over 45 per cent of GDP, in OECD countries. It has not declined significantly since the early 1980s.[9] States have lost some of their traditional powers and some weaker or collapsed states have ceased to perform their minimal modern functions. But most states do still retain and have in some cases enhanced power. States have powerful instruments to promote scientific research within their own societies, to regulate trade and to impose conditions for investment, not least for the import and export of capital. The Internet is a spin-off of US government research into secure communications begun in the 1970s. Current discussions on controlling financial instability, in which examples from recent Chilean policy play a central role, show how states can in particular manage the inflow of capital and limit short-term speculative flows. In certain respects the powers of states are greater and more intrusive than ever: regulation of the environment, of food, of personal habits such as smoking, of surveillance are all features of the contemporary world. In many cases we see states cooperating or forming international organizations to regulate the world economy, but these are, in origin and in ultimate authority, the products of states, not a supranational authority to them. Where suggestions for supranationality are made, they are unsuccessful, as the failure of proposals for a permanent peacekeeping force, for a UN army or for a minuscule degree of European taxation has shown.

In the longer term states have very important powers to shape their own societies. The example of Singapore, which in the space of a generation and with a population of four millions, became the producer of half of all the hard discs in the world demonstrates this. Paul Kennedy in his *Preparing for the Twenty-first Century* has indicated three areas vital for the economic and political performance of states in which national power remains supreme:[10] education, the participation of women in public life and the quality of political leadership. To this we can add good – i.e. honest and competent – governance. Failure in any of these, for large states and small, cannot be blamed on the world market or foreign conspiracies. If there is a deficit of political leadership in the world, something that takes many forms, this is not a result of structural factors or global trends or post-modernity but of individual and national deficiencies.

We are, therefore, far from being in a world where the market is supreme. Indeed, analytic and historical clarity, combined with observation of the contemporary world, leads us to qualify in three fundamental respects any model of an unregulated global economy, as either a description of the present or as a desirable goal. In the first place, the idea of a market without some degree of state regulation is, and always has been, a myth. States have played an essential role, in guaranteeing the physical security that trade, finance and property require, in regulating banking and commercial law, in taxing individuals and businesses, in disposing of the 40 per cent or so of national product that they control. State policies and intentions continue to play a central part in determining the prospects of markets: no market speculator, however offshore, ignores the outcome of elections or political crises or statements of economic policy. That most nebulous of all factors, the credibility of political leaders, has immense economic consequences, as events of recent years, in several countries, have shown. Equally those who suffer from economic difficulties return, again and again, to the state and its associated financial bodies for support. In the USA the bailout of Long-Term Capital Finance and the intervention by President Bill Clinton to limit cheap steel imports demonstrate this. Two other examples show the persistence of limits on free trade. Petrol prices in the USA are less than half those in Britain or France and a third those in Norway.[11] And there is a differential of about 2:1 between European and US prices for computing equipment. The question is not whether state or market rules, but what combination of the two. Neo-liberal propaganda ignored this, either by arguing for a pure, unworkable model of economic activity or by engaging in irresponsible paranoia, of a kind popularized by von Hayek, that failed to distinguish between regulatory and democratic state intervention and totalitarian abolition of the market. Nor is this just a matter of policy choices on the means of achieving an agreed goal: economics unavoidably, as Adam Smith and other classical economists were the first to assert, involves moral choices. This is the theme with which the recent Nobel prize winner in economics, Amartya Sen, is most associated.[12]

Secondly, events of the latter part of the 1990s, above all in East Asia and Russia, have underlined something that a reasonable familiarity with economic history would have helped us never to forget, namely the instability of markets. This is a central theme of classical political economy and economic history, whether Marx's theories of capitalist cycles or the work of Schumpeter and Polanyi on the in-built overreaction of markets and of state–market relations. One of many conceits of the latter part of the twentieth century has been that somehow modern capitalism has overcome these instabilities. To the cycles of productive rise and fall we can now add those enhanced and accelerated by globalization, in terms of liberalization and the electronic market-place, the instability of foreign-currency markets and, more seriously, that of investment funds. This is not an aberration, a product of overstretched Thai banks here or corrupt Russian Kremlin there. The instability is systemic and requires a systemic response: any one financial crisis may be avoidable but repeated crises are not.

Thirdly, and most seriously, the processes associated with globalization and the instabilities accompanying them have, for all their economic impact, led to a greater and greater inequality in the contemporary world. Figures released by the UNCTAD show that in the quarter century from 1965 to 1990 the share of world income owned by the richest 20 per cent rose from 69 per cent to 83 per cent. In 1965 average income per head in the richest 20 per cent was 31 times higher than in the poorest 20%, in 1990 this had risen to 60 times.[13] According to the UNDP, there has been a striking growth in price and public consumption: six times since 1950, twice since 1975, to a current total of $24,000 billion worldwide. In this sense the promise of capitalism to deliver greater volumes of good and services has been realized: but 20 per cent of the world's population account for 86% of total expenditure, while the poorest 20 per cent account for 1.3 per cent. Three-fifths of the 4.4 billion people in developing countries lack basic sanitation.[14] As the definition of what constitutes wealth and acceptable, bourgeois comfort expands to include two annual holidays, a sauna, sushi and state-of-the-art audio and computer equipment, the rest of mankind is being left further and further behind, *and knows it*. The reality and perception of inequality in the contemporary world constitute the greatest weakness of globalization and the one that contains, over the longer run, the most potential for political disruption, within and between states.

This enduring and increasing inequality must, indeed, qualify the degree to which we can talk of a globalized world at all. If most of those who live in the world do not have access to the goods of globalization, then it appears that we have an increasingly unequal, oligarchic system, in which globalization reinforces, even as it concentrates, an elite. Two obvious examples. First, labour. While capital is indeed more mobile, the opposite is true for another factor of production, namely labour. There is considerable migration in the world today but throughout the developed world there is a populist determination to limit it: it has never been more difficult than it is today for someone who is not a member of the world elite to live and work in OECD countries. A second example is information technology. This, the quintessential icon of globalization, is, of course, famously the subject of an increasingly bitter and brutal battle for monopoly control and of a cultural hegemony, by one variant of one language, over all other scripts and idioms.

This increasing hierarchization, like the instability of markets, is not something temporary or casual: it is and will remain, unless reversed by conscious and purposive intervention, a feature of globalization itself. Likewise, market instability promises to promote instability in the future. At the same time, and in contrast to hyperbole about the novelty of this process, it points to the underlying rigidity of wealth distribution in the modern world. As Giovanni Arrighi has pointed out, the group of wealthiest nations, while altering the hierarchy within itself, has remained remarkably constant for the past century and a half, only one state, Japan, entering as a full new member. This enduring hierarchy alone should give us pause about the diffusion of globalization or the ability of a world economic system based on the market to distribute wealth and generalize the benefits and opportunities it offers to its most fortunate members.

Global governance

The end of the cold war has, therefore, provided a new international political context, while the spread of globalization has altered economies and societies and will do so more in the future. The third component of the contemporary international situation is the set of institutions, official and unofficial, that we have for dealing with this context and for attempting to meet challenges and so realize shared international goals – peace, prosperity, equity. The system of inter-governmental institutions that we have today is, in large measure, a product of the reconstruction after World War II – the UN, a system that includes the IMF and the World Bank, the European Union, NATO. We have even in recent times seen significant developments of this system – the strengthening of the EU, the creation of the WTO, the growth of a concern with international humanitarian issues, be it intervention to oppose violations of human rights or the creation of an International Criminal Court. But the model of government aspired to in 1945 is in significant contrast to that 'governance' espoused today. Global 'governance', a term that also became diffused in the 1990s, is distinct from 'government' in two ways. First, it suggests an interlocking of distinct institutions rather than one convergent world government. Secondly, it suggests, as does the Commission on Global Governance's 1995 report, *Our Global Neighbourhood*, that the system of states and inter-governmental organizations should be matched by one that incorporates the 'non-state' – non-governmental organizations (NGOs), corporate bodies, social movements, the press and what has in broad if rather imprecise terms come to be termed 'global civil society'.[15] Here too the shadow of earlier decades hangs over the debate, for the idea of 'good governance' presupposes something else that has accumulated within and between states over the years since 1945, 'bad governance'. 'Governance' too, therefore, has not just a descriptive but also a normative dimension – 'good governance' in the sense of best practice, transparency, accountability.

This system can be said to rest on four broad constituent forms of support. At the top are those institutions of an inter-state or inter-governmental character. We have the UN, the EU and several dozen others, and, in keeping with the diffusion of governance rather than the concentration of government, a multiplicity of institutions in any one area: the security of Europe is, for example, the responsibility of at least eight distinct organizations.[16] The regulation of the world economy, insofar as it is the responsibility of states, and that is quite a lot, is divided between the World Bank and the IMF, the Group of 8, the Bank of International Settlements and a number of regional economic organizations of which the EU and NAFTA are the most evident examples. The newest organization on the bloc, the World Trade Organization, has had a bumpy start, more as a result of dissension between states within than because of contestation from without: but few doubt the need for regulation and adjudication of disputes procedures for world trade.

The core of the system, the entities to which most people still look for legitimacy, identity and the provision of public goods, remains states. As already indicated, these do and should retain a central role in the management of the world economy. Indeed, as some problems increase, states and inter-state cooperation may have more, not fewer, demands made on them. Three quintessential problems of the contemporary world – the drugs trade, the environment, migration – are out of hand and will remain so until and unless responsible states seek means of regulating these issues. The system of inter-governmental organization is, therefore, not yet supranational, in the sense of having authority over states, and the most powerful state of all, the USA, has indicated that it has no intention, in matters of security or economic management, of submitting to any such authority. Indeed, the greatest challenge facing this system is that of dissension between its leading members. The last great attempt at globalization, that of the decades up to 1914, failed not because of rebellion from below or the inability of states to manage the cycles and crises of the international economy, but because of competition and dissension between states. The same could, without or with war, happen again.

The third level of global governance is what is termed 'global civil society', a category in which NGOs have a special place. Much of the more optimistic, liberal literature and many of the more forward-looking reform programmes for global governance give special place to NGOs and related social movements. This is to a considerable degree justified: if we look at the development of an international liberal agenda over recent years we can see issues on which it is the non-governmental groups, sometimes social movements, sometimes a few committed and insistent individuals, who have made the running. The rise of concern with the environment and with gender rights and the campaign against anti-personnel mines are cases in point. Since its founding in 1961 Amnesty International has altered international debate and in some degree practice on human rights violations. One could indeed strengthen the argument about the 'non-state' by showing how, not just in our liberal and somewhat more democratic times, but for many decades, indeed centuries, these have been crucial. The world of today was to a considerable degree shaped by social movements of a democratic, nationalist, class-based character: the rights and freedoms of today, let alone the independence of states, including this one, were not given by benign elites and hegemons but wrested from the rulers by the ruled, sometimes at very high price.

Yet the role and potential of these NGOs and of other elements in civil society should not be exaggerated. First of all, they cannot and should not supplant states and are in many ways dependent on the collaboration and, in the case of aid agencies, the funding of states. In situations of inter-ethnic conflict the 'non-state' actors may be able to do little except act on the margins of conflict to alleviate distress: the fate of NGOs in Bosnia, and indeed in Northern Ireland, is an indication of these. Secondly, not all that is 'non-state' is liberal or benign: the most influential non-state actors in the world economy are the traders in drugs and weapons; the most powerful 'non-state' actor in the recent history of these islands goes by the name, which it has usurped, of *Oglaigh na-Eireann* (Irish for The Army of Ireland). In many European countries and in the USA we can observe widespread collective social and political action against immigrants and gender rights. The most traditional component of civil society, the press, has in large measure abandoned a commitment to fostering an educated, rational debate on international issues either in content or tone: it has become an instrument of the vapid and the sensational, inimical to, not supportive of, the consolidation of democracy and a sense of global responsibility. The globalization of Murdoch and Berlusconi is not conducive to a stronger governance system. Thirdly, in many semi- and non-democratic countries 'civil society' is controlled or suppressed. Those 'NGOs' that do exist, and which are sent to international conferences, are too often creatures of the state, if not of the secret police. 'Civil society' operates where broader democratic and legal norms also operate and where these organizations themselves operate on the basis of good internal governance.

At the basis of the whole edifice of global governance lies, however, not any collective entity, inter-state or non-state, but the individual, all six billion of us. It is the individuals who support the states, finance the economic and security policies, participate in democratic or NGO activity and, ultimately, hold to certain beliefs about how the world should be run. The rest of the edifice can and could come tumbling down if individuals do not support it or if, in matters beyond their own communities, they hold to violent or obstructive nationalism. Part of the outcome will, certainly, depend on how the upper layers of global governance function and how political leaders manage this relationship: if the latter do not seek to lead and educate, then there will be growing dissatisfaction with global governance. But the place to start is at the bottom itself, with the education and continued involvement of individuals who seek to combine their membership of particular communities and states with responsibility towards the wider world. Here trends of the past decade have not been one-sidedly reassuring. The new global elite of educated and ambitious people who claim an interest in international issues is in considerable measure marked by an exhibitionism of material achievement and a lack of normative involvement, a dot.com narcissism, that ill suits it for an international role. At the same time the horizons of citizens of many countries have narrowed, not widened, under conditions of globalization, be this through the increased trivialization of the press or through the rise of politics based on cantankerous nationalism and identity politics. It is, however, on education above all that the formation and responsibility of citizens depends, now as it has been ever since the days of the Enlightenment. In the functioning of global governance as a whole, or in such issues as peacekeeping, environmental protection or reduction in global economic inequalities, it is education and public discussion that will shape outcomes.

The alternative is a world made up of increasingly self-regarding national electorates, reduced commitment to global institutions and exacerbated international rivalry and conflict.

Conclusion: Reason and the international

We may, therefore, end, as we began, with Kant, who in another essay was well aware of the gap between aspiration and reality. 'We do not live in an *enlightened age* but we do live in an *age of enlightenment*'.[17] The world of globalization is most certainly *not* an enlightened one – the danger and, in some cases, the reality of war remains alive, inequalities between states are growing, states are struggling to meet new and old challenges. The spirit of the times is marked, on the one hand, by an apparently vital faith in the workings of impersonal forces – market, microchip, genome – on the other, by a deep pessimism about the possibilities of any rational perspective project, derived from the Enlightenment. On the other hand, the opportunities for enlightenment, for rational discourse and purposive action, collective and individual, are strong and have, in some measure, been taken in recent years. Liberal democracy and markets regulated by states do provide a broad context for benevolent development. The system of global governance, ramshackle as it may be, can be shaped and developed to meet global challenges, of which respect for human rights, broadly conceived, consolidation of democracy and increased economic equity are central components.

Enlightenment therefore remains, in international relations as in matters internal, our best guide. We have, in the two centuries since Kant wrote, learnt much about the abuses of reason and the limits of its applicability: but there is no cause to reject its continued relevance in the lives of individuals, states and humanity as a whole. This is a concern that, in its analytic and normative dimensions, concerns every social science and indeed every thinking individual. In a world where the processes of globalization appear to sweep so much before them and in which many are drawn towards the immediate and the profitable, or towards the irrational and the pessimistic, we abandon it at our peril.

12
'Islam' and the 'West': Cultural Conflict and International Relations

One of the most prevalent features of the post-cold war world is a preoccupation in international relations, as well as domestic politics, concerning the relations between the so-called 'West' on the one hand and 'Islam' on the other. Without undue simplification, it can be said that since the early 1990s there has emerged in both East and West a discourse that argues that there are here two confrontational blocks, and that there is some fundamental conflict here. On the Islamic side, this rhetoric is common to the Middle East and to other Muslim countries and it can be heard in Indonesia, in Nigeria, in Bangladesh. Its subject is confrontation with the West. Generic denunciations of colonialism, globalization, Western society, *jahiliyya* or ignorance, fuse with specific issues such as Palestine and Kashmir. In the West, the rhetoric concerns the threat, the danger and the difficulties of dealing with something called 'Islam': this very broad term covers, not only all Muslim states, but everything that happens within them. In that sense, it is a rhetoric that is shared. It is equally false in both cases, but since discourse affects politics, one has to take the rhetoric in its Eastern and in its Western variants and examine the themes and the causes. The very fact that such a rhetoric emerges from both East and West and that such diverse voices as Khomeini or Hizbullah in the Middle East and right-wing strategists in the USA, Europe or even India are all saying the same thing undoubtedly makes it much more difficult to assess and to critique this issue. It may be mistaken. It will not go away.

'Islam' versus the 'West': the illusion

There is an American saying that if you are in the middle of the road, you get run over by both sides. This is true for anybody who tries to critique the myths of both East and West. The myth about so-called 'Islam' and the so-called 'West' – as if they were unitary entities – relates to a broader theme that is also part of the intellectual climate of our times. It is to be found in Turkey and in the Middle East, as well as in the West: it concerns the relation of past to present, the power and prominence of culture and of values supposedly derived from ancient civilization in the contemporary relations between peoples and states. I term this 'faultline babble'. There is a related argument, also quite a false one, that we are witnessing a shift in the nature of conflict: relations between states were in the past, it is claimed, defined by power or by economic interests or by territory. Now discourse, ideas, the media, on the one hand, and civilizational clashes, on the other, have quite a new salience, a new power. The causes identified include the collapse of communism, globalization and the rise of the Internet. This is sometimes called 'the cultural turn'.

Behind the specific but very prevalent idea of the cultural clash, between two unitary forces, 'Islam' versus the 'West', there is another broader, social science, a thesis about the historic role of ideas, of culture, of civilization. This has received particularly clear, polemical and utterly irresponsible formulation in the writings of Professor Samuel Huntington, especially in his book, *A Clash of Civilizations*. His underlying thesis, a perfectly sensible if debatable one, is that conflict between states is inevitable in a world of sovereign states. Culture is the only thing left to argue about. This theme, central to the analysis of international relations, is not what gets discussed. All over the Middle East, especially in Saudi Arabia, and reportedly in Japan as well, Huntington finds favour among the anti-modernists, particularists, nationalists and fundamentalists. Why? Because Huntington says that East and West are separate, we are all distinct and there will inevitably be conflict. A simplistic paradigm like this has an advantage; if you want a perfect paradigm, a thing that defines its own field of investigation, that defines its concepts, that makes predictions, that even has its own concept of falsification, then the perfect example is astrology. The problem is, astrology is nonsense.

The alternative to such generalization about history and culture is more demanding analysis of what goes on in particular countries or in the relations between countries. In other words, the prime task is *disaggregation* and *explanation*, rather than invocations of the timeless essence of cultures. There will never be complete agreement even on explanation, as any great issue in social science demonstrates – the industrial revolution, the information revolution or the origins of World War I or, in the case of the Middle East, the origins of the Turkish Independence Revolution or the Iraqi occupation of Kuwait. But social scientists share the view that it is vital not just to hear what people say but to see what they actually do.

Consider the case of the Iranian Revolution of 1978–79. True, there was much talk of Islam, of *allah-u akbar*, and the Quran. But what actually happened? Eight million people were brought on to the streets, constituting the largest opposition demonstrations in human history. An army of 400,000 collapsed in three weeks. A group of clergy took control of a state. Of the three slogans of the Islamic revolution, two, *istiqlal* (independence) and *azadi* (freedom) were entirely secular, and one, *jumhuri-yi islami* (Islamic republic), a mix. What did they do about the trade unions? What did they do about women? What did they do about ethnic minorities? The answers do not come from the analysis of texts or their meanings, but from the study of actions. Of course, many people phrased these questions in an Islamic way but the solutions were not ones taken from holy texts. Whatever the nature of the discourse – be it Islamic, Marxist–Leninist, modernist–authoritarian, modernist–liberal, astrological or environmental – it is important to see what people actually do and to recognize that this is not determined by ideology.

Another obvious example of this realistic approach concerns Saddam's invasion of Kuwait in 1990. Many people at the time labelled this as a conflict between Islam and the West. Saddam habitually used Leninist language on imperialism one day and that of Muhammad the Prophet the next. First he would describe the struggle as *jihad*, the following day he would call it anti-imperialist. Why did Saddam invade Kuwait? He did so for a very simple reason: he was running out of money, so he decided to rob his neighbour. Analytically, this presents no problem: people have done this throughout history and doubtless will go on doing so. In 1882 the British occupied Egypt to recover debts. In 1902 they and others bombarded Venezuela for the same reason. There is, however, nothing distinctly Iraqi, Islamic, Marxist or un-Marxist in this; nothing other than a perfectly straightforward, secular, rational act.

In this regard I admire the work of the anthropologist Michael Gilsenan, *Recognizing Islam*.[1] He writes about what Muslims do in their societies, but never relies on any of the holy books: this is because the books do not explain what the warlords, the political leaders, the Ulema or the Hizbullahi actually do. This methodology does not try to understand situations by going to the holy texts and making interpretations, or *tafsir*. Rather, it looks at what people are doing. The same principle applies equally to, say, economics. One cannot try to explain the essentials and dynamics of the Saudi Arabian or Afghan or Malaysian economies by reference to *iqtisad-i Islami* or *iqtisad-i tawhidi*, 'Islamic economics' or 'unitary economics'. The latter is a term implying divine unity in the markets. One looks instead at people: whether they are working or not working, whether they are making money, how they receive and produce goods and services and all those other observable facts. The nineteenth-century saying applies here: 'Islam is a sea in which you can catch any fish you want.'

States

A focus on reality rather than rhetoric entails looking at the primary actors in international relations, states. For all the movements of ideas, people and money across frontiers, and for all the 'globalization' that exists, we still live and have lived for all the period in question in a world in which *states* are central. By states is meant not juridical entities but administrative bodies with armies, ministries, employment policies and so forth. Those states divide the world. There are around 195 of them at present, and attached to states are particular values and histories, which we call nationalism. Hence in analysing states in international relations, there is no one 'Islam' and there is no 'West'. There are 55 Muslim countries, members of the Organization of Islamic Conference. There are some other countries, such as Ethiopia and India, where a significant part of the population is Muslim. There are up to 16 million Muslims in Russia. There may be 60 countries in which Muslims are a significant minority. All of these states have separate interests and definitions of their national tradition. They have separate definitions of their relation to Islamic tradition when it comes to concrete questions rather than rhetoric. They also have separate policies with regard to employment, political structures, the position of women or minorities. In other words, they are distinct entities. A common 'Islam' tells us nothing: at best it is a claim. The statements of these countries often invoke the Islamic community, *umma*. In their actions, however, their relation to 'Islam' is variable. They have interests that do sometimes lead them to espouse pan-Muslim causes. The Arab states support Palestine but they do so in part to keep their own populations quiet: they do not actually *do* much for the Palestinians. Muslim states also fight *with each other*. The most important and bloody inter-state war of the twentieth century, except for the Japanese–Chinese War of 1937–45, was the war between Iran and Iraq of 1980–88. There have been many other such conflicts: Egypt and Sudan, Egypt and Libya, Morocco and Algeria. While espousing a universal discourse, states patently pursue distinct interests.

The same need to question a supposedly unitary category goes for the term 'West'. There *is* no one West – not in international relations terms, not in political terms and, most important of all, there is no one West in terms of political values. People often say that human rights or sovereignty are 'Western' concepts, yet they are concepts that did not arise from some undifferentiated West. They emerged out of conflicts between individual countries involving movements for the rights of people to vote, for the rights of women or for the rights of trade unions or other groups. It is necessary to disaggregate both so-called 'Islam' or the Muslim world and the 'West'. An international relations perspective leads one to recognize the role of a transnational community of solidarity and sentiment, which in some ways is getting stronger; it also leads to the need to differentiate. This does not entail, therefore, accepting ideologies as givens or determining factors in the Middle East or elsewhere. It leads in the opposite direction, to the questioning of such entities.

Ideologies

Only when the reality and interests of states are identified is it possible to look at ideas and symbols. The study of Middle Eastern societies, as of others, entails the study of ideologies, but there is no one approach here. There are, for example, enormous debates about nationalism, indeed a spectrum of debates between two poles. Such debate explains a lot about the approach to the question of Islam versus the West.[2] There is, at one end, the view held by most nationalists, indeed by 99.9 per cent of humanity, including some social scientists and rather more historians. This view is broadly termed 'perennialism', or primordialism. The premise is that nations have existed for hundreds, thousands of years, that they have a distinct identity, a distinct culture, a distinct language. Nationalism is the movement, the ideology that fulfils the destiny of this nation, something that already exists. This is the atavistic, sometimes called the 'sleeping beauty' theory of nationalism. The purpose of nationalism defined as such is to provide historical justification for the nation, to guard the purity of its language and to defend it against all sorts of encroachments.

At the other end is the 'modernist' approach. This argues that nationalism as movement and ideology is in fact the product of the industrial and political revolutions of the last 200 years. Its ancient historic derivation is deceptive: it reads back into the past current concerns, for example, the need to define the ethnic group, the language or the territory, and of course it also constructs the history. Everybody has to have a history. Take Qatar, which, with no disrespect to the heroic people of Qatar, is just a bit of sand on the coast of the Arabian Peninsula. Today Qatar has its own national history and its own national identity constructed for modern purposes. The modernist approach does not negate history, indeed, it makes it important to write an accurate history describing *how* nations – these particular nations – developed. It denies history as given. It is not history that determines the identity of the state or the community: it is current concerns of states and their opponents, that then run to history for validation.

The same approach to nationalism as an ideology can be applied to religion. A central point for all religions is that the past is not a set of prescriptions for the present. It is not a guidebook for running modern life. Beyond certain core principles and symbols, the past is a large range of options from which to select what is wanted to meet modern purposes: it can be compared to a menu. The perennialist approach, whether in nationalism or in religion, treats the past as a fixed menu. By contrast, the *à la carte* approach gives you dozens of choices: if your speciality, e.g. a position on management techniques or ecological controls, is not on the menu, you can ask the ideological waiter to get it for you. It is always possible to invent as well as to select. The important thing is that, whatever you choose, you must claim it was always there. A very good example has occurred in Britain. From the early 1990s or so, people began more loudly to celebrate the saint's day of St George on 23 April. Everybody knew St George as the patron saint of England (as also, incidentally, of Greece) but few took any notice of the fact until the 1990s, when people started lapel badges celebrating St George and flying pennants on their cars and so on. It was not the Union Jack that received this exposure but St George's flag. There was more than one reason for this. It may be that it is a sign of opposition to the European Community and its threatened takeover of this country, or to the autonomy of Scotland. Whatever its purpose, from the top to the bottom of society, the adoption of St George as a mascot or symbol is a modernist reinvention for current political purposes, yet disguised as a return to the past. St George is, among other things, the patron saint of shepherds: there are not many of those in England today.

We can consider religion in the same way. This is not to do with the issue of faith. In Islam there are five principles: belief in one God and Prophet, Ramadan, *zakat*, pilgrimage and prayer. Modernism does not refer to theological issues and matters of personal conviction, but to the political and social sphere. Within all major religions of the world today, Islam, Christianity, Judaism, Hinduism, there are movements that are trying to interpret them for political and social purposes. They are dipping into the reserve of religion and constructing, just as nationalists do, a set of policies for the present. This too has a modernist explanation, although, as with nationalism, most people would not accept it.

This argument can be illustrated as follows. First of all, if you look at any of the major areas of social and political activity to which religion is said to be relevant, you will see not one model but many – not the fixed menu but an *à la carte*. Religion has always been presented as the fixed menu, as 'the' answer, but in fact it is one of many answers. Take the question of political constitution or political form in the Arab world. There is an enormous variety of states that claim to be 'Muslim'. There are military dictatorships, as in Libya or in Pakistan, which espouse Islamist politics. There is tribal monarchy, as in Saudi Arabia. There are some monarchies, in Jordan and Morocco, which claim direct descent from the Prophet. Others, such as the Omani and Saudi, do not. There is a clerical regime in Iran founded on the idea that the *faqih*, the expert on *fiqh*, or Islamic jurisprudence, is able to interpret the word of God. The *faqih* is not quite infallible (*ma'sum*), but his interpretation is still the best available – and let nobody contradict it in Iran. A pluralist, democratic system exists in Turkey. There is no point in asking which of these are Islamic or not Islamic: all of them can find their own quotes in the religious texts or elements in the tradition.

On the broader question of socio-economic formation there was in the 1960s a big debate in the Arab world about whether Islam favoured communism or capitalism. Unsurprisingly, those who wished to support communism found their quotes. Among the sayings of the Prophet, the Hadith, there is one that runs, 'The people share in three things: water, grass and fire'. Marxists seized on this, saying that water, grass and fire are the equivalent in Marxist theory of the means of production in the tribal society, and therefore by extension everyone can share in industry and land tenure and so on. Others pointed to another Hadith that runs, 'Whoever takes your house, kill him', saying that this justifies the defence of private property. But that was not the end of the argument. Still others said, 'Wait! Think of the great Muslim empires, the Ummayads, the 'Abbasids, the Ottomans. What was the main form of their socio-economic formation? It was not communism. It was not capitalism. It was feudalism. Let us have feudalism (*al-iqta'iyya*).' Then a sheikh from Tunis pointed out the passage in the Quran that legitimates the possession of slaves, *raqiq*:[3] so he argued for a return to another social and economic model, slavery. Most Muslims today would of course *not* agree with that, but in the search for an Islamic form of government you can find any one of those four models and the one you have found will be the one you looked for.

Another example of such variations, for those who seek to find them, is the present debate in both Israel and Palestine about the possibility of reaching a compromise between Israel and the Palestinians. To start with the Jewish side, which is fascinating, the question has been posed, 'Can a Jewish state give away Jewish land?' For a modernist there are no surprises. If you are in favour of peace with the Palestinians, you can cite the case of King David, who gave away land to the King of Sidon. Equally, if you are against making peace with the Palestinians, you can find material in Deuteronomy 25, which enjoins war to the end, indeed the massacre of the Amalekites: if you consider the Palestinians Amalekites, there is no further argument. Now consider the Palestinian side. There is a passage in the Quran urging that 'you must fight the *kuffar* till the very end'. Yet there is also a passage relating how the Prophet came to a *hudna*, a truce, with those who were not with Islam. On that basis, a compromise with Israel is possible. Again, the text does not decide the issue. It is the reader who finds what he or she wants in it.

One further example, one that is central to the authoritarian claims of fundamentalism, is the position of women. There are plenty of lines in the holy texts of Islam, Judaism, Christianity and Hinduism that apparently suggest and endorse the inferiority of women to men. They are found in the texts and traditions of every major religion – there is nothing specific to Islam in this. Equally, there are lines that imply the opposite, that women are equal in the eyes of God. Moreover, the Quran states that no prescription of religion can be imposed – '*La ikrah fi al-din*'. You can interpret this freedom to mean equality or democracy, even the right to leave your own religion. But there is always a contrary argument. I once had a debate with some fundamentalists in Britain, *Hizb al-Tahrir*, at a meeting in Brick Lane in the East End of London, during which I asked, 'How can you adopt a fundamentalist position on texts when there is such variation? The Quran says, "if you do not believe, you will be sent to Hell", yet on the next page it forbids the imposition of religion.' A hand went up at the back of the audience. 'Professor Halliday,' said the speaker, 'it is true that there is no compulsion in religion. What that means is that you are free to go to Hell.'

So, one element of the modernist argument is that the past is variable. The interpretation is contemporary and contingent. Another point that has been well made by such scholars as Sami Zubeida, Aziz al-Azmeh and others is that the very language that fundamentalists use is not historic or traditional but reflects modernist influence and modernist concerns. Let us take Khomeini.

What was his main goal? *Inqilab-i Islami*, Islamic Revolution. The concept of *inqilab* is a modernist concept. It has nothing to do with the Quran. The *Jumhur-i Islamiyi*, Islamic Republic, is again a modernist concept. Khomeini's references to the oppressed, *mustafazin*, fighting the *mustakbarin*, or dominators, are derived from the language of populism, as found in Latin America or in any other developing country. The concept of imperialism, which he called *istikbar-i jahani*, 'world arrogance', is a modern concept, given Quranic form. Khomeini's language replicated the themes of modern radical politics. Some of the ideas were taken directly from the communists, some from radical populists, some from dependency theory. Similarly, the discourse of Algerian fundamentalists is about imperialism, cultural domination, the need to defend the nation. In that sense, the language of fundamentalism is itself modernist. It is a language that expresses modern concerns and, above all, it is a form of nationalism. When the Turkish politician Erbakan says that the West is corrupting the *ahlak*, or customs, of the Turks, he is giving expression to a theme of cultural corruption that is found in every nationalist and revolutionary context, from the Chinese revolution to the populism of Latin America. It may take a particular form, but it is the universal modernist argument. Third world demagogy about AIDS being spread by tourists, the CIA, or Jews, is one vibrant case of this.

A final example is the concept of corruption, *fasad*. In Khomeini's mouth it meant certain things that are specific to Islam. But more importantly it referred to the fact that his country had earnt large amounts of money from oil, which the Shah had stolen. This was a perfectly modernist concept, which implied that the state should be accountable and is not.

International relations: reality and myth

As Chapter 3 discusses at length, the other side of this story involves rhetoric by non-Muslims about 'Islam'. In both Western Europe and the USA, there is a lot of rhetoric about the 'threat' of Islam and the need to confront it. It is heard elsewhere too, increasingly in Israel. And it is heard in an Eastern country, namely, India. In fact, India is the country in the world where the most anti-Muslim rhetoric in public life is found. The BJP government in India is a Hindu fundamentalist government. Hindu fundamentalists are anti-secularist and anti-Muslim. Some of this involves the ease with which, in an age of globalization, ideas and stereotypes are diffused. Undoubtedly we live in a world of mass communications and ideas spreading across frontiers, but that has in some form been going on for three thousand years, as witness the spread of Islam or anti-Semitism. CNN and the Internet have merely intensified the spreading of ideas. In such a discursive context, a space is created in which people can find negative images to reinforce their own local campaigns. The allegations that Muslims are all drug-runners or all terrorists or that Muslim immigrants are all trying to swamp our society can be picked up anywhere. There is a curious similarity in the language found in India and in San Francisco or Oklahoma, or anywhere in between, not least Moscow. The threat that Muslims pose and the language of conflict have become increasingly prevalent over the last ten years or so among newspaper columnists, politicians, ministers of immigration and even certain European Union and NATO ministers. Anti-Muslim prejudice and assertions about a historic conflict have become transnational in scope and in content.

There are two questions that follow from this. Is it true? And if so, why is it so? As demonstrated in Chapter 3, it is simply not the case that in any period in the last five hundred years there has been a unified confrontation between Islamic world and the West. A small example is seen in the diplomatic relations of the Ottoman Empire. Sometimes Istanbul clashed with Western countries, sometimes it allied with them. The whole history of the Ottoman Empire from the seventeenth century onwards was one of variable involvement in the balance of power politics and shifting alliances right up to the time of World War I, when Turkey allied with Germany and Austria against all other countries. There was no timeless conflict between Islam and the West from Kaiser Wilhelm's perspective in 1914: he presented himself as the Kaiser of all the Muslims. And now, in the last ten or fifteen years, Muslim countries have conflicted with each other more than they have conflicted with the West. An extreme example was the Iran–Iraq war of 1980–88. It is an ironic fact that in the first war that NATO ever fought, it did not act in the name of NATO; yet it was a NATO operation from start to finish in command structure, in logistics and in tactics. It was a war to defend a Muslim country, namely, Kuwait. The second war that NATO fought was to defend Bosnia, also a Muslim country. Thus the facts of international relations hardly accord with the picture of Islam versus the West.

There are obvious comparable points about the real, as opposed to religious, or discursive factors affecting states. The most apparently revolutionary Islamic country, Iran, fought an eight-year war with another Muslim state, Iraq. Iran does not support Shi'ite Azerbaijan against Orthodox Christian Armenia: it supports Armenia against Azerbaijan and has good trading relations and, some say, good military relations with Armenia. Iran said nothing about Chechnya where 40,000 Muslims were killed by Boris Yeltsin in 1994, who was much loved in the West in spite of human rights violations. Iran does not support the Pakistani or *mujahid* claim to Kashmir. There is no Iranian protest about Kashmir: this is because of Tehran's good relations with India and because the Pakistanis have a bomb and the Iranians deeply suspect them.

Muslim solidarity is absent in many other cases, one of which is that of Turkey in the 1960s and 1970s. The Muslim world refused to support Turkey over Cyprus. In the Non-Aligned Movement and elsewhere for many years it supported Greece. So it is simply not the case, now or in history, that international relations are dominated or defined in cultural terms. The view of Samuel Huntington, whom I have quoted in previous chapters, is that all Muslims look at the world in terms of two categories: the world of Islam, the *Dar al-Islam,* and the enemy world or world of war, the *Dar al-Harb*. But this has not been the case since the armies of Tarik conquered Spain in the eighth century. Few Muslims, Turks, Iranians or indeed others look at the world in such generalized and starkly divisive terms. No Arab newspaper I have ever seen has sections corresponding to these categories.

On the other hand, there are cases where Muslims *are* behaving aggressively towards non-Muslims. In Indonesia the slogan in the mosques in the 1990s was, 'Death to the president, death to the IMF, death to the Chinese [traders]!' In Kashmir *mujahidin* are fomenting violence. But who was responsible in Bosnia? It was not the Muslims. Who shelled Sarajevo for 690 days and killed 20–30,000 people? In Palestine, who is responsible for the impasse in the peace process? It is not the Palestinians, whose demand for an independent state is being denied. Who is responsible in India? It is not the Muslims but the Hindu fundamentalists, who want Pakistan abolished.

As a generalization, the idea of a Muslim threat is simply invalid. Moreover, if there is a threat to the dominance of Western powers, it does not come from Muslim countries. It comes from those that were or still are, to some extent, threatening it economically, that is, the economies of East Asia, which can produce modern goods at competitive prices with much lower labour costs. They took a downturn in the late 1990s, but they will be back, probably slimmed down and with even lower wages. Singapore, with a population of three or four million, produces half of all the computer hard disks in the world, whereas thirty years ago the country was performing economically less well than Turkey or Iran. That is an amazing achievement, attributable to education directed strongly by a state. The economic performance of Muslim states is in general dismal, as the World Bank annual reports or statistics on the world distribution of foreign investment attest. The reasons have nothing to do with religion but with the kind of leadership that exists and the states they have created. There are some exceptions, such as Turkey and Malaysia. In general, however, the Islamic world is receiving little investment. There is therefore no coherent economic threat from Muslim countries: rather the opposite, as those with capital, the Gulf Cooperation Council states (GCC), have invested up to one billion dollars in Western capital markets.

Roots of anti-Muslimism

If Western rhetoric about an Islamic threat is false, why then does it recur? Certain cultural theorists claim that there is a history of verbal abuse of Muslims in the West and that this continues to shape the process. There are examples in Dante, in portrayals of the 'terrible Turk', in the utterances of later writers: some cultural theorists claim as evidence that the West has always disliked Muslims. But this is *not* an explanation. One cannot assume that what existed in the past exists now; if it does, it must be because it was reproduced. In other words, people were taught it. People are not born with prejudices about Muslims any more than they are taught knowing about international relations or the theory of inflation. The past explains the present only if its continuation can also be explained. The question that has to be answered is: why were certain prejudices, in this case anti-Muslim prejudices, reproduced?

Muslim stereotypes in the West are not unitary but very mixed.

They are an *à la carte* rather than a fixed menu. An extraordinary example is Auschwitz. As Primo Levi tells us, the weaker people, the people who gave up the right to fight and to live were known as Muslims. Why? Because the word 'Muslim' was associated with someone who was weak and submissive. It was not a term of abuse, merely a term implying lack of assertiveness. That stereotype was obviously completely different from the one that is common today. So, the past cannot explain the present. Why then has the current stereotype arisen? The standard answer is that it is connected with the end of the cold war. This is one of the most misleading ideas in international relations today. It is not half true or partially true: it is complete nonsense. The implication is that the West had an enemy in communism and once that had gone the West needed another enemy.

There are a number of things wrong with the claim that Islam has replaced communism. First of all, the communist threat, however exaggerated, however rhetorically abused, *was* a real threat. Communism set out to conquer the world. That was the aim of Lenin and Stalin, and their successors built 45,000 nuclear weapons and built up a large army in order to achieve it. Although communism did not succeed, it was a serious challenge to the West. It was not invented by the West. It was real.

Then it is claimed that some threat is needed, that Islam has filled the gap of communism. Is it true that all societies have needed threats? A very good counter-example is the conquest of the Americas by the Spaniards and the Europeans. Here there was no rival, no threat, merely the motive of making money, developing plantations and creating settlements in order to alleviate population problems back home. Is there something in the contemporary West (assuming this reified concept) that suggests that it needs to be confronted by a threat? What do people in the West want? The answer is simple. They want to make money. That is what globalization is about. It is about turning the whole world into a huge shopping arcade and an industrial production plant. Voltaire, in his sixth 'Philosophical Letter', said, 'In the marketplace, there is no Mohammedan, no Christian and no Jew. The only infidel is the bankrupt.'

The term 'Islamophobia' is also misleading. The rhetoric is 'anti-Muslim' rather than 'anti-Islamic'. The rhetoric is against people, not religion. But we still need to ask why the rhetoric is regularly coming up. The reasons are various. In Serbia, which harbours probably more anti-Muslim prejudice than any other country in Europe, it is to do with the crisis of communist ideology and the need for the authoritarian Serbian government and rulers to find a way of mobilizing people. Conspiracy theories are the Serbs' answer to their political needs.

Anti-Muslim prejudice is contingent on what has happened in the 1980s and the 1990s. In Israel, until recently, right-wing Zionists typically took their negative images from Nazism. The focus has shifted to anti-Muslimism as a result of the conflicts in Lebanon with Hizbullah and also the rise of Hamas among the Palestinians. Israelis now take the opportunity to couch their militancy in these terms. An extreme case was the rabbi who officiated at the funeral of Baruch Goldstein, the murderer of twenty-nine Palestinians, who said that the fingernail of one Jew is worth more than the lives of a thousand Arabs. Right-wing Israelis see the Islamic threat here, there and everywhere. But is a recent theme, not one that is found in classical Zionism, nor even in the Zionism of the 1960s. In France anti-Muslimism is a rhetoric against immigration and the problems of unemployment. In Britain, curiously, anti-Muslimism has, until the 1990s, been less prevalent. By chance, the British Empire had less conflict with Muslims than it did with almost any other group. It came into conflict instead with Irish Catholic terrorists, Hindu terrorists and Greek terrorists in Cyprus. One striking example: for all the thousands of people in Britain who heard of the Indian uprising, or mutiny, of 1857, and the Black Hole of Calcutta, not one could say if the Indians involved were Hindu or Muslims, or both, or Sikhs. The British Empire had a larger number of Muslims than any empire in history, more even than in the Ottoman Empire. Despite this past, however, a new anti-Muslim rhetoric has begun to grow in Britain.

There is no doubt that anti-Muslim rhetoric in Europe is related to immigration and other contemporary issues. One of the stereotypes of this issue concerns terrorism but the truth is that most terrorists in the Middle East have not been fundamentalists. They had secular ideologies. Among the Palestinians, most of the terrorist acts and the hijackings in the 1960s and 1970s were carried out by Marxist–Leninist groups. As far as Western Europe is concerned, the main terrorist problem comes not from the Muslim world: it is from Irish, Basque or Corsican terrorists, each with their own nationalistic agenda. Thus it would seem that the rhetoric has arisen in a variety of Western countries including America for contingent, very often specific, reasons. Within this rhetoric the most common theme of all – which is related to the symbol of Islam – is that the Muslims are encircling people in a strategic crescent. Geostrategy is a license for fantasy: the Indians talk about this, as do Europeans with regard to Algeria. It is, of course, demagogic.

Anti-Western militancy

Let us now look at the other side of the story, the rhetoric of anti-Western militancy in the Middle East. This is a theme that has long been present. When did Islamic fundamentalism start? Did it start with the Muslim Brothers in Egypt in 1928 or with the Wahhabis in Arabia in the eighteenth century? In contemporary politics, it has been a significant phenomenon of the last twenty-five years, from the 1970s through the Iranian Revolution and on.

What are the themes that are raised here? The first is that the West has been dominating the Muslim world, either formally through colonialism or informally. When not dominating, it has been intervening – in the Gulf, in northern Iraq, in Algeria. A second theme, which is very common and widespread, is that the West is trying to divide the Muslim world. In the Arab world, the most potent negative words are *taksim* and *infisal*. *Taksim* is partition, which is what the imperialists did after World War I when the Arabs wanted unity. *Infisal* is secession, the breaking away of a country, specifically and notably, Syria splitting from the United Arab Republic with Egypt in 1961. Arab nationalists remain very concerned on this matter: in their eyes, the autonomous Kurdish area in northern Iraq represents both *taksim* and *infisal*. Thirdly, it is argued that the West is indifferent to the oppression of the Muslims: it talks of human rights but it neglects Palestine, Chechnya, Bosnia, Kashmir and so on. Hardly anyone sees fit to mention the horrendous oppression of the Muslims of Burma, half a million of whom having been thrown out of the country in recent years. As for India, the West says little about what is going to happen or is already happening in India.

A fourth theme is that of double standards with regard to Israel. Muslim sentiments towards the West are not solely a result of the creation of Israel and the denial of the Palestinians' right to have their own state. But this issue has been a major source of concern, all the more so in the 1990s, because of the failure of the Oslo peace process to be honoured in the spirit as well as in the letter. As one who has been following and involved in the Palestinian question for thirty years, I supported and continue to support the Oslo agreement. Though certainly not ideal, it is a reasonable compromise. Any people who lost 70 per cent of their national territory in the space of two generations would have a reason to feel aggrieved. According to the agreement, the Palestinians should recognize Israel and be reasonable enough to accept 30 per cent of their national territory; that they are now being offered only half of that 30 per cent is an insult but it is the best they can get. On the other hand, the calls to return to the *intifada* and the armed struggle or to revive historic anti-Israeli rhetoric that denies Israelis the right to exist are both illegitimate and impracticable.

Fifthly, there is the widespread theme of *fesad*, or corruption, of the *ahlak* of the Muslims by the media, tourism and the large corporations and companies such as McDonald's. In some cases this widespread issue leads people into thinking that they 'would be better off without tourists'. Tunisian fundamentalists have come up with a very neat but preposterous solution: that tourists should be kept out of the mainland and confined to an island, Jerba. This idea ignores the fact that all the main tourist beaches and historic sites like Kairouan, Carthage and the Tunis *casbah*, happen to be on the mainland.

A final argument is that the West is anti-Muslim because it is maintaining dictatorial regimes in the Muslim world. This claim is made in such countries as Saudi Arabia, Algeria and Egypt and increasingly among dissident Palestinians who do not like the kind of 1950s-style dictatorship that Arafat is creating.

These themes need to be recognized but not taken at face value. First of all, to what extent are these themes specific to Muslims? The theme of foreign domination or foreign partition is not specific to the Muslim world. It has meaning for the Hindus, in regard to the partition of India. Partition is a controversial issue in Ireland. In China claims about foreign domination are made at the level of economics and politics and about interference with respect to human rights issues and cultural corruption. Chinese talk of the 'sugar-coated bullets' of capitalism and the corruptness of Western culture and consumerism has nothing to do with Islam. The same critique of the West is heard in Christian countries, not least in Latin America. The charges of imperialism, domination and cultural corruption may sometimes be phrased in a particularly Muslim way but they are not actually specific to the Muslim world. The pattern of Western domination, colonialism and military intervention over the last 50 or 100 years reveals nothing that is either specifically Islamic or anti-Islamic. It is, rather, a product of the economic and political inequality at a *global* level inherent in the modern international system. The same goes, incidentally, for the much abused concept of 'orientalism'. It may in some measure be true to say that Western writing on the Arab or the Muslim world attempted to distort or to misrepresent, even as it documented and analysed, yet the same claims arise in connection with Western works on Latin America, Africa, India, China or Japan and in writings by nationalists and fundamentalists within these countries.

What are we to conclude from all this? As academics and as intellectuals, we have a responsibility not to let this rhetoric go unchallenged. I do not imagine we shall ever win the argument. The most intelligent press in the West still carries such headlines as 'Islam and the Modern City', 'Islam and War' or 'Islam and Sport', as if this reified concept explained anything. The auction rooms sell works of many origins under the bogus category 'Islamic Art'. But we have to go on making the argument, and not let either the Khomeinis or the Huntingtons of this world gain the upper hand. Of course, ideas and words have effects and myths do often become reality. People who are attacked and oppressed and who are accused of being terrorists may start to side with real terrorists because they are the only ones who give them money and a sense of identity. They will not be as restrained as we would all wish but will start taking up guns. Events are the deciding factors, therefore, not academic debate.

Academics have a further responsibility, however, and that is to disaggregate. As social scientists we like to compare, generalize, look for laws. But we must ask whether the common generalizations are true of all Muslims or most Muslims or conversely whether they are true exclusively for Muslims. With regard to terrorism, it has to be recognized – over and over again, if necessary, that most Muslims are not terrorists and not all the terrorists are Muslims.

Thirdly, to reassess that the modernist, anti-essentialist, anti-perennialist approach is the correct one, let me give one other example. It is often said that in Islam there is no separation between religion and politics. In support of this, people quote the supposedly classical phrase, *al-Islam dinun wa dawlatun* (Islam is a religion and a state). Yet this is apparently a phrase invented in the nineteenth century. The history of any Muslim country reveals, not a fusion of temporal and spiritual powers, but a separation between the two. In the Ottoman empire, there was the Sultan and the *Sheyh-ul Islam*, representing two distinct centres of authority. In the titles of Suleyman the Magnificent, the word 'caliphate' did not appear: he regarded this as irrelevant to his authority. In Saudi Arabia there is the tribal family, Al Saud, and the religious family, Al Shaikh. So, the essentialists' assumption of continuity is mistaken and needs to be challenged.

Finally, we should remember the oldest of all social scientific prescriptions, one that the very non-idealistic, non-fundamentalist Machiavelli recommended to all of us, 'not to confuse wishes with reality'. What Muslims are doing is what people across the world are doing: trying to get power, to control their children, to learn and prosper and to make their country the most wonderful in the world. That is life and there is much conflict and inequality in it: but it is not 'Islam' versus the 'West'.

In concluding I am reminded of a fitting anecdote about the king of Afghanistan, Amanullah, a great admirer of Atatürk. He visited Turkey in 1929 where he heard that Atatürk had delivered a 'great speech', the *Buyuk Nutuk*, speaking with breaks for 36 hours to the National Assembly. Amanullah went back to Afghanistan vowing to do better and speak for two weeks. But after ten days the tribes revolted and threw him out of power. The monarchical balance that had endured since the mid-eighteenth century was broken: a group of bandits from the north under Basha-i Sago took over. That was the end of his regime and the beginning of the troubles of modern Afghanistan.

Conclusion:
Causes and Consequences

There are two frequent responses to any great historical event, both inappropriate if not downright mistaken: to say that everything has changed and to say that nothing has changed. This was true of the earlier watersheds in the modern history of the world: 1914, 1939, more recently the Iranian Revolution in 1979, the fall of the Berlin Wall in 1989, the Iraqi occupation of Kuwait in 1990. In some respects, society and relations between states went on as before. Beneath a rhetoric of change, states and people went on dealing, trading and living. Indeed, the very drama of these events, even as they precipitated people forward into a new world and into physical and psychological displacement, also drew people back to earlier themes and issues: love and hatred, fear and solidarity, enmities and causes half buried by what seemed to be progress, classic texts of politics, religion, poetry.

In this respect, 11 September 2001 is no different. Clearly, these events have unleashed a major change in international relations, between the USA and its allies and parts of the Muslim world; a realignment of diplomacy, not least with regard to the two more alienated members of the Security Council, Russia and China; and a campaign in the military, intelligence and political fields that will run for years. That this campaign is in many respects obscure, that it has no clear end or mechanisms adds to the uncertainty and to that diffuse post-11 September global melancholy, evident in everyday life as in the world economy, that promises to last far into the future. Above all, the USA has changed: two centuries of physical insulation from the conflicts of the rest of the world, a security at once individual and collective, and as such a shared value for much of the rest of the world, were shattered on that late summer morning. A sudden new insecurity, international and immediate, has affected that society.

The obscurity of this conflict is evident above all in the lack of any clear end. It is, however, equally obscure in the lack of any clear beginning. One may ask of any war when it began. World War II began for many in Europe in 1939, but for Russia and the USA it began in 1941, in China in 1937, in Spain in 1936, in Ethiopia in 1935. The Vietnam war began for the United States in 1965 and ended in 1973, but for the Vietnamese communists it started with the August 1945 uprising against the Japanese, lasted through wars with France and the USA and ended with the reunification of their country in 1975. A similar variety applies to nomenclature. What the Western world calls 'the Cuba missile crisis' of October 1962 is to the Russians the 'Caribbean crisis' and to Cubans, who point out that none of the missiles involved was 'Cuban', it is *la crise de octubre*. The Arab–Israeli war of 1973 is in the West the October war, in Israel the Yom Kippur war, in the Arab world *harb ramadan*, the war of Ramadan, the Muslim month in which Operation *Badr* was launched.

The context allows of even greater uncertainty. Many commentators in the developed and developing worlds have sought to set 11 September 2001 in a context of broader conflict and violence, costing hundreds of thousands of lives, that has beset regions of the world in recent years: in Angola, Congo, Israel/Palestine, Afghanistan and elsewhere. If the USA was innocent and unprepared on 11 September it was not without responsibility and, in some cases, complicity in these preceding conflicts. The actions of 11 September 2001, if unique in scale and impact, were not the first nor the last acts of mass terror in modern politics.

Much is made of the colonial past and of globalization in the causes of 11 September. But here it is pertinent and right to listen to what the self-proclaimed perpetrators themselves have said. They do not seem to care for global inequality as such or about what has happened in the cold war in Africa, Latin America or East Asia.

They hate their own *munafiq*, or 'hypocrite', rulers, but they also hate the Shi'ite Muslims who live in their midst in the Arab world – Iran, Pakistan and Afghanistan – and have, on the evidence, a sinister and deeply felt hatred of women. For the leadership of al-Qa'ida the conflict goes back, so they say, 80 years: this means it is dated to events, not exactly specified, in the Middle East of the 1920s. This is most likely a reference to the consequences of the fall of the Ottoman empire, including, as a possible list of starting events, the imposition of British and French mandates in parts of the Arab world in 1920, the abolition of the caliphate by Turkey in 1924, the rise of Jewish immigration to Palestine. It may include, perhaps not least, the establishment of Saudi Arabia in 1926. More immediately, the leaders of al-Qa'ida have dated the starting of their activity to the Kuwait war of 1990–91 and the stationing of US forces in Saudi territory. That this latter point is a sophistry, implying that the whole of the Arabian peninsula, rather than just Mecca and Medina and their environs, is sacred territory does not detract from its ideological appeal. It also ignores the rather significant fact that there are Americans, that is, American Muslims, in Mecca. Whatever the antecedents may be, and one may suspect that history is more pretext than cause, antecedents there are.

Looking forward, in the immediate aftermath of these events, is difficult. No one can tell how many countries will be drawn into military conflict, no one knows what the scale and geographical spread of cultural clash will be, no one can evaluate the longer-term impact on the world economy, no one can be sure how many of the regimes threatened by association with the West will still be present in, say, five or ten years. The whole world is, in different idioms and at many levels – strategic, economic, political, cultural, existential – flying blind.

Yet some things may be anticipated. The power of the USA as a military, economic and political power will not be destroyed or seriously weakened in this conflict. 11 September did not, nor was it designed to, destroy America as a power so much as to mobilize support against its Middle Eastern allies. The anger and resolve of the American people has been ensured. Whatever happens to the coalition of states, Western and other, supporting America, it will endure: alliances, like marriages, are flexible. They can survive resentment and dispute and what is overstated as 'fraying at the edges'. The downturn in the world economy, which may last for years, will be met by concerted macro-economic management by developed states: this may well provoke inflation, as fiscal and monetary support is applied to an economy in recession, but it will not lead to collapse. The same applies to internal security: there may well be more acts of terrorism, internationally organized or locally promoted, within developed states, but these societies and states will hold.

Elsewhere, the situation is less certain. Some countries, caught in the maelstrom of the conflict, may face upheaval. They include Pakistan, Saudi Arabia and Indonesia. In the Muslim world the demagogy of cultural confrontation, fuelled by political opportunism and the irresponsibility of intellectuals and leaders alike, will be much heard, matching, perhaps even far outstripping, the distortion of cultural relations heard in the West. States with their own repressive agenda will take advantage of the crisis to isolate and, where they can, destroy their enemies, while parading as allies of the West in the campaign against terrorism.

It would be comforting to believe that, whatever the costs of 11 September 2001, its consequences could be contained and some lessons learnt. One may doubt whether these outcomes will easily or speedily be attained. The root cause of this crisis is intellectual, the lack of realistic education and democratic culture in a range of countries, such that irrational hatred and conspiracy theory prevail over reasoned critique. This crisis is reinforced by the inaction and insouciance of much of the developed world in the face of the inequalities and conflicts beyond its borders. Neither of these deep cultural and psychological phenomena can, or will, be overcome in short order.

The world will be lucky to have worked through the impact of these events and dealt with their causes in a hundred years. This is not, of course, a very long time in the span of human history, but it does suggest that a strong dose of resolve, clarity and courage will be needed, in the West as in the East, in the years to come. Above all, reason and insistence on universal values and criteria of evaluation will, more than ever, be essential. The centre has to hold.

DOCUMENTARY APPENDICES

Appendix 1:
Founding Statement of al-Qa'ida
(23 February 1998)

Praise be to God, who revealed the Book, controls the clouds, defeats factionalism, and says in His Book 'But when the forbidden months are past, then fight and slay the pagans wherever ye find them, seize them, beleaguer them, and lie in wait for them in every stratagem [of war]'; and peace be upon our Prophet, Muhammad Bin-'Abdullah, who said I have been sent with the sword between my hands to ensure that no one but God is worshipped, God who put my livelihood under the shadow of my spear and who inflicts humiliation and scorn on those who disobey my orders.

The Arabian Peninsula has never – since God made it flat, created its desert, and encircled it with seas – been stormed by any forces like the crusader armies spreading in it like locusts, eating its riches and wiping out its plantations. All this is happening at a time in which nations are attacking Muslims like people fighting over a plate of food. In the light of the grave situation and the lack of support, we and you are obliged to discuss current events, and we should all agree on how to settle the matter.

No one argues today about three facts that are known to everyone; we will list them, in order to remind everyone.

First, for over seven years the United States has been occupying the lands of Islam in the holiest of places, the Arabian Peninsula, plundering its riches, dictating to its rulers, humiliating its people, terrorizing its neighbours, and turning its bases in the Peninsula into a spearhead through which to fight the neighbouring Muslim peoples. If some people have in the past argued about the fact of the occupation, all the people of the Peninsula have now acknowledged it. The best proof of this is the Americans' continuing aggression against the Iraqi people using the Peninsula as a staging post, even though all its rulers are against their territories being used to that end, but they are helpless.

Second, despite the great devastation inflicted on the Iraqi people by the crusader-Zionist alliance, and despite the huge number of those killed, which has exceeded one million . . . despite all this, the Americans are once against trying to repeat the horrific massacres, as though they are not content with the protracted blockade imposed after the ferocious war or the fragmentation and devastation. So here they come to annihilate what is left of this people and to humiliate their Muslim neighbours.

Third, if the Americans' aims behind these wars are religious and economic, the aim is also to serve the Jews' petty state and divert attention from its occupation of Jerusalem and murder of Muslims there. The best proof of this is their eagerness to destroy Iraq, the strongest neighbouring Arab state, and their endeavour to fragment all the states of the region such as Iraq, Saudi Arabia, Egypt, and Sudan into paper statelets and through their disunion and weakness to guarantee Israel's survival and the continuation of the brutal crusade occupation of the Peninsula.

All these crimes and sins committed by the Americans are a clear declaration of war on God, his messenger, and Muslims. And *ulema* have throughout Islamic history unanimously agreed that the *jihad* is an individual duty if the enemy destroys the Muslim countries. This was revealed by Imam Bin-Qadamah in '*al-Mughni*' Imam al-Kisa'i in '*al-Bada'i*', al-Qurtubi in his *Interpretation*, and the shaykh of al-Islam [not further identified] in his books, where he said, 'As for the fighting to repulse [an enemy], it is aimed at defending sanctity and religion, and it is a duty as agreed [by the *ulema*]. Nothing is more sacred than belief except repulsing an enemy who is attacking religion and life.'

On that basis, and in compliance with God's order, we issue the following *fatwa* to all Muslims.

The ruling to kill the Americans and their allies – civilians and military – is an individual duty for every Muslim who can do it in any country in which it is possible to do it, in order to liberate the al-Aqsa Mosque and the Holy Mosque [Mecca] from their grip, and in order for their armies to move out of all the lands of Islam, defeated and unable to threaten any Muslim. This is in accordance with the words of Almighty God, 'and fight the pagans all together as they fight you all together,' and 'fight them until there is no more tumult or oppression, and there prevail justice and faith in God.'

This is in addition to the words of Almighty God, 'And why should ye not fight in the cause of God and of those who, being weak, are ill-treated (and oppressed) – women and children, whose cry is "Our Lord, rescue us from this town, whose people are oppressors; and raise for us from thee one who will help!"'

We – with God's help – call on every Muslim who believes in God and wishes to be rewarded to comply with God's order to kill the Americans and plunder their money wherever and whenever they find it. We also call on Muslim *ulema*, leaders, youths, and soldiers to launch the raid on Satan's US troops and the devil's supporters allying with them, and to displace those who are behind them so that they may learn a lesson.

Almighty God said, 'O ye who believe, give your response to God and His Apostle, when He calleth you to that which will give you life. And know that God cometh between a man and his heart, and that it is He to whom ye shall all be gathered.'

Almighty God also says, 'O ye who believe, what is the matter with you, that when ye are asked to go forth in the cause of God, ye cling so heavily to the earth! Do ye prefer the life of this world to the hereafter? But little is the comfort of this life, as compared with the hereafter. Unless ye go forth, He will punish you with a grievous penalty, and put others in your place; but Him ye would not harm in the least. For God hath power over all things.'

Almighty God also says, 'So lose no heart, nor fall into despair. For ye must gain mastery if ye are true in faith.'

Appendix 2:
Tashkent Declaration on Fundamental Principles for a Peaceful Settlement of the Conflict in Afghanistan
(19 July 1999)

The Deputy Ministers of Foreign Affairs of the '6+2' group, consisting of the countries bordering on Afghanistan the People's Republic of China, the Islamic Republic of Iran, the Islamic Republic of Pakistan, the Republics of Tajikistan, Turkmenistan and Uzbekistan as well as the Russian Federation and the United States of America, having met in Tashkent on 19 July 1999 with the participation of the special envoy of the United Nations Secretary General for Afghanistan, Mr Lakhdar Brahimi, having considered the situation in Afghanistan, being sincere friends of the Afghan people and desiring peace and prosperity for Afghanistan, have confirmed the following principles:

We express the profound concern of our governments at the continuing military confrontation in Afghanistan, which is posing a serious and growing threat to regional and international peace and security.

We remain committed to a peaceful political settlement of the Afghan conflict, in accordance with the relevant provisions of resolutions and decisions of the General Assembly and the Security

Council of the United Nations, and we, in particular, recall the 'talking points' and the 'points of common understanding', adopted earlier by the Countries of the '6+2' group (*contained in annex A/52/826-S/1998/222 and annex A/53/455-S/1998/913 respectively*).

We confirm that the United Nations, as a universally recognized intermediary, must continue to play a central and impartial role in international efforts to achieve a peaceful resolution of the Afghan conflict and we affirm our full support for the efforts of the special envoy of the Secretary General to Afghanistan and the work of the United Nations special mission to Afghanistan.

We reaffirm our firm commitment to the sovereignty, independence, territorial integrity and national unity of Afghanistan.

We express our profound concern at the violations of human rights, including those against ethnic minorities and women and girls, as well as the violations of international humanitarian laws that are taking place in Afghanistan.

We are deeply distressed by the steady increase in the cultivation, production and illicit trafficking of narcotics and the illegal sale of arms, which have far-reaching unfavourable consequences, not only for the region, but beyond.

We are also concerned at the use of Afghan territory, especially areas controlled by the Taliban, to conceal and train terrorists, and the fact that dangerous consequences of such actions can be seen in Afghanistan, its neighboring countries and far beyond their borders.

In view of the foregoing, we have come to the following conclusions:

1. We are convinced that there is no military solution to the Afghan conflict, which must be settled through peaceful political negotiation in order to establish a broad-based, multi-ethnic and fully representative Government.

2. Accordingly, we urge the Afghan parties to resume political negotiations aimed at achieving these goals.

3. In order to help bring about a cessation of hostilities, which we consider essential, we have further agreed not to provide military support to any Afghan party and to prevent the use

of our territories for such purposes. We call upon the international community to take identical measures to prevent delivery of weapons to Afghanistan.

4. We express our readiness to promote direct negotiation, under the auspices of the United Nations, between the Afghan parties in accordance with the relevant resolutions and decisions of the General Assembly and Security Council of the United Nations and this Declaration, in order to conclude an inter-Afghan agreement on the implementation of paragraph 1, set forth above. As members of the '6+2' group, we are fully determined to provide our individual and collective support to this process.

5. We consider that the negotiation process must be conducted under the auspices of the United Nations and may consist of two stages:

a. The main objective of the first stage is to adopt measures for building mutual confidence. Such measures will include;

i. The signing of an agreement on an immediate and unconditional cease-fire without any pre-conditions;

ii. The holding at this stage of direct negotiations between the plenipotentiary delegations of the two main parties to the conflict – the United Front and the Taliban movement – in order to reach agreements, inter alia on:
   – Exchanging of prisoners of war,
   – Lifting internal blockades and opening roads for reciprocal trade and deliver of humanitarian assistance in the territories controlled by the various Afghan groups.

b. The main objective of the second stage is for the Afghans themselves to draw up basic principles for the future state structure of Afghanistan and die establishment of a broad-based, multi-ethnic and fully representative Government within a short period of time.

6. Those of us, who have a common border with Afghanistan, moved by a common desire to take effective and coordinated measures to combat illicit drug-trafficking, have agreed, on

a bilateral and multilateral basis, to strengthen effective and coordinated measures to combat illicit drug-trafficking. In this connection, we recall and confirm the important role played by the United Nations Drug Control Programs in this process.

7. We urge the Taliban to inform the Government of the Islamic Republic of Iran and the United Nations about the results of their investigations into the killings of the diplomatic and consular staff of the Consulate-General of the Islamic Republic of Iran in Masar-e-Sharif, and the correspondent of the Islamic Republic News Agency, and appeal to the Taliban to cooperate fully with the International investigation into their killing in order to punish the guilty parties.

8. We urge the Afghan parties, particularly the Taliban, to cease providing refuge and training to international terrorists and their organizations and to cooperate with the efforts to bring terrorists to justice.

9. We are fully determined to make every effort to encourage the Afghan parties to respect fully the basic human rights and fundamental freedoms of all Afghans in accordance with the basic norms of international law.

10. We are prepared to cooperate with the new Afghan Government that is to be established in accordance with Paragraph 1, set forth above, in all aspects, in order to strengthen security and stability in Afghanistan and the region, bring about the return of Afghan refugees to their homes and ensure the speediest rehabilitation and reconstruction of Afghanistan through support from UN agencies and programs, international financial organizations and donor countries.

11. We call upon the international community to respond to the Inter-Agency Consolidated Appeal for Emergency Humanitarian and Rehabilitation Assistance for Afghanistan, launched by the Secretary General for the period from January to 31 December 1999, bearing in mind also the existence

of the Afghanistan Emergency Trust Fund. Support for demining is of particular importance.

12. We call upon the international community to support these proposals and to take co-ordinated steps to bring about a speedy settlement of the conflict in Afghanistan and also call upon all forces in Afghanistan to demonstrate political will and wisdom, overcome their differences and mutual hostility and not miss an historic opportunity to achieve stable and long-lasting peace.

13. The present Declaration is established in two originals, in the English and the Russian languages, both texts being equally authentic.

Prepared in the City of Tashkent, the Republic of Uzbekistan, this 19th day of the month of July one thousand nine hundred and ninety nine.

For the Government
of the Islamic Republic of Iran

For the Government
of the People's Republic of China

For the Government
of the Republic of Tajikistan

For the Government
of the Islamic Republic of Pakistan

For the Government
of the Republic of Uzbekistan

For the Government
of the Russian Federation

For the Government
of the United States of America

As Observer
For the United Nations

Appendix 3:
UN Security Council Resolution 1328
(12 September 2001)

The SECURITY COUNCIL,
REAFFIRMING the principles and purposes of the Charter of the United Nations,
DETERMINED to combat by all means threats to international peace and security caused by terrorist acts,
RECOGNIZING their inherent right of individual or collective self defense in accordance with the Charter,

1. UNEQUIVOCALLY CONDEMNS in the strongest terms the horrifying terrorist attacks which took place on 11 September 2001 in New York, Washington (D.C.) and Pennsylvania and regards such acts, like any act of international terrorism, as a threat to international peace and security;

2. EXPRESSES its deepest sympathy and condolences to the victims and their families and to the People and Government of the United States of America;

3. CALLS on all states to work together urgently to bring to

justice the perpetrators, organizers and sponsors of the terrorist attacks and STRESSES that those responsible for aiding, supporting or harboring the perpetrators, organizers and sponsors of these acts will be held accountable;

4. CALLS also on the international community to redouble their efforts to prevent and suppress terrorist acts by increased cooperation and full implementation of the relevant international anti-terrorist conventions and Security Council resolutions, in particular resolution 1269 of 19 October 1999;

5. EXPRESSES its readiness to take all necessary steps to respond to the terrorist attacks of 11 September 2001 and to combat all forms of terrorism in accordance with its responsibilities under the Charter of the United Nations;

6. DECIDES to remain seized of the matter.

Appendix 4:
UN Security Council Resolution 1373
(28 September 2001)

The Security Council,

Reaffirming its resolutions 1269 (1999) of 19 October 1999 and 1368 (2001) of 12 September 2001,

Reaffirming also its unequivocal condemnation of the terrorist attacks which took place in New York, Washington, DC and Pennsylvania on 11 September 2001, and expressing its determination to prevent all such acts,

Reaffirming further that such acts, like any act of international terrorism, constitute a threat to international peace and security,

Reaffirming the inherent right of individual or collective self-defence as recognized by the Charter of the United Nations as reiterated in resolution 1368 (2001),

Reaffirming the need to combat by all means, in accordance with the Charter of the United Nations, threats to international peace and security caused by terrorist acts,

Deeply concerned by the increase, in various regions of the world, of acts of terrorism motivated by intolerance or extremism,

Calling on States to work together urgently to prevent and suppress terrorist acts, including through increased cooperation and full implementation of the relevant international conventions relating to terrorism,

Recognizing the need for States to complement international cooperation by taking additional measures to prevent and suppress, in their territories through all lawful means, the financing and preparation of any acts of terrorism,

Reaffirming the principle established by the General Assembly in its declaration of October 1970 (resolution 2625 (XXV)) and reiterated by the Security Council in its resolution 1189 (1998) of 13 August 1998, namely that every State has the duty to refrain from organizing, instigating, assisting or participating in terrorist acts in another State or acquiescing in organized activities within its territory directed towards the commission of such acts,

Acting under Chapter VII of the Charter of the United Nations,

1. Decides that all States shall:

a. Prevent and suppress the financing of terrorist acts;

b. Criminalize the wilful provision or collection, by any means, directly or indirectly, of funds by their nationals or in their territories with the intention that the funds should be used, or in the knowledge that they are to be used, in order to carry out terrorist acts;

c. Freeze without delay funds and other financial assets or economic resources of persons who commit, or attempt to commit, terrorist acts or participate in or facilitate the commission of terrorist acts; of entities owned or controlled directly or indirectly by such persons; and of persons and entities acting on behalf of, or at the direction of such persons and entities, including funds derived or generated from property owned or controlled directly or indirectly by such persons and associated persons and entities;

d. Prohibit their nationals or any persons and entities within their territories from making any funds, financial assets or economic resources or financial or other related services available, directly or indirectly, for the benefit of persons who commit or attempt to commit or facilitate or participate in the commission of terrorist acts, of entities owned or controlled, directly or indirectly, by such persons and of persons and entities acting on behalf of or at the direction of such persons;

2. Decides also that all States shall:

a. Refrain from providing any form of support, active or passive, to entities or persons involved in terrorist acts, including by suppressing recruitment of members of terrorist groups and eliminating the supply of weapons to terrorists;

b. Take the necessary steps to prevent the commission of terrorist acts, including by provision of early warning to other States by exchange of information;

c. Deny safe haven to those who finance, plan, support, or commit terrorist acts, or provide safe havens;

d. Prevent those who finance, plan, facilitate or commit terrorist acts from using their respective territories for those purposes against other States or their citizens;

e. Ensure that any person who participates in the financing, planning, preparation or perpetration of terrorist acts or in supporting terrorist acts is brought to justice and ensure that, in addition to any other measures against them, such terrorist acts are established as serious criminal offences in domestic laws and regulations and that the punishment duly reflects the seriousness of such terrorist acts;

f. Afford one another the greatest measure of assistance in connection with criminal investigations or criminal proceedings relating to the financing or support of terrorist acts, including assistance in obtaining evidence in their possession necessary for the proceedings;

g. Prevent the movement of terrorists or terrorist groups by effective border controls and controls on issuance of identity papers and travel documents, and through measures for preventing counterfeiting, forgery or fraudulent use of identity papers and travel documents;

3. Calls upon all States to:

a. Find ways of intensifying and accelerating the exchange of operational information, especially regarding actions or movements of terrorist persons or networks; forged or falsified travel documents; traffic in arms, explosives or sensitive materials; use of communications technologies by terrorist groups; and the threat posed by the possession of weapons of mass destruction by terrorist groups;

b. Exchange information in accordance with international and domestic law and cooperate on administrative and judicial matters to prevent the commission of terrorist acts;

c. Cooperate, particularly through bilateral and multilateral arrangements and agreements, to prevent and suppress terrorist attacks and take action against perpetrators of such acts;

d. Become parties as soon as possible to the relevant international conventions and protocols relating to terrorism, including the International Convention for the Suppression of the Financing of Terrorism of 9 December 1999;

e. Increase cooperation and fully implement the relevant international conventions and protocols relating to terrorism and Security Council resolutions 1269 (1999) and 1368 (2001);

f.   Take appropriate measures in conformity with the relevant provisions of national and international law, including international standards of human rights, before granting refugee status, for the purpose of ensuring that the asylum-seeker has not planned, facilitated or participated in the commission of terrorist acts;

g.   Ensure, in conformity with international law, that refugee status is not abused by the perpetrators, organizers or facilitators of terrorist acts, and that claims of political motivation are not recognized as grounds for refusing requests for the extradition of alleged terrorists;

4.   Notes with concern the close connection between international terrorism and transnational organized crime, illicit drugs, money-laundering, illegal arms trafficking, and illegal movement of nuclear, chemical, biological and other potentially deadly materials, and in this regard *emphasizes* the need to enhance coordination of efforts on national, subregional, regional and international levels in order to strengthen a global response to this serious challenge and threat to international security;

5.   Declares that acts, methods, and practices of terrorism are contrary to the purposes and principles of the United Nations and that knowingly financing, planning and inciting terrorist acts are also contrary to the purposes and principles of the United Nations;

6.   Decides to establish, in accordance with rule 28 of its provisional rules of procedure, a Committee of the Security Council, consisting of all the members of the Council, to monitor implementation of this resolution, with the assistance of appropriate expertise, and *calls upon* all States to report to the Committee, no later within days from the date of adoption of this resolution and thereafter according to a timetable to be proposed by the Committee, on the steps they have taken to implement this resolution;

7.   Directs the Committee to delineate its tasks, submit a work

programme within 30 days of the adoption of this resolution, and to consider the support it requires, in consultation with the Secretary-General;

8. Expresses its determination to take all necessary steps in order to ensure the full implementation of this resolution, in accordance with its responsibilities under the Charter;

9. Decides to remain seized of this matter.

Appendix 5:
Osama bin Laden Statement
(7 October 2001)

Transcript of a statement by Osama bin Laden, broadcast on al-Jazira television on 7 October 2001, and published the following day in the International Herald Tribune.

Here is America struck by God Almighty in one of its vital organs, so that its greatest buildings are destroyed. Grace and gratitude to God.

America has been filled with horror from North to South and East to West, and thanks be to God that what America is tasting now is only a copy of what we have tasted. Our Islamic nation has been tasting the same for more than 80 years, of humiliation and disgrace, its sons killed and their blood spilled, its sanctities desecrated.

God has blessed a group of vanguard Muslims, the forefront of Islam, to destroy America. May God bless them and allot them a supreme place in heaven. For He is the only one capable and entitled to do so.

When those who have stood in defence of their weak children, their brothers and sisters in Palestine and other Muslim nations, the whole world went into an uproar, the infidels followed by the hypocrites.

A million innocent children are dying at this time as we speak, killed in Iraq without any guilt. We hear no denunciation, we hear no edict from the hereditary rulers. In these days, Israeli tanks rampage across Palestine, in Ramallah, Rafah and Beit Jala and many other parts of the land of Islam, and we do not hear anyone raising his voice or reacting.

But when the sword fell upon America after 80 years, hypocrisy raised its head up high, bemoaning those killers who toyed with the blood, honour and sanctities of Muslims.

The least that can be said about those hypocrites is that they are apostates who followed the wrong path. They backed the butcher against the victim, the oppressor against the innocent child. I seek refuge in God against them and ask Him to let us see them in what they deserve.

I say that the matter is very clear. Every Muslim after this event, after the senior officials in the United States of America, starting with the head of International infidels, Bush and his staff who went on a display of vanity with their men and horses, those who turned even the countries that believe in Islam against us – the group that resorted to God, the Almighty, the group that refuses to be subdued in its religion.

They have been telling the world falsehoods that they are fighting terrorism. In a nation at the far end of the world, Japan, hundreds of thousands young and old were killed and this is not a world crime. To them it is not a clear issue. A million children in Iraq, to them this is not a clear issue.

But when a few more than ten were killed in Nairobi and Dar es-Salam, Afghanistan and Iraq were bombed and hypocrisy stood behind the head of international infidels, the modern world's symbol of paganism, America, and its allies.

I tell them that these events have divided the world into two camps, the camp of the faithful and the camp of the infidels. May God shield us and you from them.

Every Muslim must rise to defend his religion. The wind of faith is blowing, and the wind of change is blowing to remove evil from the Peninsula of Mohammed, peace be upon him.

As to America, I say to it and its people a few words: I swear to God that America will not live in peace before peace reigns in Palestine, and before all the army of infidels depart the land of Mohammed, peace be upon him.

God is the Greatest and glory be to Islam.

Appendix 6:
Suleiman Abu Gaith Statement
(9 October 2001)

Statement by Osama bin Laden spokesman, Suleiman Abu Gaith, published in the Financial Times, 10 October 2001.

Peace be upon Mohammad our prophet and those who follow him. I direct this message to the entire Islamic nation, and I say to them that all sides today have come together against the nation of Islam and the Muslim.

This is the crusade that Bush has promised us, coming toward Afghanistan against the Islamic nation and the Afghan people. We are living under this bombardment from the crusader, which is also targeting the whole Islamic community.

We have a fair and just case. The Islamic nation, for more than 80 years, has been suffering. The Palestinian people hate terror and the terror of the United States is only a trick. Is it possible that America and its allies would kill and that would not be called terrorism? And when the victim comes out to take revenge, it is called terrorism. This must not be acceptable.

America must know that the nation will not keep quiet any more and will not allow what happens against it. *Jihad* today is a religious duty of every Muslim if they haven't got an excuse. God says fight, for the sake of God and to uphold the name of God.

The American interests are everywhere all over the world. Every Muslim has to play his real and true role to uphold his religion and his action in fighting, and *jihad* is a duty.

I want to talk on another point, that those youths who did what they did and destroyed America with their airplanes did a good deed. They have moved the battle into the heart of America. America must know that the battle will not leave its land, God willing, until America leaves our land, until it stops supporting Israel, until it stops the blockade against Iraq. The Americans must know that the storm of airplanes will not stop, God willing, and there are thousands of young people who are as keen about death as Americans are about life.

The Americans must know that by invading the land of Afghanistan they have opened a new page of enmity and struggle between us and the forces of the unbelievers. We will fight them with the material and the spiritual strength that we have, and our faith in God. We shall be victorious.

The Americans have opened a door that will never be closed. At the end, I address the sons and the young Muslims, the men and women, for them to take their responsibility. The land of Afghanistan and the *mujahidin* are being subjected to a full crusade with the objective of getting rid of the Islamic nation. The nation must take up its response and in the end I thank God for allowing us to start this *jihad*. This battle is a decisive battle between faithlessness and faith. And I ask God to give us victory in the face of our enemy and return them defeated.

Notes

Introduction

1. Some passages in the Introduction and Chapter 1 are drawn from articles originally published in *The Observer* of 16 and 23 September 2001. Otherwise, see 'No Man is an Island', 16 September 2001; 'Beyond bin Laden', 23 September 2001.

2. 'Fundamentalism and Political Power', in Patricia Fara, Peter Gathercole and Ronald Laskey (eds), *The Changing World* (Cambridge: CUP and Darwin College, 1996); 'Violence and Communal Conflict', in Fred Halliday, *Nation and Religion in the Middle East* (London: Saqi Books, 2000); 'Anti-Muslimism: A Short History', originally published as 'Anti-Muslimism and Contemporary Politics: One Ideology or Many?', in Fred Halliday, *Islam and the Myth of Confrontation* (London: I. B. Tauris, 1996); 'Islamophobia Reconsidered', first published in *Ethnic and Racial Studies*, vol. 22, no. 5, September 1999; 'The Oslo Peace Accords', in *Mediterraneans*, no. 6, summer/fall 1994; 'A Decade after Invasion' first appeared in *MERIP Reports*, no. 215, summer 2000; 'Iran: the Islamic Republic at the Crossroads', in *Index on Censorship*, February 2001; 'Saudi Arabia 1997: A Family Business in Trouble', in Fred Halliday, *Nation and Religion in the Middle East* (London: Saqi Books, 2000); 'The Other Stereotype', in *Marxism Today*, August 1991; 'Global Inequality and Global Rancour', first published as 'Globalization and its Discontents', *Irish Studies in International Affairs*, vol. 11, 2000. Chapter 12 is based on a lecture given at the Middle East Technical University, Ankara, in March 1997.

Chapter 1

1. The discussion on cold war comes from his *Libro de Estados* in which

a wise man gives moral advice to a young prince on the conduct of warfare against the Muslim foe: *Escritores en Prosa Anteriores al Siglo XV* (Biblioteca de Autores Españoles de Rivadeneira: Madrid, 1952), p. 362.

2. Olivier Roy, *The Failure of Political Islam*, London: I.B. Tauris, 1994.

3. On the origins of the Taliban see John Cooley *Unholy Wars: Afghanistan, America and International Terrorism* London: Pluto, 1999; Ahmad Rashid, *Taliban* London: I.B.Tauris, 1999; Michael Griffin, *Reaping the Whirlwind: The Taliban Movement in Afghanistan*, London: Pluto, 2001.

4. Samuel Huntington, 'A Clash of Civilizations?, *Foreign Affairs*, summer 1993; *The Clash of Civilizations and the Remaking of World Order* (London: Simon & Schuster, 1997).

5. *Surat al-baqara*, no. 2, Verse 190. See John Kelsay and James Johnson (eds), *Just War and Jihad: Historical and Theoretical Perspectives on War and Peace in Western and Islamic Traditions* (New York, 1991).

Chapter 3

1. Part II, 'Humane Treatment', in 'Protocol Additional to the Geneva Conventions of 12 August 1949, and Relating to the Protection of Victims of Non-International Armed Conflicts (Protocol II), of 8 June 1977.'

2. Conor Gearty, *The Future of Terrorism* (London: Phoenix, 1997). See also his *Terror* (London: Faber & Faber, 1991) and his edited collection *Terrorism* (Aldershot: Dartmouth, 1996).

3. For one discussion in terms of Western law, see Tony Honoré, 'The Right to Rebel', in Gearty, (ed.), *Terrorism*. Within the Islamic tradition rebellion against those rulers guilty of oppression – *dhulm* or *istibdad* – is legitimate, as it is against those accused of betraying the principles of Islam – *kufr* or *ilhad*. For an eloquent summary of Western political traditions, see Fidel Castro, *History Will Absolve Me*, a justification of the 1953 attack on the forces of dictator Batista, which ranged across mediaeval and modern Western thought.

4. Alex Schmid, in Alex Schmid and Albert Jongman, *Political Terrorism: A New Guide to Actors, Authors, Concepts, Data Bases, Theories and Literature* (Amsterdam: North-Holland Publishing Company, 1988).

5. I have analysed US 'anti-terrorist' or preventive and 'counter-terrorist' or retaliatory policies, in Fred Halliday, *Cold War, Third World* (London: Hutchinson Radius, 1989), ch. 3. See also my entry on terrorism in Joel Krieger (ed.), *The Oxford Companion to Politics of the World* (New York: Oxford University Press, second edition, 1999).

6. Trotsky's 1920 text, *Terrorism and Communism*, was a reply to Karl Kautsky's 1919, *Terrorism and Communism: a contribution to the natural history of revolution*. The British translation was *In Defense of Terrorism*. See George Kline, 'The defense of terrorism: Trotsky and his major critics', in Terry Brotherstone and Paul Dukes (eds.), *The Trotsky Reappraisal* (Edinburgh: Edinburgh University Press, 1992).

7. An example of the distortion produced by such a perspective is contained in Edgar O'Balance, *Islamic Terrorism, 1979–95. The Iranian Connection* (London: Macmillan, 1997). O'Balance rightly identifies acts of political violence carried out by pro-Iranian groups – kidnappings in Lebanon, assassinations in Western Europe, bomb attacks in a number of countries. But in casting the net wide in search of a single international logic he includes groups which have no connection with Iran, such as the highly secular PKK in Turkey, and omits those groups that were organized by Iran's opponents – notably the Sunni fundamentalists in Afghanistan, backed by the USA and Pakistan, and the Mujahidin-i Khalq, supported by Iraq. For a scholarly treatment of the issue, see Mehdi Mozafhari, *La violence Shi'ite contemporaine, évolution politique*, Institute of Political Science, Aarbus, 1988.

8. Adrian Guelke, *The Age of Terrorism and the International Political System* (London: I.B. Tauris, 1995), ch. 3, 'The poverty of general explanations'.

9. Here I draw on Walter Laqueur, *The Age of Terrorism* (London: Weidenfeld & Nicolson, 1987) and Guelke, *The Age of Terrorism*.

10. João Quartim, *Dictatorship and Armed Struggle in Brazil* (London: New Left Books, 1971); Jorge Castañeda, *Utopia Unarmed. The Latin American Left after the Cold War* (New York: Alfred Knopf, 1993).

11. For one alarmed, but not necessarily alarmist, account 'The New Terrorism: coming soon to a city near you', *The Economist*, 15 August 1998.

12. 'Fight in the cause of God, those who fight you. But do not transgress limits, for God loves not the aggressors.' For a general discussion, see John Kelsay and James Johnson (eds.), *Just War and Jihad: Historical and Theoretical Perspectives on War and Peace in Western and Islamic Traditions* (New York, 1991).

13. *Protocols Additional to the Geneva Conventions of 12 August 1949* (International Committee of the Red Cross, Geneva, 1977). Protocol II of 8 June 1977 concerns 'the Protection of Victims of Non-International Armed Conflicts'. The latter are defined in Article 1 (p. 90) as armed conflicts between a state and 'dissident armed forces or other organized armed groups which, under responsible command, exercise such control over a part of its territory as to enable them to carry out sustained and concerted military operations and to implement this Protocol.' Article 4 (pp. 91–2) lays out the 'fundamental guarantees' concerning humane treatment.

14. The distinction *ad bellum/in bello*, despite its Latinate form, was developed in the League of Nations discussions of the 1920s and 1930s. See Robert Kolb, 'Origins of the twin terms *jus ad bellum/jus in bello*', *International Review of the Red Cross*, no. 320, September/October 1997.

Chapter 4

1. Samuel Huntington, 'The Clash of Civilizations?', *Foreign Affairs*, summer 1993.

2. In this context, the writer Salman Rushdie does not qualify as a proponent of 'anti-Muslimism', whatever his critics may say. Rushdie satirized the early history of Islam, but did not incite or promote prejudice against living Muslims. Indeed one of the several strands in his book is a critique of British racism towards immigrants from (partly Muslim) South Asian societies.

3. Judith Herrin, *The Formation of Christendom* (Oxford: Basil Blackwell, 1987).

4. Contingency is rife in these areas: the Croatian Roman Catholic propaganda about the need to defend 'European' values was directed against the Orthodox Serbs and cast them as the Oriental 'Byzantines'. (I am grateful to Gabriel Partos for this point.)

5. This was also a common perception among enemies of the Ottoman empire in Western Europe during World War I, not least the British intelligence officer T. E. Lawrence. However, British medical examination of Turkish prisoners captured during that war failed to show any above-average incidence of sexually induced disease.

6. For a brilliant evocation of the multi-ethnic history of Bosnia, see the novel by the Serbian writer Ivo Andric, *The Bridge Over the Drina* (London: Harvill, 1994). As this shows so well, animosity, suspicion and occasional killing there certainly was, but at the same time a degree of coexistence and tolerance prevailed for much of the last few centuries. Andric himself at one point seems to give support to the image of an eternal, and particularly Bosnian, animosity: 'Everything else was flushed away in that dark background of consciousness where live and ferment the basic feelings and indestructible beliefs of individual races, faiths and castes, which, to all appearances dead and buried, are preparing for later far-off times unsuspected changes and catastrophes without which, it seems, peoples cannot exist and above all the peoples of this land.' (pp. 173–4). The rest of his novel, and the history of Yugoslavia, not least the record of intermarriage in the post-1945 period, are in conflict with this perennialist, and partisan terms, see Robert Donia and John Fine, *Bosnia and Hercegovina, A Tradition Betrayed* (London: Hurst and Company, 1994).

7. Misha Glenny, *The Fall of Yugoslavia* (London: Penguin, 1992).

8. A similar charge is contained in the Irish Catholic claim that the Protestants are 'soupers', i.e. not a legitimate community because they were Catholics who converted to Protestantism to get economic benefits from the English.

9. Norman Cigar, *Genocide in Bosnia. The Policy of 'Ethnic Cleansing'* (College Station, Texas: Texas A & M University Press, 1995), ch. 3.

10. The Martinovic case has become the subject of much Serbian nationalist poetry. Thus one ran: 'With a broken bottle / On a stake / As though through / a lamb / but alive, / they went through Drordje

Martinovic / As if with their first and heavy steps into their future field they treaded ... / When out of the opium and pain / Drordje Martinovic came round / As if from the long past / Turkish times / He woke up on a stake.' (From 'Kosovo, 1389, Kosovo 1989', *Serbian Literary Quarterly*, Serbian Writers Association, 1989, p. 94.) Note the 'Ottoman' themes – opium, kebabs, torture.

11. According to Abdulah Skaljic's *Turkisms in Serbo-Croat* the *balija* originally referred to a particularly poor and primitive clan or tribe, or to a group of Muslims settled in part of Herzegovina. The *Matica srpska* dictionary gives it as 'a simple and uneducated Muslim peasant'. (I am grateful to my colleague Bernard Johnson for these reference.)

12. See the weekly *Information about Yugoslavia*, published by the Yugoslav embassy in London. Characteristic headlines include 'Isarbegovic's Forces Go to Battle on Plum Brandy', 'Muslim Authorities in Sarajevo to Ban Pork', '20,000 Mujaheddin Are Fighting in Bosnia'.

13. *The Guardian*, 2 August 1993.

14. For a critical view of this issue, see Shkelzen Maliqi, 'Athens' Anti-Albanian Campaign', *Balkan War Report*, September 1994, issue no. 28.

15. *Eleftheros Tipos*, 24 May 1993.

16. *Le Monde*, 26 June 1993.

17. This, *inter alia*, confused the difference between Bulgarian Tuks, i.e. Bulgarian citizens who were Muslims and had Turkish as their first language, and the Pomaks, the Bulgarian-speaking converts to Islam.

18. Hugh Poulton, *Balkans: Minorities and States in Conflict* (London: Minority Rights Group, 1991), chs 10 and 11.

19. 'Les Turcs de Bulgarie entre l'espoir et la méfiance', *Le Monde*, 21 December 1994.

20. Akbar Ahmed provides a perceptive account of the Indian case, eliciting connections with that of Bosnia, '"Ethnic cleansing": a metaphor for our time?', *Ethnic and Racial Studies*, vol. 18, no. 1, January 1995, pp. 12–16.

21. Tapan Basu and others, *Khaki Shorts, Saffron Flags* (Hyderabad: Orient Longman 1993); Sitaram Yechury, *What is this Hindu Rashtra?* (Madras: Frontline, 1993).

22. 'The Road to Ayodhya', *The Economist*, 6 February 1993.

23. 'Muslims have no right to complain about demolition in Ayodhya, says Nirad. C. Chaudhuri', *The Organiser* (weekly paper of RSS), 12 September 1993.

24. Under the influence of European fascism, Golwalkar played up the threat of Jews to Hinduism: these sections of his work have been suppressed by the RSS and BJP, who now look to Israel as a potential ally against the Muslim threat. Golwalkar's anti-Semitism is explained away as a fashion of the times.

25. See on this Romila Thapa, in Sarvepalli Gopal (ed.), *Anatomy of a Confrontation* (New Delhi: Penguin Books, 1991).

26. The concept of Hindutva was expounded during the 1920s in the influ-

ential text by V. D. Savarkar, *Hindutva, who is a Hindu?* This conception of Hindutva was wider than that of the Hindu religion, since it included those who equated their fatherland and a holy land: Hindus, Buddhists and Sikhs were included, Christians, Parsis, Jews and, of course, Muslims were excluded.

27. *Shri Guruji, The Man and His Mission* (Deli: B. N. Bhargava, n.d.), p. 70.
28. *Shri Guruji*, pp. 67–8.
29. Anthony Elenjimmitam, *Philosophy and Action of the RSS for the Hind Swaraj* (Bombay: Axmi Publications, 1951), p. 61.
30. Kamal A. Mitra Chenoy, 'Citizen's Inquiry Reports on Ayodhya and Its Aftermath', *South Asia Bulletin*, vol. XIV, no. 2, 1994.
31. M. S. Golwalkar, *Bunch of Thoughts* (Bangalore: Vikrana Prakashan, 1966), ch. 12.
32. *The Organiser*, 12 September 1993.
33. 'Hindu Extremist Fans Bombay Hatred', *International Herald Tribune*, 14–15 August 1993.
34. *Le Monde*, 29 March 1995, quotation retranslated from the French.
35. For more extensive analysis, see *Khaki Shorts*.
36. Norman Daniel, *The Arabs and Mediaeval Europe* (London: Longman, 1975), provides a masterful survey or history, war, theology and literature.
37. Albert Hourani, *Islam in European Thought* (Cambridge: Cambridge University Press, 1991), pp. 28–30.
38. There is no clear etymology for 'Saracen'. Some suggest it refers to the descendants of Biblical Sarah, others that it is a Greek variation on the Arabic *sharqi*, eastern. One other possibility is that it is derived from the world *sirkashi*, Arabic 'Circassian', an ethnic group with a strong military record.
39. 'On War Against the Turk', *Martin Luther: Selected Political Writings*, ed. J. M. Porter (Lanham London: University Press of America, 1988), p. 126.
40. Paul Coles, *The Ottoman Impact on Europe* (London: Thames and Hudson, 1968), pp. 145–8. See also Norman Daniel, *The Arabs and Mediaeval Europe*.
41. *Le Monde*, 9 December 1993.
42. Curiously, one of the borrowings from the Muslim foe, the abusive term 'cretin', is of course but the word for Christian deployed on that side as an epithet. Another term that has followed a curious semantic journey is the term *kafir*: originally the Arabic word for an unbeliever, it re-entered Dutch and English via South Africa, where it was a term of abuse for the indigenous populations. The result is that in spoken Dutch of today the most common form of abuse of Moroccan immigrants is *stumme kaffir*, stupid kaffir. The French word *giaour* for a North African soldier may be derived from the same source.
43. The theme of the Muslims as sea-borne marauders, threatening the Corsican coast, especially in the Sartenes region, is widespread. See

Dorothy Carrington, *Granite Island, A Portrait of Corsica* (London: Penguin, 1971). Yet, as she points out (p. 118) 'North African piracy flourished at this period precisely because it was run by Europeans.'

44. 'This world *"Musselmann"*, I do not know why, was used by the old ones of the camp to describe the weak, the inept, those doomed to selection.' Primo Levi, *If This Is A Man, The Truce* (London: Sphere Books, 1987), p. 94.

45. On this US background, see Laurence Michalak, *Cruel and Unusual. Negative Images of Arabs in American Popular Culture*, American-Arab Anti-Discrimination Committee (ADC), Issue Paper no. 15, third edition. Washington, 1988; Suha Sabbagh, *Sex, Lies and Stereotypes*, ADC Issue Paper no. 23, 1990.

46. The term 'raghead' appears to have originated in the 1920s in reference to turbaned Asian students at the University of California, who would, presumably, have as likely been Hindus or Sikhs as Muslims. *Oxford English Dictionary*, 2nd ed., vol. XIII, p. 114.

47. 'Rising Islam May Overwhelm the West', *NewHampshire Sunday News*, 20 August 1989.

48. Thus *The Economist*, 4 April 1992, headed an article on three Islamist movements with the title 'Islam Resumes its March'. See also Charles Krauthammer, 'The New Crescent of Crisis: Global Intifada', *Washington Post*, 16 February 1990. Former French President Valéry Giscard d'Estaing struck a similar note in his interventions in the French press: 'L'immigration, l'invasion', *Le Figaro Magazine*, 21 September 1991.

49. For accounts of anti-Muslimist responses to the Oklahoma bombing, see 'Rush to Judgement Alarms U.S. Arabs', *International Herald Tribune* 25 April 1995; 'Camel Jockeys Killed Your Kids', *Village Voice* 2 May 1995; 'One Man's *Jihad*', *The Nation* 15 May 1995; 'The Oklahoma City Bombing: the Jihad that Wasn't' by Jim Nanreckas, *Extra"* July/August 1995. Among other incidents an Iraqi refugee living in Oklahoma City, Sahar al-Mawsawi, lost a baby after her home was attacked, a mosque in the city was attacked by a man with a shotgun, and a US citizen of Arab extraction, long resident in Oklahoma, was arrested and aggressively questioned after taking a flight to London.

50. *Bulletin of the Jerusalem Institute for Western Defense*, vol. 6, no. 3, October 1993, quoted in *Information about Yugoslavia*, 10 November 1993.

51. *International Herald Tribune*, 9 November 1993.

52. Christopher Husbands, '"They Must Obey Our Laws and Customs!": political debate about Muslim assimilability in Great Britain, France and The Netherlands', in Alec Hargreaves and Jeremy Leaman (eds.), *Racism, Ethnicity and Politics in Contemporary Europe* (Aldershot: Edward Elgar, 1995).

53. 'France's Not-so-Veiled Message: It Will Not Tolerate Multiculturalism', *International Herald Tribune* 6 December 1993; Harlem Desire, *SOS Racisme* (Paris: Calmann-Lévy, 1987), pp. 33–4, discusses the relation between racism and hostility to Muslims in France.

54. French terms of abuse for Arabs are many: *bicot, melon,* literally 'melon' (with the implication of 'idiot'), *raton,* 'rat', *bougnoul,* 'wog', *crouille* (Foreign Legion slang from the Arabic *ya-akhi,* 'my brother'), again 'wog' but definitely meaning North African.

55. *Le Monde,* 26 April 1995.

56. *International Herald Tribune,* 3 May 1995.

57. *Le Monde,* 4 May 1995.

58. See my *Arabs in Exile, Yemeni Communities in Urban Britain* (London: I. B. Tauris, 1992).

59. 'Strongest among men in enmity to the Believers wilt, thou find the Jews and Pagans', sura 5, verse 85, *The Holy Qur'an,* translation and commentary by Abdullah Yusuf Ali (London: the Islamic Foundation, 1975), p. 268.

60. Exodus 17: 14–16; Deuteronomy 25: 17–19.

61. In contrast to the mainstream of Judaism, which stresses pre-ordained fate, the kabbala asserts that human beings can help God and can therefore anticipate redemption by their actions: Gush Emunim and Meir Kahane argued that by expelling Arabs from the land of Israel, and never retreating from an inch of Jewish land, Jews could be seen to be doing God's work. Such work might itself destroy the pious believer who carried it out: here a central figure was Samson, who is held to have said: 'I shall perish with the philistines.' In the aftermath of the Hebron killings, Goldstein was widely hailed as a new 'Samson'. Other titles bestowed on him were 'Kennedy' and 'Martin Luther King' (*The Independent,* 28 February 1994).

62. Israel Shahak, *Jewish History, Jewish Religion. The Weight of Three Thousand Years* (London: Pluto Press, 1994), p. 98.

63. Ibid.

64. Information from Israel Shahak.

65. Ken Brown, 'Iron and a King: The Likud and Oriental Jews', *MERIP Reports,* vol. 13, no. 4, May 1983.

66. The Hebrew poet Haim Nahman Bialik (d. 1934) is reputed to have said: 'I hate Arabs because they remind me of Franks.' This is a saying that was often quoted, against Ashkenazim, by militant Sephardim of the Black Panther movement, but there are many who doubt whether this is an accurate attribution. I am grateful to Israel Shahak and Udi Adiv for elucidation on this point.

67. Louis Marton, 'Destroying the Amalekites', *Israel and Palestine Political Report* (Paris), no. 129, December 1986.

68. *Hared,* literally 'fearful', hence 'religiously observant'.

69. According to Kahane, the Arabs are 'an enemy whose hatred for Jews is an obsession; an enemy whose entire culture and tradition is filled with vicious barbaric cruelty against others and against himself … an enemy whose origin was already foretold in the Bible'. *The Jewish Press,* 2 March 1990.

70. *The Jewish Press,* 12 January 1990.

71. Robert Friedman, *The False Prophet: Rabbi Meir Kahane – from FBI*

informant to Knesset member (New York: Lawrence Hill Books, 1990), p. 260.

72. Ehud Sprinzak, *The Ascendance of Israel's Radical Right*, (Oxford: Oxford University Press, 1991), p. 239. Kahane's ideas were expressed in his regular column in the New York-based *Jewish Press*. See also his interview in Raphael Mergui, *Israel's Ayatollahs: Meir Kahane and the Far Right in Israel* (London: Saqi Books, 1987).

73. As quoted in Israel Shahak, *Report no. 130*, 10 December 1993.

74. Settler support for Goldstein was widely reported at the time of his crime. 'Islam is the poison of humanity ... This is not killing. This is revenge,' one Israeli told reporters ('They Hate Us, and We Hate Them', *International Herald Tribune*, 28 February 1994).

75. *Yerushalaim*, 30 July 1993, translated by Israel Shahak.

76. Baruch Goldstein, in an interview with Israeli radio some weeks before he died, denounced 'the Arab Nazi enemy, who strives to attack any Jew just because he is a Jew in the land of Israel'.

Chapter 5

1. A Book Review for *Ethnic and Racial Studies*: Browning, David, *Building Bridges between Islam and the West*, Wilton Park Paper no. 138, 1998. Hafez, Kai, ed., *Der Islam und der Westen: Anstiftung zum Dialog*, Fischer Verlag, 1997. Hafez, Kai, ed., *Islam and the West in the Mass Media: Fragmented Images in a Globalizing World*, Hampton Press, 1999. Pope, Nicole and Hugh, *Turkey Unveiled: Atatürk and After*, London, John Murray, 1997. The Runnymede Trust, *Islamophobia: A Challenge for Us All*, The Runnymede Trust, 1997. Said, Bobby S., *A Fundamental Fear: Eurocentrism and the Emergence of Islamism*, Zed Books, 1997.

2. Runnymede, p. 8, lends credence to this.

3. For a cogent critique of the way in which well-meaning British politicians have colluded in such conservative renderings of Islam, see Lucy Carroll, 'Muslim Women and "Islamic Divorce" in England', *Women Living under Muslim Laws*, Dossier 19, October 1997.

4. Interview on BBC 'Today' programme, 12 January 1999.

5. I have tried to explore this in my study of the first Muslim community in the UK, *Arabs in Exile: Yemen Migration in Urban Britain* (London: I. B. Tauris, 1992).

6. I have argued the case at greater length in 'Anti-Muslimism in Contemporary Politics', *Islam and the Myth of Confrontation* (London: I. B. Tauris, 1996), reprinted here as Chapter 4. For an alternative, and itself dissident approach, see Michael Banton, 'Islamophobia: A Critical Analysis', *Dialogue*, December 1998.

7. The front page of the *Daily Mail* (22 February 1996) headlined the decision of the then Minister of Education, Gillian Shephard, to permit separate religious education for Muslims in Birmingham: 'Shephard gives way on segregation. Moslems win their separate lessons'. Similarly, *The Sun* (24 November 1998) ran a front-page story on a British

women who abandoned her children on holiday: 'Worst mum in world. She dumps kids in Turkey to run off with Arab lover'.

8. *International Herald Tribune*, 17 November 1997.

9. For an account of the policing of women in British Muslim communities by young males and hostility to those who question their authority, see Yasmin Alibhai-Brown, 'God's own vigilantes', *The Independent*, 12 October 1998.

10. Membership of the Runnymede Commission gives striking evidence of this, by inclusions and by those whose voices were not heard – Women Against Fundamentalism, dissident Muslims, sympathetic but secular critics of both camps. It also ties itself into a knot (p. 60) by arguing for an extension of the blasphemy law: would they ban the Quran, which argues, *inter alia*, that Christ was not the son of God, that he was not crucified and that he did not rise from the dead – all propositions that would be considered blasphemous by Christians?

11. See the regular reports of *Women Living under Muslim Laws* and the documents of Amnesty International and Human Rights Watch: Said is silent, arguably complicit, on such issues.

Chapter 9

1. Technically the English translation of the state, the Kingdom of Saudi Arabia, is misleading. There is no Arabic word corresponding to English 'Arabia' – it is normally referred to as *al-jazira*, 'the peninsula'. The title of the country *al-mamlaka al-arabia al-saudia* literally means 'the Arab Saudi Kingdom'.

2. Hasan Abdulla al-Qurashi, *Spectres of Exile* (Echoes); Abd al-Rahman Munif, *Cities of Salt* (Vintage); Ghazi Algosaibi, *An Apartment Called Freedom* (Routledge).

3. *Voices of Change, Short Stories by Saudi Arabian Women Writers* (Lynne Reinner).

Chapter 11

1. Immanuel Kant, *On History* (New York: Bobbs-Merrill, 1963), 'Idea for a Universal History from a Cosmopolitan Point of View', thesis 8, p. 23.

2. I have developed these arguments in my *Rethinking International Relations*, London, Macmillan, 1994.

3. *International Herald Tribune*, 24 November 1998.

4. Carlos Castañeda, *Utopia Unarmed: The Latin American Left after the Cold War* (New York: Knopf, 1993); François Furet, *Le passé d'une illusion: Essai sur l'idée communiste au XXe siècle* (Paris: Laffont, 1995); Francis Fukuyama, *The End of History and the Last Man* (London: Hamish Hamilton, 1992).

5. For all the appeal to a seventh-century religious authority, the Qoran, the rhetoric of Ayatollah Khomeini reproduced many of the characteristic themes of twentieth-century third world populism – an appeal to the masses against a corrupt and dependent elite, anti-imperialism, a

planned economy, autonomous industrialization, redistribution of wealth. See Ervand Abrahamian, *Khomeinism* (London: I. B. Tauris, 1990).

6. I have discussed this further in *Revolution and World Politics. The Rise and Decline of the Sixth Great Power* (London: Macmillan, 1999), ch. 12.

7. In what follows I draw heavily on the work of analysis and clarification of others: Paul Hirst and Graham Thompson, *Globalization in Question. The International Economy and the Possibilities of Governance* (Oxford: 1996); Harry Gelber, *Sovereignty through Interdependence* (London: Kluwer, 1997); Jonathan Perraton, David Goldblatt, David Held and Anthony McGrew, 'The Globalization of Economic Activity', *New Political Economy*, vol. 2, no. 2, 1997; the 'Schools Brief' series on globalization in *The Economist* beginning 18 October 1997.

8. Susan Strange, *States and Markets* (Oxford: Blackwell, 1988); *Mad Money*, 1998.

9. Even the US figure runs at 33.3%, up from 8.6% in 1938. See 'The Future of the State', *The Economist*, 20 September 1997.

10. London: HarperCollins, 1993.

11. $0.4 a litre, as against $1.0, $1.1, $1.25 respectively. Second quarter 1997 prices, as given in *The Economist*, 26 July 1997.

12. Amartya Sen, *On Ethics and Economics* (Oxford: Blackwell, 1987).

13. *The Economist*, 20 September 1997, p. 172.

14. *Financial Times*, 10 September 1998.

15. *Our Global Neighbourhood. The Report of the Commission on Global Governance* (Oxford: OUP, 1995).

16. UN, EU, NATO, OSCE, WEU, Council of Europe, Partnership for Peace, ESDP.

17. *On History*, 'What is Enlightenment?', p. 8. *New Political Economy*, vol. 2, no. 2, 1997; the 'Schools Brief' series on globalization in *The Economist* beginning 18 October 1997.

Chapter 12

1. London: Croom Helm, 1982.

2. For an overview see the work of Umut Ozkirimli, *Theories of Nationalism* (London: Palgrave, 2000).

3. On slavery in the Quran see 4.40, 16.73, 24.33, 47.4. Reuben Levy, *The Social Structure of Islam* (Cambridge: Cambridge University Press, 1965), pp. 73–89.

Index